AN ANTHOLOGY OF RELIGIOUS TEXTS FROM UGARIT

RELIGIOUS TEXTS TRANSLATION SERIES

NISABA

VOLUME SIXTEEN

AN ANTHOLOGY OF RELIGIOUS TEXTS FROM UGARIT

BY

JOHANNES C. DE MOOR

TUTA SUB AEGIDE PALLAS · EJB ·

E.J. BRILL
LEIDEN · NEW YORK · KØBENHAVN · KÖLN
1987

NISABA is the name of the Sumerian goddess of vegetation and writing, whose symbol is the calamus (the instrument with which the writing was impressed on the soft clay) on an altar. The Sumerians were the first people to use writing, for keeping accounts and, by extension, inter alia, as a substitute for the oral tradition. For this reason, the goddess has been given pride of place here.

Library of Congress Cataloging-in-Publication Data

An Anthology of religious texts for Ugarit.

(Nisaba, ISSN 0169-930X; v. 16)
Includes indexes.
1. Ugarit (Ancient city)—Religion. 2. Ugaritic literature. I. Moor, Johannes Cornelis de, 1935- II. Series.
BL1640.A58 1987 299'.26 87-22410
ISBN 90-04-08330-8 (pbk.)

ISSN 0169-930x
ISBN 90 04 08330 8

PRINTED IN THE NETHERLANDS BY E. J. BRILL

TABLE OF CONTENTS

PREFACE

The first clay tablets from the ancient kingdom of Ugarit were discovered in 1929. Soon afterwards several people succeeded in deciphering the relatively easy cuneiform script. It turned out to be an alphabetic script which had been used to record ancient Canaanite and, to a far lesser extent, Hurrian myths, epics, rituals, letters and administrative documents. Ever since, the religious texts of Ugarit have continued to fascinate philologists, historians of religion and Bible scholars alike, because they constitute the most authentic and extensive corpus of religious literature from the Canaanite world to date. Because in later centuries the peoples of Canaan used to write mostly on papyrus and leather, which usually decomposed in the soil, it is unlikely that comparable finds in later Canaanite dialects, such as Phoenician, will ever turn up, and it remains to be seen whether the much older tablets of Ebla really will eclipse the rich legacy of Ugarit.

Ugarit is the name of a city hidden in a tell called Ras Shamra, about 12 kilometres North of Latakia on the coast of Syria. Its port was Ma'hadu, present-day Minet el-Beida. Ugarit was the capital of a kingdom of the same name. Most of the tablets were found during the many archaeological campaigns at Ras Shamra, Minet el-Beida and Ras Ibn Hani, ancient Appu, where the queen of Ugarit had her own residence.[1]

[1] For a short survey of the *excavations* of Ugarit see: A. S. Kapelrud, in: Interpreter's Dictionary of the Bible, vol. 4, Nashville 1962, 724-732; J. C. de Moor, in: Supplement to IDB, Nashville 1976, 928-931. More extensive information offers the excellent review article Ras Shamra, in: Supplément au Dictionnare de la Bible, t.9, Paris 1979, 1124-1466.

Useful *bibliographical tools* are: J. P. Lettinga, in: J. H. Hospers (ed.), A Basic Bibliography for the Study of the Semitic Languages, vol. 1, Leiden 1973, 127-145;

The Ugaritic tablets date from the period between 1400 and 1200 B.C. when Ugarit was a flourishing metropolis with extensive international contacts. The Ugaritians conversed and traded with Babylonians, Assyrians, Hittites, Hurrians, Cretans, Cypriots, Arabs from the Syrian desert, other Canaanites from the South and last but not least, the Egyptians. Small wonder that the religious texts from Ugarit reflect this international orientation.

This book is intended to disclose the more important religious texts from Ugarit to a broad audience. For that reason it was provided with extensive notes trying to explain as far as possible the religious background of this literature. The text on which the translations were based has been published separately.[2] In order not

M. Dietrich, O. Loretz, P.-R. Berger, J. Sanmartín, W. C. Delsman, Ugarit-Bibliographie 1928-1966, 4 Bde., Neukirchen 1973; Ugarit-Bibliographie 1967-1971, Neukirchen 1986.

Information on *recent publications* can be found in: Ugarit-Forschungen (annual), Ugaritic Newsletter, Elenchus Bibliographicus Biblicus (of Biblica), Archiv für Orientforschung, Keilschriftbibliographie in Orientalia.

The most complete *edition* of the alphabetic texts of Ugarit is: M. Dietrich, O. Loretz, J. Sanmartín, Die keilalphabetischen Texte aus Ugarit, Bd. 1, Neukirchen 1976 (transliteration only).

At the moment the best tools for the study of the *Ugaritic language* are: S. Segert, A Basic Grammar of the Ugaritic Language, Berkeley/London 1984 with R. E. Whitaker, A Concordance of Ugaritic Literature, Cambridge, Mass. 1972 (incomplete and in certain respects obsolete). A complete *dictionary* of the Ugaritic language is being prepared by M. Dietrich and O. Loretz of Münster. The present author hopes to publish a comprehensive *syntax* of literary Ugaritic in the near future.

Other noteworthy recent *translations* of sizeable portions of Ugaritic literature are: A. Caquot, M. Sznycer, A. Herdner, Textes ougaritiques, t.1, Paris 1974; J. C. L. Gibson, Canaanite Myths and Legends, Edinburgh 1978; G. del Olmo Lete, Mitos y Leyendas de Canaan segun la tradición de Ugarit, Madrid 1981; Interpretación de la Mitología Cananea, Valencia 1984.

[2] J. C. de Moor, K. Spronk, A Cuneiform Anthology of Religious Texts from Ugarit (CARTU), Leiden 1986 (with glossaries). The only significant category not represented in this selection are the omina on livers and lungs of clay. They were left out deliberately because a new edition of these was about to appear when the manuscript of this book had to be closed.

to burden the non-specialist with the innumerable philological puzzles which had to be solved before this translation could be published the number of references and notes of a technical nature has been kept to the absolute minimum. I have tried to justify my interpretations in numerous publications over the past fifteen years. There I have discussed other scholarly opinions which because of its format had to be skipped in this publication.

In the translations non-italic words indicate a relatively high grade of uncertainty. Square brackets indicate that part of the text had to be restored. These brackets were omitted, however, whenever there can be no reasonable doubt as to the correctness of a restoration. Words between normal parentheses were added for the sake of clarity or because they were required in English. Usually the nature of the original text fully justifies these additions. A few major emendations are indicated by < >.

Many people have helped me during the long years of preparation of this book. Dr Meindert Dijkstra, Dr Pieter van der Lugt, Dr Klaas Spronk and Drs Marjo Korpel all contributed in one way or another to earlier drafts of parts of the book. Often we published our results as joint authors of articles in the specialized journals. Klaas Spronk drew the cuneiform text for the separate text edition. His constructive criticism often helped me to make better decisions on difficult readings. Special thanks are due to Miss Marjo Korpel who provided many detailed comments and valuable suggestions during the last few arduous months of copy editing.

I am particularly grateful to Mervyn Richardson of Manchester who undertook the exacting task of correcting my English style. I hope he can forgive me that I decided to maintain a few Semiticisms for clearness' sake. These and any other flaws should be attributed entirely to me as the author of this book.

It was Dr Thieu Heerma van Voss who invited me to prepare this volume. Later on he and Dr F. Th. Dijkema of Brill's encouraged me time and again to persevere. To both of them I owe thanks.

Finally I pay tribute to the board of governors and the council of the "Theologische Hogeschool" at Kampen for their generous support, and to the personnel of our library for their patience with my endless requests which sometimes must have looked rather exotic.

Kampen, September 1986

LIST OF ABBREVIATIONS

AASF	Annales Academiae Scientiarum Fennicae, Series B.
AcOr	Acta Orientalia.
AHw	W. von Soden, Akkadisches Handwörterbuch, 3 Bde., Wiesbaden 1965-81.
AJBI	Annual of the Japanese Biblical Institute.
ANEP	J. B. Pritchard (ed.), The Ancient Near East in Pictures Relating to the Old Testament, Princeton 1954.
ANET	J. B. Pritchard (ed.), Ancient Near Eastern Texts Relating to the Old Testament, 3rd ed., Princeton 1969.
AnOr	Analecta Orientalia.
AOAT	Alter Orient und Altes Testament.
AOATS	Alter Orient und Altes Testament, Sonderreihe.
ASKT	P. Haupt, Akkadische und sumerische Keilschrifttexte, Leipzig 1882.
AuS	G. Dalman, Arbeit und Sitte in Palästina, 7 Bde, Gütersloh 1928-1942.
b	Babylonian Talmud.
BAfO	Beiheft Archiv für Orientforschung.
Barthélemy	A. Barthélemy, Dictionnaire Arabe-Français: Dialectes de Syrie, Paris 1935-54.
BASOR	Bulletin of the American Schools of Oriental Research.
Bibl	Biblica.
BiOr	Bibliotheca Orientalis.
BJRL	Bulletin of the John Rylands Library.
BMS	L. W. King, Babylonian Magic and Sorcery, London 1896.
BRM	Babylonian Records in the Library of J. Pierpont Morgan.
BWL	W. G. Lambert, Babylonian Wisdom Literature, Oxford 1959.
BZ	Biblische Zeitschrift, Neue Folge.
BZAW	Beiheft zur Zeitschrift f.d. Alttestamentliche Wissenschaft.
CAD	The Assyrian Dictionary of the University of Chicago.
CH	Codex Hammurapi.
CT	Cuneiform Texts from Babylonian Tablets in the British Museum.
CTA	A. Herdner, Corpus des tablettes en cunéiformes alphabétiques découvertes à Ras Shamra-Ugarit de 1929 à 1939, 2 tomes, Paris 1963.
DaM	Damaszener Mitteilungen.
Denizeau	C. Denizeau, Dictionnaire des parlers arabes de Syrie, Liban et Palestine, Paris 1960.
EA	El Amarna tablets.

En.el.	Enuma Elish, cited after W. G. Lambert, S. B. Parker, Enuma eliš. The Babylonian Epic of Creation, Oxford 1966.
GAG	W. von Soden, Grundriss der akkadischen Grammatik, 2. Aufl., Roma 1969.
Gilg.	Epic of Gilgamesh, cited after A. Schott, W. von Soden, Das Gilgamesch-Epos, Stuttgart 1958.
GLECS	Comptes Rendus du Groupe Linguistique d'Études Chamito-Sémitiques.
HAL	W. Baumgartner et al., Hebräisches und aramäisches Lexikon zum Alten Testament, Leiden 1967-
HTR	Harvard Theological Review.
JANES	Journal of the Ancient Near Eastern Society of Columbia University.
JAOS	Journal of the American Oriental Society.
JBL	Journal of Biblical Literature.
JCS	Journal of Cuneiform Studies.
JEA	Journal of Egyptian Archaeology.
JEOL	Jaarbericht van het Vooraziatisch-Egyptisch Genootschap Ex Oriente Lux.
JNES	Journal of Near Eastern Studies.
JQR	Jewish Quarterly Review.
JRAS	Journal of the Royal Asiatic Society of Great Britain and Ireland.
JSS	Journal of Semitic Studies.
KAI	H. Donner, W. Röllig, Kanaanäische und aramäische Inschriften, 3 Bde, Wiesbaden 1962-64.
KAJ	E. Ebeling, Keilschrifttexte aus Assur juristischen Inhalts, Leipzig 1927.
KAR	E. Ebeling, Keilschrifttexte aus Assur religiösen Inhalts, 2 Bde, Leipzig 1915-1923.
KAV	O. Schroeder, Keilschrifttexte aus Assur verschiedenen Inhalts, Leipzig 1920.
KTU	M. Dietrich, O. Loretz, J. Sanmartín, Die keil-alphabetischen Texte aus Ugarit, Bd. 1, Neukirchen 1976.
KUB	Keilschrifturkunden aus Boghazköi.
LÄ	Lexikon der Ägyptologie.
Lane	E. W. Lane, Arabic-English Lexicon, 8 vols., London 1863-93.
LXX	Septuaginta.
m	Mishna.
MIO	Mitteilungen des Instituts für Orientforschung.
MLC	G. del Olmo Lete, Mitos y Leyendas de Canaan, Madrid 1981.
MLE	Materiali Lessicali ed Epigrafici.
NYCI	J. C. de Moor, New Year with Canaanites and Israelites, 2 vols., Kampen 1972.
OBO	Orbis Biblicus et Orientalis.
OIP	Oriental Institute Publications.

OLP	Orientalia Lovaniensia Periodica.
Or	Orientalia.
OrAnt	Oriens Antiquus.
OTS	Oudtestamentische Studiën.
PEQ	Palestine Exploration Quarterly.
PJ	Palästina Jahrbuch.
PRE	Paulys Real-Encyclopädie der classischen Altertumswissenschaften.
QS	Quaderni di Semitistica.
RÄR	H. Bonnet, Reallexikon der ägyptischen Religionsgeschichte, Berlin 1952.
RAI	Comptes Rendus de la Rencontre Assyrologique Internationale.
RB	Revue Biblique.
RIH	Ras Ibn Hani tablets.
RLA	Reallexikon der Assyriologie.
RSP	Ras Shamra Parallels.
SEL	Studi Epigrafici e Linguistici.
STT	The Sultantepe Tablets.
SVT	Supplement to Vetus Testamentum.
TCS	Texts from Cuneiform Sources.
ThWAT	Theologisches Wörterbuch zum Alten Testament.
TO	A. Caquot, M. Sznycer, A. Herdner, Textes ougaritiques, tome 1, Paris 1974.
UF	Ugarit-Forschungen.
VT	Vetus Testamentum.
WO	Die Welt des Orients.
YOS	Yale Oriental Series, Babylonian Texts.
ZA	Zeitschrift für Assyriologie.
ZÄS	Zeitschrift für Ägyptische Sprache und Altertumskunde.
ZAW	Zeitschrift für die Alttestamentliche Wissenschaft.
ZDPV	Zeitschrift des Deutschen Palästina-Vereins.

CONVERSION TABLE KTU-ARTU

MYTH: BAAL

Baal I, fragment a

KTU 1.101, *obv.*

The beginning of the great myth of Baʿlu has been preserved on this relatively small fragment of a tablet. Originally the myth covered six large tablets and, according to the present writer, described the mythological prototype of the normal agricultural and cultic year of the people of Ugarit.[1] The narrative starts with a description of the supposed first autumnal New Year festival when Baʿlu celebrated his victory over Death and his return to his holy mountain.

1 *Baʿlu was seated, as immovable as a mountain,*[2]
Haddu r[ested][3] *like the ocean,*
on his mountain, the divine Sapanu,[4]
[*on*] *the mountain of victory.*

[1] See J. C. de Moor, The Seasonal Pattern in the Ugaritic Myth of Baʿlu (AOAT, 16), Neukirchen 1971; New Year with Canaanites and Israelites (Kamper Cahiers, 21-22), Kampen 1972. Both publications need to be updated. In the present translation and commentary a number of improvements has been incorporated. See also Myth and Ritual I, II, IV; Ritual I, III; Incantation V; Aqhat, notes 78ff., 100ff., 170ff., 236, 241ff., 263ff., 275ff. as well as the comprehensive table pp. 101ff.

The seasonal interpretation was criticized by L. L. Grabbe, UF 8 (1976) 57-63, 14 (1982) 89-92.

For attempts to elucidate the "theology" of the myth see J. C. L. Gibson, Or 53 (1984) 202-219; J. C. de Moor, OTS 24 (1986) 1ff.

[2] Cf. Ps. 125:1, also Isa. 14:13 and Ps. 9:12.

[3] According to a different restoration "*Haddu the S*[*hepherd*]", Shepherd being an epithet of Baʿlu. Cf., however, Gen. 49:25; Deut. 33:13.

[4] Sapanu was the name of the mountain of Baʿlu, Mt. Kasios/Casius of Hellenistic times, the present day Jebel Akra (1759m), about 40 km north of Ugarit. All Canaanites oriented themselves toward this holy mountain so that its name became tantamount to "North".

Seven lightnings [he had],
eight storehouses of thunder,[5]
the shafts of lightning he [ ].
Tallayu[6] *stroked his head,*
the thin-haired spot between his eyes.
She rubbed his legs,[7]
the horns that were on him,
his head with snow[8] *from heaven.*
[It] *was asked*: "*Is there a* meal?
His mouth is [craving] *for bowls of milk,*
[(his) lip]*s surely for the wine from the jars,*
his heart [ ].
[ ] let bring wreaths"
(broken)

Baal I

KTU 1.3

About 15 lines are missing between KTU 1.101, obv. (fragment a) and the first column of KTU 1.3.

I.1* [ ],
1 *let not sink down* [ ],"
Then Radmanu[9] *served Baʿlu, the Almighty.*
he regaled his Highness, the Lord of earth.

[5] Compare Ps. 29:3,4a,4b,5,7,8,9 (7 times!) and Rev. 10:3-4. See J. Day, VT 29 (1979) 143-151. Cf. Job 38:22 and Baal IV (KTU 1.4):vii.59f.

[6] Daughter of Baʿlu, one of the goddesses of the dew. See note 18 below.

[7] Compare the Descent of Ishtar, 128, as read by W. von Soden, ZA 58 (1967) 193. See also Ritual I, note 16.

[8] Cf. Job 9:30.

[9] The interpretation is uncertain. If *Rdmn* is really the name of a god, he might be identical to the Greek Radamanthys, a deity of foreign origin who was thought to rule over the Elysiac fields.

He rose, set (the table) to offer him food,
he divided a suckling[10] *before him,*
with a salted knife he carved a fatling.
He stood up, made preparations to offer him drink,
he put a cup into his hands,[11]
a beaker into both his hands,
the large goblet, grand to behold,
the vat of the men of heaven,[12]
the holy cup which no married woman may look at,[13]
the beaker which not (even) Athiratu[14] *may see.*
He took a thousand pitchers of foaming wine,[15]
ten thousand he mixed in his mixture.

[10] In the offering lists of Ras Ibn Hani *ṯd* is a specific type of sacrificial meat. The parallelism of our text renders it unlikely that we are dealing with the homograph *ṯd* "udder".

In August and September many calves were born and the gods received their due in the form of sacrifices, cf. AOAT 16,80.

[11] Cf. Gen. 40:13; Iliad XVIII.545f.; Odyssey III.51,53.

[12] A designation of the male deities.

[13] This mirrors the rules of a *mrzḥ* on earth. A *mrzḥ* was a cultic society devoted to the drinking of wine and to the communication with the spirits of dead ancestors and friends. The members were men. Only "virgins" (young women who had not yet born a son) were admitted occasionally, not married women. For further information see Aqhat, note 265.

With regard to the holy vessel which may not be looked at, cf. M. W. Green, JCS 30 (1978) 136f., IV.9.

[14] Wife of Ilu, the head of the pantheon.

[15] Freshly fermented new wine which was prepared during the New Year festival in autumn. Note the mythological exaggeration of the quantities consumed. In the actual cult everybody was allowed to drink his fill on the first day of the festival which lasted seven days and was celebrated around the time of the autumnal equinox. Cf. below, Myth and Ritual I, note 25; II, note 39; Ritual I, note 56; Incantation V; Aqhat, notes 81, 293.

The Sabians of Harran who still worshipped a form of Baal Zaphon in the Middle Ages celebrated a festival on the 3rd of Aylul (September) on which date every man drank seven cups of wine ((al-Nadim, Fihrist, IX.1). A similar festival is attested in Egypt, cf. H. F. Lutz, Viticulture and Brewing in the Ancient Orient, Leipzig 1922, 107. The offering of grapes and wine was also an element in the Egyptian New Year festival, cf. J. F. Borghouts, Nieuwjaar in het Oude Egypte, Leiden 1986, 17f.

He rose, improvised a poem and sang,
the gracious lad[16] *(held) the cymbals in his hands,*
the sweet-voiced youth sang
before Baᶜlu in the highlands of Sapanu.[17]
Baᶜlu looked for his daughters,
he saw Pidrayu, the girl of the honey-dew,
then also Tallayu, the girl of the mist.[18]
"Pidru,[19] *you certainly know*
whether the brides are [respectab]le,[20]
and [ ].
A covenant [ ]

(broken)

About 40 lines are missing. Before she goes to battle,[21] ᶜAnatu, the

[16] The word "gracious lad" as a designation of the minstrel recurs in 2 Sam. 23:1.

[17] A sweet-voiced youth also features in a ritual for the New Year festival (Myth and Ritual I (KTU 1.23):14). It is one of many indications that the Ugaritic myths were actualized in the cult of Ugarit.

The episode described in Baal I:i is alluded to in the Legend of Aqhat, cf. Aqhat, notes 100-102. The following passage from Hesiod may be compared: "Verily wise Zeus carried off golden-haired Ganymedes because of his beauty, to be amongst the Deathless Ones and pour drink for the gods in the house of Zeus" (Hesiod, Homeric Hymns, V.201ff.; cf. Homer, Iliad, XX.232ff.).

[18] These minor goddesses, daughters of Baᶜlu (cf. Myth and Ritual IV (KTU 1.24):26ff.), represented certain types of dew which had disappeared with Baᶜlu during the mythological episode corresponding to the summer. Cf. Baal V (KTU 1.5):v10f. It is noteworthy that Arsayu, the goddess of the ample dew of summer, did not go with Baᶜlu and is not mentioned here when his return is celebrated. On honey-dew see UF 7 (1975) 590f. For the connection between dew and resurrection see below, note 38.

[19] The reading is uncertain. Perhaps Pidru was a minor deity. It is also possible to assume haplography: *pdr⟨y⟩. ydᶜ [ydᶜ]t* "Pidrayu, you certainly know". In that case Pidrayu, being the eldest of the two, had to vouch for their chastity during their absence.

[20] An allusion to their usual epithet "the respectable brides".

[21] Why she has to go to battle is unclear, perhaps out of frustration over her inability to bear (cf. Myth and Ritual IV). Parallels of goddesses fighting or even

wife of Baᶜlu, who does not live with her husband,[22] has herself made-up by her attendants.

II.

They put n[ard] *on her,*
the seven girls[23] *(put) henna (on her),*
scent of coriander and murex-dye.[24]
ᶜAnatu closed the doors of the mansion
and went to meet the lads at the base of the mountain.
And look! ᶜAnatu fought in the plain,
she slaughtered between the two cities.[25]
She smote the people of the sea-shore,
silenced the men of the east.[26]
Heads were under her (feet) like clods of earth,
on her were hands like locusts,
like scales of a plane-tree the hands of the warriors.

wading in the blood of their victims are abundant. Cf. M. H. Pope, Song of Songs (Anchor Bible, 7C), Garden City 1977, 605-612.

It is very likely that the episode is a mythological reflection of a sham combat during the New Year festival. Not only the strange episode about the arranging of tables and chairs for the "victims" points in that direction, but also the circumstance that this combat of ᶜAnatu was actualized in the cult according to Myth and Ritual IV (KTU 1.13). Perhaps the pressing of the grapes by a girl formed part of that ritual. Cf. Isa. 63:1-6 and AOAT 16,94f.; NYCI 2,8; UF 12 (1980) 305ff. It may be noted that such a mock battle also took place during the Egyptian New Year, cf. Borghouts, *op. cit.* (n. 15), 18f. Finally it may be pointed out that exactly such a mock battle was enacted during the autumnal festival for the Hittite weather god, cf. O. R. Gurney, Some Aspects of Hittite Religion, Oxford 1977, 27,31,40. In Deut. 32:42; Ps. 68:22 and Ps. 110:6 it is YHWH who crushes the heads of his enemies.

[22] Like the earthly queens of Ugarit, most of the time.

[23] Cf. Esth. 1:10; Song of Songs 4:13f.

[24] The purple snail was used as a dye or paint. Autumn was the season for the fishing of purple snails, cf. AOAT 16,85ff.

[25] Ugarit and its harbour in mythological disguise, cf. AOAT 16,94, n. 3.

[26] Possibly "the men of the east" are Arab mercenaries whose presence at the festivities for the New Year would seem to be attested by Myth and Ritual I (note 13).

She attached the heads to her chest,
tied up the hands with her girdle.
She plunged her knees in the blood of the guards,
her buttocks in the gore of the warriors.[27]
With a staff she chased the old men,
with the stave of her bow the veterans.[28]
And look! ʿAnatu arrived at her house,
the goddess proceeded to her palace.
But she was not sated with her fighting in the plain,
the slaughtering between the two cities.
She arranged chairs for the warriors,
arranged tables for the soldiers,
stools for the heroes.[29]
ʿAnatu fought hard and looked around,
slaughtered and watched.
Her liver shook with laughter,[30]
her heart was filled with joy,[31]
the liver of ʿAnatu with triumph,
as she plunged (her) knees in the blood of the guards,
(her) buttocks in the gore of the warriors,
until she was sated with fighting in the house,
slaughtering between the tables.
The blood of the guards was wiped from the house,
oil of pacification was poured from a bowl.[32]

[27] Cf. Isa. 63:1-6; Rev. 14:18-20; 19:13,15.

[28] Possibly the veterans represented the Old Year. Cf. note 21.

[29] Clearly a feast for the army.

[30] Compare ANET, 580, line 40; Descent of Ishtar, 31.

[31] Cf. Ps. 16:9.

[32] The word translated by "pacification" is actually a type of oil-offering. See Ritual IV (KTU 1.119):24f. as compared to lines 20-22 of the same text (for the expression "former kingship" cf. Mic. 4:8). The pouring of oil was a rain-charm performed in autumn, cf. AOAT 16,100; UF 11 (1979) 645f.

The Virgin[33] *ʿAnatu washed her hands,*
the Wanton Widow of the Nations[34] *her fingers.*
She washed her hands of the blood of the guards,
her fingers of the gore of the warriors.
She stacked chairs on chairs,
tables on tables,
stools she stacked on stools.
She scooped up water and washed herself
with[35] *dew of heaven,*
oil of earth,[36]
with the drizzle of the Rider on the Clouds,[37]
dew that heaven poured out for her,
drizzle that the stars[38] *poured out for her.*

[33] The translation is inaccurate since ʿAnatu did have some sort of intercourse with her husband Baʿlu. See Loves II-III, Myth and Ritual IV. The term has a more specific meaning for which no proper equivalent exists in English. It designates a young woman who did not yet bring forth male offspring.

[34] Again a technical term, describing the goddess of love as the harlot of the world, like her Babylonian counterpart Ishtar. ʿAnatu received this epithet because she became a nubile widow when Baʿlu had died, cf. Baal VI (KTU 1.6):i.30f. The nearest male kin of her husband had to marry her according to the custom of the time. We know from the Bible that men obliged to marry such a young widow were often unwilling to fulfil their duty (Gen. 38:9; Deut. 25:7-10; Ruth 4:6). Women in this position had to go pretty far in trying to seduce the man (Gen. 38:14ff.; Ruth 3). As a result the *ybmt* acquired a reputation of lewdness. This is why ʿAnatu is the patroness of wanton love, the harlot of the world who virtually denies her widowhood (cf. Ez. 23:8, 21; Isa. 60:16; Rev. 17:2,15; 18:3,7, all patterned after the Canaanite goddess of love).

[35] Cf. Ex. 30:20.

[36] Cf. Gen. 27:28,39; Ps. 133:2f. Cf. H. J. Zobel, ZAW 82 (1970) 209-216. See note 31.

[37] Epithet of Baʿlu, depicting the weather god as the charioteer of the clouds. Cf. En.el. IV.50; Ps. 68:5,34; 104:3, Isa. 19:1; Deut. 33:26; AOAT 16,98; M. Dijkstra, Gods voorstelling, Kampen 1980, 293, n. 80. Also, in apparent opposition to the Canaanite conception, Job 38:28-38.

ʿAnatu is washing herself here in the first rain-like dew of autumn which signifies the return of Baʿlu from the Nether World. Possibly this episode corresponded to the rite of the Rain Bride in the actual cult of Ugarit. Cf. Aqhat, notes 181, 246, 249, 263; Myth and Ritual II, note 45.

[38] For the stars as a source of dew see CAD (K) 46; W. G. E. Watson, UF 9

III.

1 *She made herself up with the murex*
whose habitat covers a thousand acres in the sea.
(broken)

About 15 lines are missing. When the text resumes Baᶜlu is giving instructions to his servants. The first part of the column can partially be reconstructed with the help of another fragment.

3a [" [39] *on the herbs,*]
[*an effusion for her, the shower of the Most Graceful,*[40]]
[*abundant rain for her*].
[*Oil of pacification will be poured from a bowl.*]
[*The Virgin ᶜAnatu will wash her hands,*]
[*the Wanton Widow of the Nations her fingers.*]
[*She will take her lyre in her hands,*]
5 [*p*]*ut the beloved instrument*[41] *to her breast.*
She will sing of the love of Baᶜlu the Almighty,
the affection of Pidrayu, the girl of the honey-dew,
the passion of Tallayu, the girl of the mist,
the love of Arsayu, the girl of the ample flowing.[42]
Then, o lads, enter!

(1977) 274; A. Caquot et al., Textes ougaritiques, t.1., Paris 1974, 161f. Compare the "dew of lights", Isa.26:19, which is connected with resurrection.

[39] The text of lines 3^a-3^e can be restored on the basis of KTU 1.7:19ff. and 1.101:11ff.

[40] Because of the parallel Baal I (KTU 1.3):ii.40 "The Most Graceful" (*nᶜmn*) must be an epithet of Baᶜlu here. Compare Isa. 17:10, and note 353 below.

[41] Cf. KAR no. 16, Rev.6 (SAHG, 70).

[42] See note 18. During the Ugaritic New Year festival the sacred marriage was concluded. Even in ancient Israel the autumnal festival was still connected with the fertility of women. See the commentary on Myth and Ritual I (KTU 1.23). Among the Arab peasants autumn is the ideal time for weddings. Love-songs are heard almost daily. Cf. H. Granqvist, Marriage Conditions in a Palestinian Village, vol. 2, Helsingfors 1935, 32-39. It is possible that this joyful period is reflected in this episode of the myth.

Bow at the feet of ʿAnatu and fall down,
prostrate yourselves, honour her.
And say to the Virgin ʿAnatu,
repeat to the Wanton Widow of the Nations:
'A message from Baʿlu the Almighty,
a word from the Mightiest of heroes:
Oppose war on earth,[43]
put love-fruit in the ground,[44]
pour peace in the middle of the earth,[45]
tranquillity in the middle of the fields.
Hurry! Move on! Make haste![46]
Let your feet run to me,
let your legs rush to me!
For I have a word, which I want to speak to you,
a message which I want to communicate to you,
a word of trees and a whisper of stones,[47]
a groaning of the heavens to the earth,
of the Flood to the stars:

[43] Cf. CH col. XLVII.32f.; YOS, No.11:ii.1; Hos. 2:20; Ps.46:10. Warfare stopped in autumn, cf. AOAT 16,157f. The translation, however, is not entirely certain. A plausible alternative is "Put an offering of bread in the earth".

[44] This is probably the mythological prototype of a ritual act performed in connection with the season of ploughing (late autumn). The aphrodisiac involved is the mandrake, cf. Gen. 30:14-16; M. H. Pope, Song of Songs, Garden City 1977, 647ff.

[45] Probably corresponding to the pouring of the oil of pacification in the actual ritual. See notes 32, 36. For the idea of peace on earth: Lev. 26:6; Isa, 2:4; 57:19; Ps. 72:3; 85:10f.; Luke 2:14; Hesiod, Work and Days, 228; H. Gross, Die Idee des ewigen und allgemeinen Weltfriedens, 2.Aufl., Trier 1967; S. N. Kramer, in: Gesellschaftsklassen im Alten Zweistromland, München 1972, 113-121.

[46] The translation of this verse is uncertain. For a possible Akkadian parallel see W. G. E. Watson, UF 9 (1977) 274.

[47] The mysterious signs of nature announcing an impending change, an "electrified" atmosphere. Cf. Hos. 2:23f.; Ps. 19:2; 42:8; 96:12.

I understand the lightning which the heavens do not know,
a matter that mankind does not know,[48]
and the multitudes of the earth do not understand![49]
Come, I pray,
towards my mountain, the divine Sapanu,[50]
to the holy one, to the mountain of my heritage,[51]
to the lovely one, the hill of victory.'"[52]

[53]

Look! ᶜAnatu saw the two gods,[54]
with her, the feet began to totter,[55]
at her back the spine loosened,[56]
her face above began to sweat,
the joints of her spine shook,
the small of her back too.
She raised her voice and cried:
"Why have Gupanu and Ugaru arrived?

[48] Cf. Job 28:13; 37:5; 38:35.

[49] For the chiastic construction "understand" / / "do not understand" see Job 32:8f.; Prov. 28:5; Dan. 12:10. According to the beginning of the myth Baᶜlu possessed seven lightnings (Baal I, fragm. a (KTU 1.101):3, above p. 2). Apparently he now understands what to do with them (cf. Job 38:35).

Thunderstorms do not occur in summer. Only late in September they announce the arrival of the rains. So this too reflects the Syrian autumn (cf. AOAT 16,108).

[50] See note 4.

[51] Cf. Ex. 15:17; Deut. 32:8f.; Ps. 78:54.

[52] Presumably the victory which entitled Baᶜlu to take possession of Mt. Sapanu.

[53] At this point the scribe deliberately omitted the repetition of III.3^a-8. He indicates such omissions by a double line. This clearly implies that the texts were not meant to be read aloud, but had to be learnt by heart. See also notes 251, 317.

[54] Gupanu-and-Ugaru, the messengers of Baᶜlu. Messengers used to travel in pairs.

[55] A sign of fear, in Akkadian with the verb *tarāru*.

[56] She lost her composure. Cf. Ezek. 21:11; Dan. 5:6. Note the beautiful description of the coursing of the shiver, first upwards, then downwards.

What enemy has risen against Baʿlu?
What foe against the Rider on the Clouds?
Did I not slay Yammu, Beloved of Ilu?[57]
Did I not destroy River, the god of the Big Ones?[58]
Did I not muzzle Tunnanu?[59]
Did I not stop his mouth?
I did slay the coiling serpent,[60]
the tyrant with the seven heads!
I did slay Arishu,[61] *Beloved of Ilu!*
I silenced ʿAtiku,[62] *the bull-calf of Ilu!*

[57] God of the sea and rivers, son of Ilu. Compare Baal II-III (KTU 1.1-1.2). According to Baal III (KTU 1.2):iv and Baal V (KTU 1.5) (below pp. 69) the victory over Yammu and his monstrous helpers was Baʿlu's. See also Incantation I and II (KTU 1.82-83), as well as the following notes. For similar lists of defeated monsters see J. S. Cooper, The Return of Ninurta (AnOr 52), Roma 1978, 141ff.

[58] *I.e.*, the big monsters supporting the sea-god. Compare Baal VI (KTU 1.6): v. 1-4, as well as Enuma elish, IV.107ff., the Greek Hydra and the biblical Rahab, Isa. 51:9; Ps. 89:11; Job 9:13; 26:12, also Ps. 29:3; 74:13f., 93:4. Cf. O. Kaiser, Die mythische Bedeutung des Meeres in Ägypten, Ugarit und Israel (BZAW, 28), 2.Aufl., Berlin 1962; J. Day, God's Conflict with the Dragon and the Sea, Cambridge 1985; C. Kloos, Yhwh's Combat with the Sea, Leiden 1986.

[59] Our word "tuna", Hebrew Tannin. Cf. Job 38:8ff.; Ps. 74:13ff.; 89:10f.; Rev. 13:1ff.

The translation of *šbm* by "to muzzle" is practically certain. The Egyptian Apophis-serpent was kept on a leash, cf. E. Hornung, Ägyptische Unterweltsbücher, 2.Aufl., Zürich 1984, 284, 300f. See also Enuma elish IV.117; Job 40:29; 41:5.

The parallel *ʾištm.lh* should not be emended to *ʾištm*dh (so D. Pardee, UF 16 (1984) 252, after collation), but should be maintained as *lectio difficilior*. For the correct interpretation see G. del Olmo Lete, MLC, 634.

[60] Compare the partial quotation from Baal V (KTU 1.5):iff. in Isa. 27:1. Also Lugal-e, 133, and note 325 below.

[61] Cf. Baal VI (KTU 1.6):vi.51 where it is Kotharu who has to vanquish this monster. The text is uncertain, however, and "the Beloved of Ilu, Earth" is a plausible alternative. Cf. UF 16 (1984) 248.

[62] Cf. Incantation V (KTU 1.108):11f.

I did slay Ishatu,[63] *the bitch of Ilu!*
I did destroy Dhubabu,[64] *the daughter of Ilu!*
I shall battle for the silver,
(and) gain possession of the gold

IV.

of anyone who tries to expel Baʿlu from the heights of Sapanu,
who tries to make (him) fly up like a bird from his aerie,
who tries to chase him from the chair of his kingship,
from the seat of the throne of his dominion!
What enemy has risen against Baʿlu?
What foe against the Rider on the Clouds?"
The lads answered,
they answered her:
"No enemy has risen against Baʿlu!
No foe against the Rider on the Clouds!
A message from Baʿlu the Almighty,
a word from the Mightiest of heroes:
'Oppose war on earth,[65]
put love-fruit in the ground,
pour peace in the middle of the earth,
tranquillity in the middle of the fields.
Hurry! Move on! Make haste!
Let your feet run to me,
let your legs rush to me!
For I have a word which I want to speak to you,
a message which I want to communicate to you,
a word of trees and a whisper of stones,
a word that mankind does not know,
and the multitudes of the earth do not understand,

[63] Literally "Fire". Compare Baal III (KTU 1.2):i.32 for other fiery helpers of Yammu. Cf. Ps.29:7.

[64] A monstrous fly whose name has been preserved in Baal Zebub, 2 Ki. 1:2-17. Cf. JEOL 27 (1981-82) 114ff.

[65] See notes 43-45.

a groaning of the heavens to the earth
of the Flood to the stars:
I understand the lightning which the heavens do not know!
Come, I pray,
towards my mountain, the divine Sapanu,
to the holy one, to the mountain of my heritage!'"
And the Virgin ʿAnatu answered,
the Wanton Widow of the Nations replied:
"Should I oppose war on earth?
Put love-fruit in the ground?
Pour peace in the middle of the earth?
Tranquillity in the middle of the fields?
Let Baʿlu put his thunderbolt [in the sky],
let [the god Haddu] kindle his flash!
Then I will oppose war on earth,
put love-fruit in the ground,
pour peace in the middle of the earth,
tranquillity in the middle of the fields.
And I have still something else to say:
Go, go, attendants of the gods!
You should depart, and I too will leave
Ughra,[66] *(heading) for the remotest of the gods,*[67]
Inbubu, (heading) for the remotest of the ghosts,
two layers below the furrows of the earth,
three strata of the lowest realms!"
Then she headed straight
for Baʿlu in the heights of Sapanu.

[66] The vocalisation of Ughra and Inbubu is uncertain. The latter toponym might mean "the Flute". Both are designations of the mountain where ʿAnatu dwells (see Myth and Ritual IV (KTU 1.13):9).

[67] The deities were able to travel by air or, if they preferred to go unnoticed, by subterranean routes.

Over a thousand acres,
ten thousand square miles,[68]
Baᶜlu saw his sister[69] *coming,*
(*saw*) *the Wanton Widow of his father*[70] *approaching.*
He removed the women from his presence.
He set an ox before her,
a fatling right in front of her.
She scooped up water and washed herself
with dew of heaven,
oil of earth,[71]
dew that heaven poured out for her,
drizzle that the stars poured out for her.[72]
She made herself up with the murex[73]
whose habitat covers a thousand acres in the sea.
(broken)

About 15 lines are missing. During their conversation Baᶜlu complains to ᶜAnatu about his miserable quarters.[74]

47a "*Now there is no house for Baᶜlu like the* (*other*) *gods* (*have*),
no residence like the sons of Athiratu (*have*)!

[68] Actually the measures mentioned in the text are both about 600 square metres. The Ugaritic poets often stress the extraordinary powers of vision of gods and legendary heroes.

[69] "Sister" and "brother" were designations of lovers. ᶜAnatu is the wife of Baᶜlu. Cf. Song of Songs 5:1f.

[70] An important variant reading of her more common epithet "the Wanton Widow of the Nations". Baᶜlu's father Daganu and his male offspring were under the obligation to marry "the Wanton Widow" when her husband Baᶜlu had died without giving her a son. See UF 12 (1980) 308f. and notes 33-34 above.

[71] Cf. notes 35-37.

[72] See note 38.

[73] See note 24.

[74] Compare Baal IV (KTU 1.4):iii.12ff.

Ilu's dwelling is the shelter of his son,[75]
the dwelling of Lady Athiratu of the Sea,
the dwelling of Pidrayu, the girl of the honey-dew,
the shelter of Tallayu, the girl of the mist,
the dwelling of Arsayu, the girl of the ample flowing,[76]
the dwelling of the respectable brides!"
And the Virgin ᶜAnatu answered:
"The Bull Ilu, my father, will return to me,
he will return to me, and I shall return to him![77]

I shall make sure I drag him like a lamb to the ground,[78]
I shall make his grey hair run with blood,[79]
the grey hair of his old age[80] *with gore,*
if he does not give a house to Baᶜlu like the (other) gods (have),
and a residence like the sons of Athiratu (have)!"
She shuffled her feet and flew up from the earth.
Then she headed straight
for Ilu at the fountain-head of the two Rivers,
in the middle of the bedding of the two Floods.[81]

[75] "His son" is actually "his son-in-law" Baᶜlu who was lodged with Ilu before he was able to build his own house. The temple of Ilu in Ugarit was older than that of Baᶜlu.

[76] See note 18.

[77] A standard phrase in Ugaritic, as in Hebrew: Zech. 1:3; Mal. 3:7; 2 Chr. 30:6. Ilu shares the title of "Bull" with the Egyptian high god Amun-Re. It indicates their potency as creator-gods. Cf. Gen. 49:24; Isa. 49:26; 60:16; Ps. 132:2,5; Jer. 46:15.

[78] *I.e.*, to slaughter him in the manner lambs were slaughtered.

[79] Cf. 1 Ki. 2:9.

[80] Cf. Isa. 46:4.

[81] Like the Babylonian god Marduk (Enuma elish IV.135ff.) and YHWH/El the God of Israel (cf. Gen. 1:6; 2 Sam. 22:16; Ps. 36:7; Job 28:11; 38:16; Prov. 3:19f.) the Ugaritic Ilu was held responsible for the separation of the cosmic waters. The Canaanites distinguished an Upper Flood above the firmament from the Lower Flood below the earth. Ilu dwelt at the confluence of the two *i.e.* at the horizon of the habitable cosmos. Cf. Gilg. XI.195f.; Koran XVIII.61f.; Ps. 29:10.

She appeared in the encampment of Ilu[82]
and entered the camp of the King, the Father of Years,[83]
she entered the stronghold,
the encampment of the Creator and Lord of the gods.[84]
The Bull Ilu her father heard her voice.
From the seven chambers[85] *Ilu answered,*
from the eight entrances of lockable rooms:
"*The shadow [o]ver him is gr[eat],*
[ ] *my eye espies.*
[ ]
over him [ ]
[ ]
at the feet of the lads [of Yammu]
[ ][86]
I am really a[fraid]!
What [enemy will rise] against him?
The Lamp of the gods, Shapshu, has a dusty colour,
the heavens are soiled by Motu, the son of Ilu!"[87]

[82] In the texts of Ugarit "encampment" is a metaphor for territory and "tent" a metaphor for dwelling. Cf. Job 5:24; Ps. 15:1, etc. In the case of Ilu it is possible that he is depicted as a tent-dweller because it was he who stretched out the heavens like a tent. Cf. Isa. 40:22; Ps. 19:5. It is clear, however, that Ilu owned a palace of his own. See also V.26ff. It is certain that this episode, too, was actualized in the cult of Ugarit. See Myth and Ritual IV, notes 30-35.

[83] An epithet describing Ilu as the oldest among the gods. Cf. Ps. 90:2-4; 102:25,28; Job 10:5; 36:26.

[84] The Ugaritic term for Lord is *ʾadn*, related to Hebrew *ʾādōn* and *ʾădōnay*. Cf. O. Eissfeldt, ThWAT 1,65. See also: The Bible World. Essays in Honor of C. H. Gordon, New York 1980, 171ff. Baʿlu received the same title, cf. note 435 and Keret, note 83.

[85] For the chambers and lockable rooms of God, cf. Job 37:9.

[86] Although the tablet is badly damaged at this point it would seem that Ilu foresees the misfortunes which will befall Baʿlu. Just as he dreams about the resurrection of Baʿlu later on in Baal VI (KTU 1.6:III-IV). Ilu is omniscient.

[87] A bad omen, cf. Baal IV (KTU 1.4):vii.56f.;viii.21ff.; Baal VI (KTU 1.6):ii.24f. Motu is the god of death who will summon Baʿlu to descend into his dreary realm in Baal V (KTU 1.5).

And the Virgin ʿAnatu answered:
"Let not the sons of your mansion, o Ilu,
let not the daughters of your mansion rejoice,
let not the children of your palace rejoice![88]
I shall make sure I seize them with my right hand,[89]
I shall strike them with my long, mighty arm![90]
I shall strike you on your skull,
make your grey hair run with blood,
the grey hair of your old age with gore!"
And Ilu answered from the seven chambers,
from the eight entrances of lockable rooms:
"I know you, my daughter, (I know) that you are like a man,[91]
(and) that among goddesses your scorn is unequalled!
What do you want, o Virgin ʿAnatu?"
And the Virgin ʿAnatu answered:
"Your judgment, Ilu, is wise.[92]
May your wisdom last forever!
Long live the sharpness of your judgment!
Baʿlu the Almighty is our king,
our judge - nobody is over him.[93]

The interpretation of this verse is disputed, but from a purely philological point of view the translation chosen is the most plausible one.

Motu is the god of the sirocco, a hot desert wind obscuring the sun with dust. It blows in spring and occasionally in autumn when it is not really dangerous any more. See AOAT 16,114f., 173ff., 187ff. and note 470 below.

[88] Not only declared enemies of Baʿlu like Yammu and Motu, but also other members of Ilu's family used to rejoice in the misfortunes of their brother-in-law. Cf. Baal VI (KTU 1.6):i.39ff.

[89] Cf. Enuma elish IV.37.

[90] Cf. Ex. 15:16; Num. 11:23; Isa. 50:2; 59:1; Ps. 79:11 and for some Babylonian parallels UF 7 (1975) 193.

[91] Like her foreign counterparts the Babylonian Ishtar, the Hurrian Shaushka and the Phoenician Tinnit, the goddess ʿAnatu has androgynous traits.

[92] Cf. 1 Ki. 3:28; Isa. 31:2; Jer. 10:12; 51:15; Ps. 104:24; Job 11:6; 12:13; 28:23; 37:16; Prov. 3:19; 8:22ff.; Dan. 2:20.

[93] Cf. Enuma elish IV.21,28; Isa. 33:22; Ps. 95:3.

All of us must bring him gifts,[94]
all of us must bring him the cup!"
The Bull Ilu, his father, groaned (and) cried out,
Ilu, the King who had created him,[95]
Athiratu and her sons cried out,
the Goddess and the troop of her kin:
"Now there is no house for Baʿlu like the (other) gods (have),
no residence like the sons of Athiratu (have)!
Ilu's dwelling is the shelter of his son,
the dwelling of Lady Athiratu of the Sea,
the dwelling of Pidrayu, the girl of the honey-dew,
the shelter of Tallayu, the girl of the mist,
the dwelling of Arsayu, the girl of the ample flowing,
the dwelling of the respectable brides!"
(broken)

Only a few illegible traces remain in the next 25 lines between column V and column VI.[96] It seems that it is Athiratu who sends her personal attendant Qidshu-and-Amruru to the divine technician, Kotharu-and-Khasisu.[97] Since she was with Ilu in column V it is possible that Ilu and Athiratu decided to consult the builder on the matter of costs in the missing part of the text.

[94] Cf. Baal III (KTU 1.2):i.19; Baal I (KTU 1.3):iii.46f.; Enuma elish IV.44; V.80; VII.110, as well as 4 R 61:IV.52 proving that presents could be offered in a cup.

[95] Not "her" because before Baal IV (KTU 1.4):iv.47 Athiratu, the wife of Ilu, is speaking. Even though Daganu was the physical father of Baʿlu, his father-in-law was still regarded as his creator. Compare Deut. 32:6 and the discussion in: The Bible World. Essays in Honor of C. H. Gordon, New York 1980, 173.

[96] The proposal of M. Dijkstra, BiOr 39 (1982) 151f. and UF 15 (1983) 28-30 to insert the fragment KTU 1.8 at this point is untenable. There is no way to make the fragment KTU 1.8 match the traces of CTA, Pl.V. Moreover, it is Qidshu-and-Amruru who is sent to Kotharu, not Gupanu-and-Ugaru.

[97] For that reason we read the damaged signs in line 24 as *ṯḥm ʾad*[*ty*].

"[*Ca*]*rr*[*y my message in*] *your head,*
[*my words*] *between your eyes.*[98]
[*And pass*] *over a thousand* [*acres of*] *sea,*
ten thousand [*square mile*]*s of the two Rivers.*[99]
Pass Byblos,
pass Qaʿilu,
pass the islands of Noph.[100]
Cleave the skies,
o Fisherman of Athiratu,
come on, o Qidshu-Amruru!
Then you must head straight
for all Divine Egypt.
Kaphtor is the throne he sits on,
Egypt the land of his inheritance.[101]
Over a thousand acres,
ten thousand square miles,
bow at the feet of Kotharu and fall down,
prostrate yourselves and honour him,
and say to Kotharu-and-Khasisu,
repeat to the Skilful, the Craftsman:
'*A message from* [*my*] *Mistress,* [*Lad*]*y* [*Athiratu:*]' "
(broken)

[98] Cf. Deut. 6:8; 11:18; Y. Avishur, UF 12 (1980) 125ff.

[99] The two streams enclosing the abode of Ilu. See note 81.

[100] The messenger flies bird-like, first crossing the sea between the abode of Ilu in the West and the mainland, then taking a route from North to South over Canaan and the "islands of Noph (= Memphis)", *i.e.* finally crossing the delta of the Nile. A reference to bird-migration? Cf. note 301.

[101] Kaphtor is Crete. Like many of his earthly colleagues the divine artisan was equally at home at the two centres of art and technology of that period.

The expression "land of his inheritance" is interesting from the viewpoint of the history of religion. Cf. Deut. 32:8f. Also Baal I (KTU 1.3):iii.30.

Baal II

KTU 1.1

The second tablet of the series is KTU 1.1. Between KTU 1.3:VI and KTU 1.1:II (the first column is lost) 90 to 140 lines are missing. As far as the fragmentary col. II allows us to form an idea about the action, it seems that ᶜAnatu has complained about other gods harassing her, presumably in connection with the building plans of her husband Baᶜlu, which understandably excited envy. Ilu promises help and asks ᶜAnatu to come to him with a list of materials needed for Baᶜlu's palace.

II.

''*Hurry*! *Move on*! *Make haste*! [102]
  Let your feet run to me,
    let your legs rush to me,
      in the middle of Khurshanu! [103]
[*For I want to spea*]*k a* [*mess*]*age to you*:
[*I*] *will put* [*a spell on your enemies*],
  [*sorcery*] *o*[*n*] *those who harass you*!
[*Take a list of l*]*apis-stones* [*in your hand*],
  [*a list of gold in your right hand*],
[*so that they can be c*]*arried into* [*your palace*],
  [ ].
I shall bind [ ],
  [ ]*s*,
    may die [ ]!

[102] See note 46.

[103] Or: ''mountain range''. In any case it designates the region at the edge of the world where Ilu lives. In Baal II (KTU 1.1):iii.12 it is called ''the mountain of the cup'', possibly the cup of destiny which Ilu takes in his hand when he is going to bless someone. Cf. UF 7 (1975) 177f.

[Let his soul go forth like wind],
[his life] like spittle!"
[Ilu] did put [a spell] on the earth,
[on the ground],
[s]orcery he put [on   ].
[One day, two days] passed,
[then Qidshu-and-Amruru li]stened.[104]
Then [Qidshu headed straight]
[for] Inbubu.[105]
Over a thousand residences,
[ten thousand mansions],
[Amruru bowed at the fe]et of ʿAnatu [and fell down],
he prostrated himself and honoured her.
He raised his voice and cried:
"A message from the Bull Ilu, your father,
a word from the Benevolent, your sire:
'Oppose war on earth,[106]
put love-fruit in the ground,
pour peace in the middle of the earth,
tranquillity in the middle of the fields.
Hurry! Move on! Make haste!
Let your feet run to me,
let your legs rush to me,
in the middle of Khurshanu!
[For I must speak a message to you:]
[Take] a list [of lapis-stones] in your hand,
[a list of gold in] your [r]ight hand,' "
(broken)

[104] Units of time do not have literal meaning in the myth, cf. note 122.
[105] See note 66.
[106] See notes 43-46.

About 35 lines are missing between the fragments of KTU 1.1:II and III. It seems that the preparations are now complete and that the actual building is commissioned to Kotharu, the architect and technician of the gods. Ilu is speaking:

III.

"Kaphtor is the throne he sits on,
Egypt the land of his inheritance.[107]
Over a thousand acres,
ten thousand square miles,
bow at the feet of Kotharu and fall down,
prostrate yourselves and honour him.
And say to Kotharu-and-Khasisu,
repeat to the Skilful, the Craftsman:
'A message from the Bull Ilu, your father,
a word from the Benevolent, your sire:
[Ha! Kotharu, (you) builder]!
Ha! Kotharu, (you) buil[der of homes for the gods]!
(You) who sets [costly stones] in the construction of dwel[ling places],
who founds dwel[lings of] on the rock![108]
Hurry! Move on! Make haste!
Let your feet run to me,
let your legs rush to me,
in the middle of Khurshanu, the Mountain of the Cup![109]
For I have a word which I want to speak to you,
a message which I want to communicate to you,

[107] See note 101.

[108] Cf. Num. 24:21; Matth. 7:24f. Apparently Ilu wants to stress that Kotharu has to start with laying the foundation. Late autumn was a suitable time to start excavation work for the foundations of a building because in summer the soil was too dry and hard (cf. AOAT 16,112f.). It should be noted that "to lay a foundation" was equivalent to "to build a house" (cf. S. Krauss, Talmudische Archäologie, Bd. 1, Leipzig 1910, 22) so that there is no contradiction between this passage and the actual commissioning of Kotharu in col. III.26-29.

[109] Cf. note 103.

a word of trees and a whisper of stones,
a groaning of the heavens to the earth,
of the Flood to the stars,
a word that mankind does not know,
and the multitudes of the earth do not understand.[110]
Come, I pray,
towards Khurshanu!' "
And Kotharu-and-Khasisu answered:
"Go, go, attendants of the gods!
You should depart, and I too will leave
Kaphtor, (heading) for the remotest of the gods,[111]
Egypt, (heading) for the remotest of the ghosts,
two layers below the furrows of the earth,
three strata of the lowest realms!"
Thereupon he headed straight
for the Benevolent, Ilu the good-natured,
on Khurshanu, the Mountain of the Cup.
He appeared in the encampment of Ilu[112]
and entered the camp of the King, the Father of Years.[113]
At the feet of Ilu he bowed and fell down,
prostrated himself and honoured him.
And the Bull Ilu, his father, said:
["Ha! Kotharu, (you) builder!]
[Build] a man[sion] quickly,
[set up a palace quickly]
in the middle of [the highlands of Sapanu[114]*],*
[on the mountain of Ba^{c}lu],
[on the hill of the son of Daganu]!
(broken)

[110] Cf. note 49.
[111] Cf. note 67.
[112] Cf. note 82.
[113] Cf. note 83.
[114] Cf. note 4.

50 to 70 lines are missing between the end of column III and the beginning of column IV. This lacuna is much too small for any serious building activities to have taken place. Little more than the foundations (cf. III.8-9) can have been laid. In column IV, however, Baʿlu seems to have fallen into disgrace. Acting on the complaints of a goddess, probably Athiratu, Ilu decides to appoint his own son Yammu, god of the sea, as viceroy instead of Baʿlu. It seems that the inconvenience caused by the ground-work provided Athiratu with a suitable excuse to lay this plot against Baʿlu. Yammu is invited to take over the unfinished palace of Baʿlu. The omniscient Ilu knows beforehand, however, that Baʿlu will ultimately defeat Yammu (IV.26-27).

On the one hand this reconstruction of the events described in column IV explains why Ilu, without a qualm, hands over the seemingly unsuspecting Baʿlu to the lackeys of Yammu in KTU 2:I. On the other hand it hints at the fact that soon afterwards Yammu himself has to surrender to Baʿlu without receiving any support from his father Ilu (2:IV).

The goddess (Athiratu) is complaining:

IV.

"[heigh]ts of Sapanu [ ].
Cry aloud to those near[*by*],
[ ] *to those far away,*
to [ ] *cry* [*aloud*]!
Ilu is sitting with his dr[*inking society*],
[Ilu does not notice] *the shameful conduct of the usurper*! [115]

[115] "Usurper": literally "child-of-whom?", *i.e.* a nonety. Here it is apparently a derisive designation of Baʿlu. Ilu is similarly chided for lack of concern in Myth and Ritual III (KTU 1.114). Baʿlu's offense seems to be that he walks hurriedly around (see note 413 below), creating a mess of mud and overflowing sludge by his rains. December is the month with the highest amount of rainfall. The roads become muddy, and all building activities have to stop temporarily (cf. AOAT 16,121).

You should [ ] the gods,
the house of Baᶜlu surely [ ].
[ ]
so that he cannot walk around in a hurry.
On the e[arth],
on the ground a mess of mud!
He gives [us loam to eat],
gives masses of sludge to drink!
He puts [a cup (of it) into our hands],
a beaker into both our hands.
[ ] *like crumbs,*
like gravel are gathered [ ].
Ilu should appoint his son as his deputy,
the Bull [Ilu should appoint Yawwu[116] *as his deputy]!"*
And the Benevolent, Ilu the good-natured, answered:
"*My son [shall not be called] by the name of Yawwu, o goddess,*
[but Yammu shall be his name[117]*]!"*
So he proclaimed the name of Yammu.
[Lady Athiratu] *answered:*
"*For our maintenance [you are the one who has been proclaimed],*
you are the one who has been proclaimed 'master'!"[118]
[And the Bull Ilu answered:]

[116] It is not very likely that this name has anything to do with that of YHWH, the God of Israel (cf. AOAT 16,118f.). From a philological point of view, however, the connection is possible, because verbs from roots primae-H could loose the H in the imperfect. If it is true that in southern Canaan YHWH was a rival of Baal whereas in northern Canaan Baal prevailed (so J. C. de Moor, Uw God is mijn God. Over de oorsprong van het geloof in de ene God, Kampen 1983), the equation of YHWH with Yammu was a possible way to explain his demise theologically, because in the end Baᶜlu defeated Yammu (Baal III (KTU 1.2):iv).

[117] Renaming took place at important turns of the life of the persons renamed, cf. Gen. 17:5,15; 32:29; Enuma elish V.109f.; Atra-hasis I.245f.; O. Eissfeldt, in: P. R. Ackroyd—B. Lindars (eds.), Words and Meanings. Essays ... D. Winton Thomas, Cambridge 1968, 69-79.

[118] Cf. Enuma elish IV.11; VI.88; VII.7.

"I myself, the Benevolent, Ilu the good-natured,
[have taken you] in my hands,[119]
I have proclaimed [your name].
[Yammu is your name],
your name is Beloved of I[lu Yammu].
[And I shall give you] a house of my own silver,[120]
[a palace] of [gold].
[You may take it] from the hand of Baʿlu the Almighty,
[from the hand of the son of Daganu],
because he has reviled us [ ],
[ ].
Chase him away from the chair of his kingship,
from the seat of the throne of his dominion,
make (him) fl[y up like a bird from his aerie]!
But if, however, [you do] not [chase him away],
he will beat you like [ ],
[ ]!"
Ilu sacrificed [in his house],
[gave a banquet for] the naming of [his] son,
[ ].
He slaughtered oxen,
and small stock as well.
He slew bulls
and the fattest of rams,
yearling calves,
sheep, a multitude of lambkins.[121]
(broken)

[119] Cf. Hos. 11:3; Ps. 91:12.
[120] Ilu had paid for the palace of Baʿlu, cf. Baal II (KTU 1.1):ii-iii.
[121] Many lambs and calves were born in November-December, cf. AOAT 16,122f. Even the author of Enoch 82:19 knew that the sexual activity of sheep increases with the decreasing length of the days.

Not only are some 35 lines missing between the end of column IV and the beginning of column V, but what remains of column V is badly damaged so that its interpretation is very uncertain. Baˁlu seems to sense that Ilu is plotting against him and he will be imprisoned in the dreary realm of the sea-god "bound between the stones of the stream-bed". In Baal IV (KTU 1.4:VII) Baˁlu has a similar vision, and feels he will soon be threatened by Motu, the god of death.

[ ]
  [ ]
And one day, two days passed,
  (another) month came.[122]
The soul of [Baˁlu scrutinized him (Ilu)[123]*],*
  [the heart of Had]du scrutinized him.
[Baˁlu prepared a young deer*] on Sapanu,*
  [ ] *a haunch.*
In the spring [ ],
  [in the f]ountains.
[Baˁlu the Almighty] said:
"I know [for sure],
  [I perceive with certainty]
[that you] would imprison me, [Bull Ilu the good-natured],
  that you would bind [your son between the stones],
    [be]tween the stones of the stream-bed!

[122] In the myth, everything that takes only a few days or weeks on earth is taking months or even years, and *vice versa*. Cf. AOAT 16, 33.

We have now arrived in the part of the myth representing the winter. Baˁlu prepares a deer or a doe for himself. The cold season, especially when snow made it easy to track down the game, was the preferred time for hunting. Cf. KTU 1.92 (UF 17 (1986) 225ff.); 2 Sam. 23:20; G. Jacob, Altarabisches Beduinenleben, Berlin 1897, 117f.; A. Jaussen, Coutumes des Arabes au Pays de Moab, Paris 1907, 282.

[123] *I.e.*, his father-in-law Ilu.

[You re]quest [the right to enter my house],
and [you covet] the mountain I have been given,
[you want to take over the c]ella[124] *on the crest!*
Can anybody protecting what has been given to him
[comply with your request?]
[ ]?''
And one day, two days passed,
(another) month came.
The soul of [Baʿlu scrutinized him],
[the hear]t of Haddu scrutinized him.
[Baʿlu prepared] a young deer *on Sapanu,*
[ ] *the* leg *of a doe.*
[In the spring],
[*in] the fountains.*
[Baʿlu the Almighty] said [to Ilu:]
''*I know for sure, [o Ilu],*
[I perceive with certainty]
[that] you would imprison me, Bull Ilu [the good-natured],
[that you] would bind [your son] between the stones,
[between the stones] of the stream-bed.
[You request] the right to enter [my house],
[and] you covet the mountain I have been given,
[you want to take over the cella on its crest]!
Can anybody protecting what has been given to him
comply with [your re]quest?
How you covet it! How you want to take it over!
[ ]
[ ] *on earth*''
(broken)

[124] If the reading *prq* ''cella'' is correct, it appears that up to this episode of the myth only a relatively small structure had been erected.

Baal III

KTU 1.2

The third tablet of the Baal series is KTU 1.2, written by the same scribe Ilimilku, but here he chose to divide the tablet into four instead of the usual six columns (Baal, I, II, V, VI; Baal IV has eight columns). As a result the lines on this tablet are abnormally long.

Between Baal II (KTU 1.1) and Baal III (KTU 1.2) about 100 normal lines (Baal II) and up to 20 long lines (Baal III) are missing. Yet we have no reason to suspect any major development has taken place. Baᶜlu is still quarreling with Yammu over the latter's right to assume power and take over Baᶜlu's property after Ilu appointed him as his steward and promised him Baᶜlu's palace (Baal II:iv).

The struggle between Yammu, the sea-god, and Baᶜlu, the god responsible for rain, storms and fertility, represents the mythological prototype of the short Syrian winter with its gales, rain, hail and occasional high tides.[125]

[ ]
[ ]
[ ]
"*You were the one who rebell*[*ed*]
[ ]
[ ]
You were the one who rose against [ ]
[ ]
[ ]".
[*And*] *Baᶜlu the Almighty* [*answered*:]
"[ ]

[125] See AOAT 16,140-142, with some additions and corrections below.

[ ] *your dominion,*
[your] ruler[ship]!
[Yagrush[126] *will strike you on the shoulder],*
Ayyamur (will strike) you on the head!"
[And his Highness Yammu answered],
Judge Naharu[127] *[replied]:*
*"O Ba*ʿ*lu, Horonu*[128] *break -,*
Horonu break your head,
(and) ʿ*Athtartu, consort of Ba*ʿ*lu, your skull!*
[May you go] down [to the p]lace of death,[129]
may you fall down at the height of your years,
in the prime of your strength, and yet be humbled![130]
[Like the F]ather of Years[131] *you [take] two wives,*[132]
[ ]!"
Yammu sent messengers,
Judge Naharu an envoy.

[126] Again Baʿlu gives a fine example of his ability to foresee future developments (cf. Baal II:v and IV:vii). Yagrush and Ayyamur are the names of the magic weapons he will eventually use to defeat Yammu (Baal III (KTU 1.2):iv).

It is likely that the speech of Baʿlu in lines 4-6 was related to Yammu by messengers because according to line 21 Baʿlu is in the assembly of the gods at this moment.

[127] Naharu means "River, Stream". Possibly he was also called "Judge" because the deceased were thought to be judged on the bank of the River of Death. Compare Baal V (KTU 1.5):i.18-22 where it is Naharu who mixes the cup of Motu (Death). In the cup is the "clay" (flesh) of mortals.

[128] God of black magic, master of evil demons.

[129] Cf. Deut. 28:43; Prov. 15:24. On *mmt* as a designation of the realm of death see Job 33:22 and AOAT 16,186. Cf. note 385 below.

[130] A shorter version of the same curse occurs in Keret III (KTU 1.16):vi.54ff. Cf. Isa. 38:10; 65:20; Ps. 102:25; Job 15:32; Descent of Ishtar, 34-36.

[131] *I.e.*, the head of the pantheon Ilu. See note 83.

[132] Ilu has amorous affairs with two women at the same time in Myth and Ritual I (KTU 1.23):30ff. and II (KTU 1.12):i.5ff. The consorts of Baʿlu were ʿAnatu and her double ʿAthtartu. According to column III Yammu resented the fact that he did not have a wife.

With jubilant cries they flew heavenwards,[133]
[ ],
the bills of their beaks (open) to a span.[134]
"Depart, lads, do not tarry!
Then you shall head straight
for the Congregation assembled[135]
on Lelu's[136] *mountain.*
Do not fall at the feet of Ilu,[137]
do not prostrate yourselves in the Congregation assembled.
Stand (and) tell what you have to tell,
repeat what you know.
And say to the Bull, my father Ilu,
repeat to the Congregation assembled:
'A message from Yammu, your lord,
from your master[138], *Judge Naharu:*
Give up, o gods, him whom you protect,
him whom you protect, o crowd!
Give up Baʿlu and his attendants,
the son of Daganu whose gold I am to inherit!' "[139]
The lads did depart, they did not tarry.
Then they headed straight
for Lelu's mountain,
for the Congregation assembled.

[133] The messengers took the form of birds. See note 100, O. Keel, Vögel als Boten, Freiburg 1977, and Keret, note 96.

[134] A description of their terrifying hawk-like appearance.

[135] Of the gods. The somewhat pleonastic expression has parallels in Ugaritic (*pẖr qbṣ*) and Hebrew (*qhl ʿdt*, Ex. 12:6; Num. 14:5).

[136] Probably the god of the night who acted as the nominal president of the assembly of the gods, like Nusku in some Mesopotamian traditions, cf. AOAT 16,128.

[137] Un unbelievable effrontery.

[138] Yammu had been proclaimed master of the gods in Baal II (KTU 1.1):iv.17.

[139] Ilu had promised him the gold in Baal II:iv.20. Daganu is the father of Baʿlu.

The gods were seated eating,
the sons of Qudshu[140] *were dining.*
Baʿlu was standing by Ilu.
Look! The gods saw them,
they saw the messengers of Yammu,
the envoys of Judge Naharu.
The gods lowered their heads
on to their knees[141]
and on to their exalted thrones.
Baʿlu rebuked them:
"*Why, gods, do you lower your heads*
on to your knees
and on to your exalted thrones?
Alone I will answer, gods,
the (words on the) tablets[142] *of the messengers of Yammu,*
of the envoys of Judge Naharu.
Gods, lift up your heads
from your knees,
from your exalted thrones!
For I am going to answer the messengers of Yammu,
the envoys of Judge Naharu."
The gods lifted up their heads
from their knees,
from their exalted thrones.
Then the messengers of Yammu arrived,
the envoys of Judge Naharu.
They did not fall at the feet of Ilu,
did not prostrate themselves in the Congregation assembled.

[140] Name of Athiratu, mother of the gods. Both Athiratu and Qudshu mean "holy place, sanctuary".

[141] Cf. 1 Ki. 18:42; Lam. 2:10; J. B. Bauer, Hermes 87 (1959) 383f.

[142] Messengers brought along tablets confirming their orally delivered message.

They stood (and) told what they had to tell,
repeated what they knew.
They looked like fire, two fires,[143]
their t[ongue] was a sharpened sword.[144]
They said to the Bull Ilu, his father:
"A message from Yammu, your lord,
from your master, Judge Naharu:
Give up, (o) gods, him whom you protect,
him whom you protect, (o) crowd!
Give up Baʿlu and his attendants,
the son of Daganu whose gold I am to inherit!"
And the Bull Ilu, his father, answered:
"Baʿlu is your slave, o Yammu,
Baʿlu is your slave, Naharu,
the son of Daganu is your prisoner![145]
He also must bring you tribute, like the (other) gods,
he also must bring you gifts, like the sons of Qudshu!"[146]
His Highness Baʿlu became angry.
[And he too]k a slaughtering-axe in his hand,
he ra[ised] a slayer of lads in his right hand.
[ʿAna]tu took [his hand],
ʿAthtartu took his left hand:[147]

143 Cf. Maqlû VI.121f.; Ps. 104:4; Job 41:11. In Ex. 3:2 the messenger ("angel") of YHWH appears in flames of fire. See also Judg. 13:20; 2 Ki. 2:11; 1 Cor. 3:13; 2 Thess. 1:8; Rev. 9:17f.; 11:5; and note 63.

144 Cf. Ps. 57:5, also 52:4; 64:4; 140:4.

145 This treacherous act is the outcome of the plot laid against Baʿlu in Baal II:iv, cf. II:v.9f.,22f. (KTU 1.1:iv-v). Prisoners of war were employed as slaves by their captors. Cf. Ps. 79:10f.

146 As in the human world (*e.g.* Ps. 72:10), all gods were obliged to pay tribute to the overlord of the moment. In Baal I (KTU 1.3):v.33f. it was still Baʿlu himself who enjoyed this privilege. See note 94.

For a different restoration of the passage see D. Pardee, BiOr 37 (1980) 272. The position of *kʾilm* at the beginning of a colon is rather awkward, however.

147 It is noteworthy that ʿAnatu and her double ʿAthtartu turn against their husband Baʿlu on several occasions. See also IV.28ff. and the Legend of Aqhat.

"How dare [*you slay a messenger*]*?*
[*An en*]*voy of Judge Naharu?*
A messenger hol[*ds*] *the staff of a free man,*[148]
[*so would you slay*] *a messenger?*
Between his shoulder-blades is the word of his lord, [149]
and he [ ]."
His Highness Baʿlu became angry:
"*The terraces with the vin*[*es* will wither],[150]
[*the f*]*ields, messengers of Yammu,*
envoys of Judge Naharu!
[*But*],
I say to Yammu, your lord,
[*to your*] *mas*[*ter Judge Naharu*:]
['*He*]*a*[*r*] *the word of Haddu the Champion*:
[*I am*] *a follower of Yammu,*
[*Judge Naharu*], *I walk behind him*!' "[151]
The mes[*sengers of Yammu*] *did not bow,*
(broken)

Just a few fragmentary words are preserved in column II, and at present no sensible reconstruction is possible. This means that in effect about 115 long lines are missing between the point where col-

[148] The "staff of the free man" was probably a status symbol, guaranteeing the messengers immunity. Cf. UF 14 (1982) 168, n. 126.

[149] Letters were carried in a despatch-bag slung round the neck.

[150] The tentative restoration is based on Isa. 16:8, see also Deut. 32:32 and KTU 1.23:9f. for the combination of *šdmt/h* with *gpn(m)*. In January the growth of the vegetation comes to a temporary halt because of the cold, cf. Genesis Rabba XIII.12; G. Dalman, Arbeit und Sitte in Palästina, Bd.1, 249f.; H. Klein, ZDPV 37 (1914) 224f.; J. Weulersse, Le pays des Alaouites, t.1, Tours 1940, 193, 237. During the short Syrian winter the leaves of the vine fall off, cf. Dalman, Arbeit und Sitte, Bd. 4, 293. Frost could damage the vines, cf. R. H. Rodgers, JAOS 100 (1980) 4f.

[151] As in Baal V (KTU 1.5):ii.12ff. the "Champion" surrenders immediately and abjectly. If one considers the narrative as a seasonal nature myth, this is perfectly understandable - nature has to take its inexorable course.

umn I ends and the first lines of column III. Presumably Yammu ousted Baᶜlu and took possession of the latter's mansion on Mt. Sapanu.

But what remains of column III suggests that subsequently Yammu was unable to occupy the throne on Mt. Sapanu. A similar development takes place in Baal VI:i.56ff. (KTU 1.6:I.56ff.). Then ᶜAthtaru, the irrigation-god, was too small to fill the place of the rain-god Baᶜlu. Here the sea-god Yammu may well have been too big. Perhaps his attempt to take up residence on Mt. Sapanu led to the destruction of the relatively small structure that had been erected there for Baᶜlu (see note 124), and so Kotharu is now summoned to build a new palace for Yammu in a more suitable place.

[ ]*father*[ ]
  [ ]
[ ][152]
  [ ] .... [ ]
[ ]
  [ ] .... [ ]
[ ]
  [ ]
Then he[153] *headed straight*
  for Ilu at the fountain-head of the two Rivers
    in the middle of the bedding of the two Floods.[154]
He appeared in the encampment of Ilu
  and entered the camp of the King, the Father of Years.[155]
At the feet of Ilu he bowed and fell down,
  he prostrated himself and honoured him.

[152] The restoration proposed by the editors of KTU is incompatible with the traces in Virolleaud's early copy of the tablet.

[153] Kotharu, the builder-technician among the gods.

[154] See note 81.

[155] See notes 82-83.

After this the Bull Ilu, his father, said:
"Depart, Kotharu-and-Khasisu!
Build a mansion for Yammu,
set up a palace for Judge Naharu,
a house for Naharu in the middle of the sea!
Depart, Kotharu-and-Khasisu!
Build a mansion for his Highness Yammu quickly,
set up a palace for Judge Naharu,
in the middle of the be[d of the] de[ep sea]!
Build his house quickly,
set up his palace quickly!
The house should cover a thousand acres,
the palace ten thousand square miles.[156]
For [Yammu] desires a house in the dark,
in the bitter field of the sea![157]
Let [Baᶜlu (?)] die in the deepest sea!"[158]
ᶜAthtaru confronted him.[159]
"Because you have become k[ing, Yammu,]
fever[160] *and r[ui]n*[161] *[are yours]!*
I will set [your] pa[lace on] fire,[162]
[in the middle of] the fire my [lads] will carry it!
You do [not] even [have] a child,
[you do] no[t have a wife],
[n]or a son!"[163]

[156] Mythological exaggeration. See note 68. Later on the same measures are given for the palace of Baᶜlu, cf. Baal IV (KTU 1.4):v.56f.

[157] Lit. "the field of the bitterness of the sea", referring to its saltiness. Cf. Akkad. *marratu* and Ex. 15:23; Num. 5:18ff.

[158] Lit. "in the sea of sea", cf. Mic. 7:12. At the beginning of column IV Baᶜlu is relating his experiences in the deep sea.

[159] Text uncertain, cf. Akkad. *pūta ummudu* "to be obstinate".

[160] Cf. Deut. 28:22.

[161] "Perdition" or "Ruin" is a name of the Nether World. Cf. note 287 below.

[162] Cf. Baal IV (KTU 1.4):v.22ff.

[163] Cf. Aqhat I (KTU 1.17):i.18ff. and line 22 below.

Shapshu[164]*, the Lamp of the gods, answered him,*
she raised her voice and cried:
"You over there, listen!
The Bull Ilu, your father, has granted
his favour to his Highness Yammu,
to Judge Naharu.
How can the Bull Ilu, your father,
fail to hear you?
He is sure to pull out the door-posts from your residence,
he is sure to overturn the chair of your kingship,
he is sure to break your judicial sceptre!"[165]
But ʿAthtaru answered:
"Should he who is [kin]g [t]ake [everything]?[166]
I beg you, Bull Ilu, my father!
I do have no house like the (other) gods (have),
no residence like the sons of Qudshu.[167]
I have to get out of my underwear alone,
nimble lads have to wash me.[168]
Should then his Highness Yammu be dwelling in a house,
Judge Naharu in a palace?
Should the Bull Ilu, his father, grant
his favour to his Highness Yammu,
to Judge Naharu?
(Yammu,) whether you are king or not,
you have no wife, like the (other) gods (have),
[no lass, like the fa]mily of Ilu!"

164 The sun-goddess.

165 Set phrases, cf. Baal IV (KTU 1.6):vi.26ff.; CH Rev. XXVI.50f.; KAI, no.1:2; Hag. 2:22, cf. J. C. Greenfield, in: H. Goedicke (ed.), Near Eastern Studies in Honor of W. F. Albright, Baltimore 1971, 253-268.

166 Cf. 2 Sam. 19:31, also Josh. 11:19; 1 Ki. 14:26.

167 Clearly a reminiscence of Baal I (KTU 1.3):iv.

168 Translation uncertain, but probably a reference to the circumstance that ʿAthtaru, too, does not have a loving wife who undresses and washes him at night.

His Highness Yammu answered,
Judge Naharu [replied:]
[“*The Bull Ilu will give me a wife*],
he will send me [*a lass*].”
But ʿAthtaru said:
(broken)

20-30 long lines are missing here. In view of the poem's circumstantial style this is a relatively short interval. It may be assumed that Kotharu took advantage of the confusion created by the quarrel between ʿAthtaru and Yammu to make contact with his friend Baʿlu. The preserved part of column IV resumes with Baʿlu describing his terrible situation to Kotharu.

IV.

“[ ]
[*my*] *arms became weak.*
[*I am sure I suffered*] *the state of death,*[169]
I was unable to extricate the life of (my) s[*oul*].[170]
When [*I*] *saw the nose,*[171] [*I was afraid*],
and my repose perished in the sea.
There are m[*aggots*] *crawling in Yammu,*
there are worms [*in*] *Naharu!*[172]
There I was put to the test of the sword,
I had to kiss both [*ed*]*ges.*

[169] Cf. Baal V (KTU 1.5):v.16f., with note 376.

[170] Cf. 1 Sam. 17:55, etc., also Ps.107:28.

[171] It seems that Yammu is depicted as a god who is suffering from the vermin living in his own body, the sea. For worms infesting the nose see Gilg. M. II.9 and E. Neufeld, Or (49) 1980, 37f. with Plate II,3-4. Cf. Acts 12:23.

[172] Cf. Ex. 16:20; Isa. 14:11; Job 25:6. Cf. KTU 1.9:14f.

The strength of the two of us[173] *fell to the ground,*
and the power of the two of us to the earth.''
His words had scarcely left his mouth,
his speech, his lips,
when she cried out,
(and) he cowered under the chair of his Highness Yammu.[174]
But Kotharu-and-Khasisu said:
''Truly I say to you, o Highness Ba^{c}lu,
I repeat, o Rider on the Clouds:[175]
Now, o Ba^{c}lu, your enemies –
now you should slay your enemies,
now you should silence your foes![176]
Take your eternal kingship,
your everlasting dominion!''[177]
Kotharu took down a double-headed axe
and proclaimed its name:
''You – your name is Yagrush![178]
Yagrush chase away Yammu,
chase Yammu away from his chair,
Naharu from the throne of his dominion!

[173] It appears that Ba^{c}lu had taken someone with him into the sea. The next line seems to indicate that this person was a woman standing guard while Ba^{c}lu was whispering to Kotharu. According to line 28 ^{c}Athtartu was present during the ensuing fight so it is logical to assume that it was she who had accompanied Ba^{c}lu. Perhaps not of her own will but because Ilu had given her to Yammu as his wife (see column III).

[174] Defeated kings had to crawl under the furniture of their victors to pick up the crumbs. Cf. KTU 1.114:5ff.; Judg. 1:7.

[175] See note 37.

[176] Cf. Ps. 92:10; 143:12.

[177] Cf. Ps. 145:13; Dan. 3:33; 4:31; 7:14; Rev. 11:15; 22:5, and note 473 below.

[178] For the naming of weapons see *e.g.* Enuma elish IV.57ff.; V.87ff.; VI.82ff.; UF 7 (1975) 182, n. 110. Yagrush means ''Let him chase away''. See also ''the chasen sea'' in Isa. 57:20, and Mark 4:41 (par.).

Leap from the hand of Baʿlu,
like an eagle from his fingers![179]
Strike the shoulder of his Highness Yammu,
Judge Naharu between the arms!"[180]
The axe leapt from the hand of Baʿlu,
like an eagle from his fingers.
It struck the shoulder of his Highness Yammu,
Judge Naharu between the arms.
Yammu was strong,[181] *he did not fall down,*
his joints did not quiver,
his pelvis did not shake.[182]
Kotharu took down (another) double-headed axe
and proclaimed its name:
"You – your name is Ayyamur![183]
Ayyamur, expel Yammu,[184]
expel Yammu from his chair,
Naharu from the throne of his dominion!
Leap from the hand of Baʿlu,
like an eagle from his fingers!
Strike the skull of his Highness Yammu,
Judge Naharu between the eyes![185]
Let Yammu collapse
and fall to the earth!"

[179] The magic weapon strikes automatically because Baʿlu lacks the strength to hurl it himself. The simile is derived from falconry, cf. Aqhat II (KTU 1.18):iv.

[180] Cf. Zech. 13:6; 2 Ki. 9:24; Y. Avishur, UF 12 (1980) 125ff.

[181] The same is said of Baʿlu's other formidable adversary, the god of death Motu: Baal VI (KTU 1.6):vi.17ff. See also Isa. 43:16; 51:9f.; Ps. 74:13.

[182] Cf. Eccl. 10:18; UF 12 (1980) 425f.

[183] The name means "Expel anyone!".

[184] Perhaps the name of Miriam is a quotation ("Expel the sea") from the Yahwistic account of the battle with the sea (cf. Ex. 15:21). Compare note 446 below on the name of Jezebel.

[185] See note 98. Also 1 Sam.17:49.

And the axe leapt from the hand of Baᶜlu,
like an eagle from his fingers.
It struck the skull of his Highness Yammu,
Judge Naharu between the eyes.
Yammu collapsed,
he fell to the earth.
His joints quivered,
and his pelvis shook.[186]
Baᶜlu wanted to drag away
and put Yammu down,
he wanted to finish off Naharu.[187]
ᶜAthtartu rebuked the Name:[188]
''*Be ashamed, o Baᶜlu Almighty*!
Be ashamed, o Rider on the Clouds!

[186] So Baᶜlu ''defeated'' the Sea. Cf. note 57. It is typical of the half-hearted recognition Baᶜlu receives in the religious texts of Ugarit that his victory had to be a Pyrrhic one. This circumstance will be exploited by Motu in Baal V (KTU 1.5):i.1ff. and is the mythological explanation for the fact that the sea continued to constitute a menace. Baᶜlu himself concedes that he did not have any strength left in his arms (lines 1,5). He owes his victory entirely to the magic weapons of Kotharu. In apparent contrast to this the Hebrew tradition speaks emphatically of the strong arm of YHWH (see *e.g.* Ex. 15:6,12f.; Isa. 51:9f.; Ps. 89:11; 93:1-4; Job 26:12). The very special weapon with which the weather-god defeated the sea is also mentioned in a Hurrian version of a Canaanite myth, cf. I. Wegner, AOAT 36 (1981) 68.

[187] See for the imperfect expressing intention GK § 107n. No other interpretation of these imperfects is feasible because a past tense would render the ensuing discussion meaningless.

Perhaps *yšt* may be translated ''wanted to dry up'' (if we adapt the proposal of J. A. Montgomery, JAOS 55 (1935) 276; see also C. Kloos, Yhwh's Combat with the Sea, Leiden 1986, 86-88), cf. Isa. 19:5. However, En.el. IV.104 argues in favour of a derivation from *šyt* ''put down'', and in Myth and Ritual III (KTU 1.114):4f. the verb *qṯ* ''to drag, tear out'' is paired with *ᶜdb* ''to put down''.

[188] Because of the offensive context the name of Baᶜlu is replaced here by ''the Name'' (*par excellence*), cf. Lev. 24:11.

For his Highness Yammu is our captive,
[for] Judge Naharu is our captive!''[189]
And when the word had left her mouth,
Baᶜlu the Almighty was ashamed for her.
But [Kotharu-and-Khasisu said:]
''Yammu, to death!
May Baᶜlu be king![190]
[ ]
[ ] heat for the stalks.[191]
And [ ]
[ ]
[ ] *he answered*:
''Yammu, to death!
May Baᶜlu be king!
[heat] for the stalks.''
And [ᶜAthtartu ans]wered:
''[ ]
[ ] *Baᶜlu will* [ ] *them.*
[ ]
[heat] for the stalks.
Put [ ]
[the crown] on his head.[192]
[ ]
[ ] *his enemies.*
Anoi[nt]

[189] Captives ought not be put to death (cf. 2 Ki. 6:22). See the notes 145, 147-148 above, and Ps. 68:22. The protest would be meaningless if Baᶜlu had already finished off Yammu, as some scholars assume.

[190] Cf. Enuma elish IV.28, with R. Frankena, Tākultu, Leiden 1954, 64. See also Ex. 15:18; Ps. 93:1-4.

[191] The stalks of the grain sprouting in the fields about this time of the year. Yammu is defeated, winter is over. Compare note 150.

[192] The restoration is uncertain, but cf. Ps. 21:4; Zech. 6:11; Est. 2:17; 6:8.

[ ] *between his eyes.*''[193]

(broken)

Of Baal III:iv (KTU 1.2:IV) no more than twenty (perhaps only ten) lines are lost and at the beginning of Baal IV:i (KTU 1.4:I) another 20 lines have been destroyed. It follows from Baal IV:iii.1ff. and vi.10ff. that Yammu was not put to death but was only held captive. Because elsewhere Yammu and his monstrous helpers are more or less identified (Baal I:iii.38f.; Incantation II [KTU 1.83]), these helpers too may have been punished, possibly in a joint effort of Baᶜlu and ᶜAnatu (see also Incantation I, KTU 1.82). The lost part of Baal III:iv is large enough to accommodate such an episode. In the Babylonian Epic of Creation the punishing of the helpers of Tiamat takes only 17 lines (En.el. IV.105-122).

It is also possible that it is only Yammu who is punished in Baal III:iv. In that case the episode is a partial repetition of an earlier struggle, not necessarily involving Baᶜlu, which may have taken place in connection with the creation of the world. This struggle was commemorated at the end of the year (see p. 99 below).

In the last few lines of Baal III:iv Kotharu was discussing the enthronement of Baᶜlu with ᶜAthtartu and /or her double ᶜAnatu (see Baal III:i.40 for the pair of them). It is logical to suppose that in the course of that discussion the question of a proper palace for Baᶜlu cropped up again. On the basis of Baal IV:v.13f. (KTU 1.4:V.13f.) it may be concluded that at the time when the actual building started some kind of structure which could be called a ''house/palace'' did already exist, as we have assumed all along. So what takes place in Baal IV is a *resumption* of the building activities, not a totally new project. In this connection it is worth noting that in many Semitic languages the verb ''to build'' is also used for rebuilding, repairing or adding wings to an existing building.

[193] Cf. Baal I, fragm. a (KTU 1.101):4.

In Baal IV:i.19ff. Kotharu is instructed to make the presents intended to persuade Athiratu to intercede with Ilu so that he would give his permission to resume the building activities. If KTU 1.4 follows KTU 1.2, the deterioration of the relation between Ilu and Baᶜlu offers a ready explanation for such a discreet approach. At first Athiratu fears that Baᶜlu and ᶜAnatu have come to slay more of her sons (Baal IV:ii.23ff.), which is a natural reaction after KTU 1.2:IV. If KTU 1.4 should follow KTU 1.3, or should be a partial duplicate version of the latter, however, all this would be very hard to explain. Moreover, the place of KTU 1.1 in the story would become totally uncertain. Finally it should be observed that the command to make the presents is given in person and not through the intermediary of messengers. Kotharu does not confirm his willingness to cooperate, as would have been customary if messengers had been involved.[194] Therefore it is *not* an argument in favour of the sequence KTU 1.3-KTU 1.4 that at the end of the former messengers are sent to Kotharu.

But who ordered the presents to be made, Baᶜlu or ᶜAnatu?[195] The latter is a more attractive possibility. In Baal I (KTU 1.3) it was she who took the initiative, and, being a daughter of Ilu and Athiratu she would have known better how to approach the old couple. Since Baᶜlu is spoken of in the third person in Baal IV:i.9,13 it is less likely that he was the one who instructed Kotharu. ᶜAnatu is probably, therefore, reminding Kotharu at the beginning of tablet IV that earlier Ilu and his family had recognized Baᶜlu's right to own a palace for himself (Baal I:iv-v). She did this because Kotharu would naturally object that, since Baᶜlu had just defeated Ilu's favourite son Yammu, Ilu would never give his approval to the plan to rebuild the palace for Baᶜlu.

[194] Cf. Baal I (KTU 1.3):iv.31ff.; Baal II (KTU 1.1):iii.17ff.; Baal V (KTU 1.5):i.

[195] See Baal IV (KTU 1.4):ii.12ff.

Baal IV

KTU 1.4

"[ ]
[ ] my [ ]
[ ]
The Bull Ilu, his father, groaned (and] cried out,
Ilu, the King who had created him,[196]
Athiratu and her sons cried out,
the Goddess and the troop of her kin:
'Now there is no house for Baʿlu like the (other) gods (have),
no residence like the sons of Athiratu (have)!
Ilu's dwelling is the shelter of his son,
the dwelling of Lady Athiratu of the Sea,
the dwelling of the respectable brides,
the dwelling of Pidrayu, the girl of the honey-dew,[197]
the shelter of Tallayu, the girl of the mist,
the dwelling of Arsayu, the girl of the ample flowing!'
And I have still something else to say to you:
Please make a present for Lady Athiratu of the Sea,
a bribe for the Creatress of the gods!"[198]
The Skilful One[199] *went up to the bellows,*
the handles were in the hands of Khasisu.
He poured silver,
smelted[200] *gold.*

[196] See note 95.

[197] For the goddesses of dew see note 18.

[198] Creating, begetting and bearing were all part of the same creative process. See Gen. 4:1 as well as: The Bible World. Essays in Honor of C. H. Gordon, New York 1980, 171ff.

[199] Kotharu-and-Khasisu, the craftsman.

[200] Cf. the Peshitta on Ex. 25:12 and perhaps Hebr. *šlḥ* in Prov. 6:14,19. The enormous quantities are exaggerations of the mythopoet.

He poured silver by the thousands (of shekels),
gold he poured by the ten-thousands.
He poured a baldachin and a resting-place,[201]
a tremendous socle[202] *of twenty thousand (shekels),*
a tremendous socle overlaid with silver,
polished with gold-blood,[203]
a tremendous throne,
with a cushion on it,
a tremendous foot-stool,
covered with electrum,
a tremendous couch,
with a head-rest on it,
the support of which was of gold,
a tremendous table,
filled with all kinds of winged monsters
from the foundations of the earth,[204]
a tremendous bowl,
as delicate as one from Amurru,
shaped like one from the Yam'anu country,[205]
with ten thousand wild oxen within.[206]

---

[201] Normally these pieces would not be made from metal. However, divine furniture is totally different from human furniture, just as a god's house is different. See notes 262ff. below.

[202] The dais where the throne stood. Cf. Myth and Ritual IV (KTU 1.13):10,12. The Hebrew equivalent is *mkwn ks*ʾ, Ps. 89:15; 97:2.

[203] Apparently a metaphor designating a coating of gold, possibly liquified with mercury. It is also attested in Akkadian.

[204] A description of the elaborate decoration of the table. Contrast Ex. 20:4.

[205] Apparently Amurru and Yamʾanu were regions of Canaan which from the poet's viewpoint were foreign countries. See note 25; Myth and Ritual I, note 9.

[206] A description of the decoration inside the bowl. The detailed mythological account of the work of Kotharu tallies with the situation on earth in winter when the men often seek the warmth of a smithy, sitting around idly and watching the skill of the artisan. Cf. J. Pairman Brown, VT 19 (1969) 152.

Between column I and column II about 16 lines are missing in which Baˁlu and ˁAnatu leave Kotharu with the presents for Athiratu whom they find busy with her domestic chores.

[ ] *house* [ ]
on the stone [ ]
She took her spindle in her hand,
(and) the spindle fell from her right hand.[207]
She carried her clothing into the sea,
her skirts, the covering of her body,
her two skirts into the river.[208]
She placed a cauldron on the fire,
a washing-copper on the coals.
She wanted to charm the Bull Ilu, the good-natured,
she wanted to please the Creator of creatures.[209]
When she raised her eyes, she saw –
Athiratu was sure she saw Baˁlu coming,
(saw) the Virgin ˁAnatu coming,
the Wanton Widow of the Nations[210] *advancing.*
With her, the feet began to totter,[211]
at her back the spine loosened,
her face above began to sweat,

[207] This traditional way of spinning is still practised in Palestine, cf. S. Weir, The Bedouin, Westerham 1976, 32-34, Pl. VIII.

[208] Women used to wear double skirts. During the winter they had little opportunity to do the washing. People disliked it intensely that their clothes were often stained by mud during the rainy winter (cf. Aqhat I (KTU 1.17):i.34 and Baal II (KTU 1.1):iv.1-10). So it was a relief to them when the weather finally cleared to allow them to clean and dry their garments. Now that the sea (*i.e.* the god Yammu "Sea"/Naharu "River") has calmed down (Baal III.iv) the women can use its water safely for rinsing (compare Odyssey VI.91). Afterwards the laundry is boiled in a large cauldron.

[209] Cf. The Bible World. Essays in Honor of C. H. Gordon, New York 1980, 182f., and with regard to the verb Prov. 6:25.

[210] See notes 33-34.

[211] See notes 55-56.

the joints of her spine shook,
the small of her back too.
She raised her voice and cried:
"Why is Baˁlu the Almighty approaching?
Why is the Virgin ˁAnatu approaching?
To slay me, or to slay my sons?[212]
To destroy the troop of my kin?"
Athiratu was sure she saw the glitter of silver,[213]
the glitter of silver and the sheen of gold.
Lady Athiratu of the Sea rejoiced.
Then she cried aloud to her lad:
"Look, succesful explorer of the bottom [of the sea],
fisherman of Lady Athiratu of the Sea!
Qi[dshu], take a net in your hands,
[Amruru], (take) a large (net) in your hands!
[Cast] (it) in Yammu, Beloved of Ilu,[214]
in Yammu, the god of [ ],
in Naharu, the god of ...[ ].
[Offer] Baˁlu the Almighty [food],
[offer] the Virgin ˁAnatu [drink].
[ ] what that [ ]
[ ] *and you* [ ]
[ ]."
Athira[tu]
by becoming k[ing]
not for [ ]

[212] Athiratu's apprehension is understandable because Baˁlu and ˁAnatu have discovered her scheming (Baal II:iv) and have slain her son Yammu only a short time ago (Baal III (KTU 1.2):iv).

[213] Cf. Eccl. 7:12.

[214] Yammu is the sea. Cf. Mark 1:16; Matth. 4:18; Luke 5:4; John 21:6. This mythological passage reflects the re-opening of the fishing season which in antiquity took place in the first days of March when the winter gales were over. Compare note 208, Plutarch, De Iside et Osiride 16,357D, and AOAT 16,144f.

king [ ]
of [ ]
by ... [ ]
aloud [ ]
he [ ]

About 12 lines are lost now. It seems that Athiratu is still speaking at the beginning of col. III. She urges Baᶜlu not to let some male adversary, who is probably none other than the sea-god Yammu, escape.

"[ ]
[ ] *you shall judge*
[*Yammu, Be*] *loved of* [*Ilu*]
[ ] ... *like* ...
[ ]
let not [*Naharu*] *escape!*[215]
[*Ilu*] *will establish you* [*forever*],[216]
and [*the days of*] *your* [*li*]*fe will be everlasting,*[217]
and the spirit that is [*in you*],[218]
o god who is king!"[219]
A[*gain*] *Baᶜlu the Almighty* [*spo*]*ke up,*
the Rider on the Clouds repeated (*his words*)
when he arose and scoffed,
stood up and spat
in the assembly of the sons of Ilu.[220]

215 Cf. Ps. 114:3,5; Enuma elish IV.110,140; Prov. 8:29.
216 Cf. Ps. 78:69; 119:52.
217 Cf. Gen. 3:14,17; Deut. 4:9; Ps. 23:6; 27:4; Eccl. 5:19, etc.
218 Cf. Gen. 6:17; 7:15; Num. 27:18; Josh. 5:1; 1 Ki. 10:5, etc., also Isa. 11:2.
219 See Baal III (KTU 1.2):iv.32ff. with the comment. See also Isa. 52:7; Ps. 47:9 and note 190.
220 Spitting in the middle of the assembly was an outrageous act, cf. 1QS VII.13: "The man who spits into the session of the many, shall be fined for thirty days".

"F[oul meat][221] *has been placed on my table,*
I have had to drink filth from my cup!
Now there are two sacrifices Baʿlu hates,
three[222] *the Rider on the Clouds:*
A sacrifice with shameful conduct,
and a sacrifice with strife,[223]
and a sacrifice with handmaids' lewdness.[224]
Indeed there is shamefulness to be seen,
and there is handmaids' lewdness!"
Then Baʿlu the Almighty approached,
the Virgin ʿAnatu approached.
They gave Lady Athiratu of the Sea the presents,
offered the Creatress of the gods the bribes.
And Lady Athiratu of the Sea said:
"Why do you give presents to Lady Athiratu of the Sea,
do you offer bribes to the Creatress of the gods?
Did you give presents to the Bull, Ilu the good-natured?
Or did you offer bribes to the Creator of creatures?"
And the Virgin ʿAnatu answered:
"To you, Lady Athiratu of the Sea, we give the presents,
we offer the bribes to the Creatress of the gods!
[Later] we will give him presents (too)."

[221] Cf. Mal. 1:7,12. Cf. Loven en geloven. Fs Nic. H. Riddderbos, Amsterdam 1975, 211-226.

Apparently Baʿlu complains about being quartered with the lower ranks of Ilu's household. The obvious implication is that he needs a dwelling of his own.

[222] Cf. Prov. 6:16, also Isa. 17:6; Job 33:29; Prov. 30:15; Eccl. 4:12.

[223] Cf. Prov. 17:1.

[224] Slave girls had a reputation of lewdness because their masters were entitled to disregard their matrimonial status. Because in this case the "handmaids" belong to the family of Ilu their offensive behaviour was a form of incest, called "wickedness" (Hebr. *zimmāh* = Ugar. *tdmmt*) in Lev. 18:17 and Ezek. 22:9f.

Baʿlu the Almighty [sat down],
Lady Athiratu of the Sea [sat down],
the Virgin ʿAnatu [sat down].[225]
[And again] they ate, the gods drank,
and they were supplied with a suckling,[226]
with a salted knife they carved a fatling.
They drank beakers of wine,
from golden cups blood from the trees.[227]
[ ]
[ ]
[ ]
[ ]
[ ]
[ ]
[ ]
[ ] *on us*
[ ] *for us*
(broken)

The next 12 lines, containing Baʿlu's plea for help, are missing.

V.

"[ ] *the Bull [Ilu, our father].*"
And Lady Athiratu of the Sea answered:
"*Hear, o Qidshu-and-Amruru,*[228]
o fisherman of Lady Athiratu of the Sea!

[225] If the verbs have been restored correctly, it is worth noting that Baʿlu is the first to take a seat.

[226] The herds grew substantially in March and April. The gods received their due share of the young in the form of lavish sacrifices. See in addition to AOAT 16,146f.: T. Canaan, ZDPV 36 (1913) 281f., and RS 1957.4 mentioning 68 spring lambs (L. R. Fisher (ed.), The Claremont Ras Shamra Tablets, Roma 1971, 27).

[227] Cf. Ugar. *dm zt* "blood of the olive" = olive juice. Also Gen. 49:11; Deut. 32:14. Similar metaphors are used in Akkadian, Hittite and Ethiopic.

[228] Her personal attendant. See Baal I (KTU 1.3):vi and Baal IV (KTU 1.4):ii.

Saddle a he-ass,
harness a male (animal).
Put on the reins[229] *of silver,*
the straps of gold,
prepare the reins of my donkey!"
Qidshu-and-Amruru obeyed.
He saddled a he-ass,
harnessed a male (animal).
He put on the reins of silver,
the straps of gold,
he prepared the reins of her donkey.
Qidshu-and-Amruru embraced (her),[230]
he put Athiratu on the back of the he-ass,
on the most comfortable part of the male (animal)'s back.
Qidshu took the lead,[231]
Amruru trailed like a star.
The Virgin ʿAnatu followed,
but Baʿlu left for the heights of Sapanu.
Then she headed straight
for Ilu at the fountain-head of the two Rivers,
in the middle of the bedding of the two Floods.[232]
She appeared in the encampment of Ilu
and entered the camp of the King, the Father of Years.[233]
At the feet of Ilu she bowed and fell down,
prostrated herself and honoured him.
Look! When Ilu saw her,

229 Actually "vine-tendrils", a metaphor. See for some Akkadian parallels W. G. E. Watson, UF 10 (1978) 398f.

230 To lift her on the back of the animal.

231 Others: "took a torch" or "kindled a torch".

232 See note 81.

233 See notes 82-83.

his frown disappeared and he laughed,
he placed his foot on the foot-stool
and drummed with his fingers.
He raised his voice and cried:
"*Why have you arrived, Lady Athiratu of the Sea?*
Why have you come, Creatress of the gods?
Are you very hungry? You have only to ask!
Or are you very thirsty? I will do (anything)![234]
Eat and drink!
Eat bread from the tables,
drink wine from the beakers,
from a golden cup blood from the trees!
If only the love of Ilu, the King, could stimulate you,
the affection of the Bull could arouse you!"[235]
But Lady Athiratu of the Sea answered:
"*Your judgment, Ilu, is wise.*[236]
May you be wise forever!
Long live the sharpness of your judgment!
Baʿlu the Almighty is our king,
our judge – nobody is over him.
All of us must bring him gifts,
all of us must bring him the cup!"
The Bull Ilu, his father, groaned (and) cried out,
Ilu, the King who had created him,
Athiratu and her sons cried out,
the Goddess and the troop of her kin:
"*Now there is no house for Baʿlu like the (other) gods (have),*
no residence like the sons of Athiratu (have)!

[234] Cf. Ex. 8:26f.

[235] Note the irony in the choice of words. Ilu is depicted here as an old charmer whose overtures are brusquely ignored.

[236] See with this and the following lines notes 92-95 and 75-76.

Ilu's dwelling is the shelter of his son,
the dwelling of Lady Athiratu of the Sea,
the dwelling of the respectable brides,
the dwelling of Pidrayu, the girl of the honey-dew,
the shelter of Tallayu, the girl of the mist,
the dwelling of Arsayu, the girl of the ample flowing!"
And the Benevolent, Ilu the good-natured answered:
"Am I a slave then,
an attendant of Athiratu?
Am I a slave then,
to hold the brick-mould?
Or a slave-girl of Athiratu,
to make bricks?

V.

Let a house be built for Baʿlu[237] *like the (other) gods (have),*
and a residence like the sons of Athiratu (have)!"
And Lady Athiratu of the Sea answered:
"You are great, o Ilu!
Surely the greyness of your old age is wisdom,
surely the compassion[238] *which is in your breast instructs you!*
Also it is the prime time[239] *for his rains,*
Baʿlu should designate the time of the barque with snow,
and of the giving forth of his voice in the clouds,
of his letting loose the lightnings to the earth.[240]

[237] Cf. 1 Ki. 3:2; Zech. 1:16; Prov. 24:3. The circumstance that Ilu now says "let it be built" does not preclude that some kind of (ruined ?) construction did exist already (see p. 43 and note 124).

[238] Cf. Ex. 34:6, etc., with J. C. de Moor, Uw God is mijn God. Over de oorsprong van het geloof in de ene God, Kampen 1983, 17, 31, 54. Also R. Borger, BAfO 9,42, Nin A I.30.

[239] Lit. "the nose of time".

[240] A clear reference to the seasonal background of the myth. The goddess is referring to the so-called "latter-rains" in early spring (first half of March). The timing of these rains is of crucial importance to the standing crops. Cf. Deut. 11:14; Jer. 3:3; 5:24; Job 29:23. These rains arrive with thunderstorms and occasionally take

A house of cedars[241] *– let him complete it!*
Or a house of bricks – let him construct it![242]
Let Baᶜlu the Almighty be told:
'Call a caravan[243] *to your mansion,*[244]
merchandise[245] *into your palace!*
Let the mountains bring you[246] *silver in plenty,*
the hills the choicest of gold,[247]
let the slopes bring you nuggets.[248]
Then build a mansion of silver and gold,
a mansion of purest lapis!' "
The Virgin ᶜAnatu rejoiced.
She shuffled her feet and flew up from the earth.
Then she headed straight
for Baᶜlu in the heights of Sapanu.
Over a thousand acres,
ten thousand square miles,[249]
the laughing of ᶜAnatu was heard.
She raised her voice and cried:
"You have good news, o Baᶜlu,
I bring you good news![250]

the form of snow and hail. Cf. Job 37:3. For further details consult AOAT 16,150f. The holy voice of Baᶜlu is the thunder, cf. 2 Sam. 22:14; Ps. 29; RSP I, i.17. Only in vii.27-29 Baᶜlu decides the time is ripe for it.

241 Cf. 2 Sam. 7:2,7; 1 Ki. 7:2.

242 Cf. Neh. 4:11.

243 Again a seasonal phenomenon. Early spring was the best time for caravans to depart. Cf. D. O. Edzard, RLA, Bd. 5, 415.

244 See note 124 and p. 43 above.

245 Cf. Ezek. 27:12,14,16, etc.

246 Cf. Job 40:20, also Job 28.

247 Cf. Hos. 9:6; Ezra 8:27.

248 Cf. UF 14 (1982) 159, nn. 55-56. Hebrew uses a different word for "nuggets" in Job 28:6.

249 Cf. note 68.

250 Cf. 2 Sam. 18:19-27. With a message implying the rebuilding of Zion Isa. 52:7, cf. 52:1,9.

A house has been given to you, like your brothers (have),
and a residence like your kin (has)!
Call a caravan to your mansion,
merchandise into your palace!
Let the mountains bring you silver in plenty,
the hills the choicest of gold.
Then build a mansion of silver and gold,
a mansion of purest lapis!"
Ba^{c}lu the Almighty rejoiced.
He called a caravan to his mansion,
merchandise into his palace.
The mountains brought him silver in plenty,
the hills the choicest of gold,
the slopes brought him nuggets.
He did send (messengers) to Kotharu-and-Khasisu.

And repeat the recitation of how
the lads were sent.[251]

Afterwards Kotharu-and-Khasisu arrived.
He set an ox before him,
a fatling right in front of him.
He placed a chair and made him sit down
at the right hand of Ba^{c}lu the Almighty.[252]

[251] The scribe becomes impatient with the elaborate style of the narrative and omits a portion of standard text relating how the messengers were sent out, how they delivered their message and what Kotharu did answer. All in all a substantial part of text was left to the improvisation of the reciting priest. See note 53.

[252] The place of honour. See Ps. 45:10; 110:1; Matt. 26:64 (par.); Acts 7:55f.; Rom. 8:34; Eph. 1:20; Col. 3:1; Hebr. 10:12; 1 Petr. 3:22.

Again they ate, the gods drank.
And Baˁlu the Almighty said:
"[*Look*! *De*]*p*[*art, Kotharu-and-Khasisu*]!
Quickly, o Kotharu, a mansion –
  quickly set up a palace![253]
Build a mansion quickly,
  set up a palace quickly
    in the middle of the highlands of Sapanu![254]
The house should cover a thousand acres,
  the palace ten thousand square miles!"[255]
And Kotharu-and-Khasisu answered:
"*Listen, o Baˁlu Almighty,*
  pay attention, o Rider on the Clouds:
Should I not put a window in the mansion,
  a lattice in the middle of the palace?"[256]
But Baˁlu the Almighty answered:
"*Do not put a window in the mansion,*
  (*not*) *a lattice in the middle of the palace*!"

A very small number of lines might be missing between column V and column VI.

And Kotharu-and-Khasisu said:

[253] Cf. Ezra 9:9.

[254] Cf. Baal II (KTU 1.1):iii.25ff.; Baal III (KTU 1.2):iii.7ff. March and April were neither too dry nor too hot and thus provided ideal weather to resume building operations.

[255] Cf. note 156.

[256] Later on the window will appear to be a rift in the clouds (vii.19). So the poet, even though he is mentioning very earthly materials for the construction of the palace of Baˁlu, is fully aware of the fact that he is only speaking in metaphors.

It may be assumed that the opening of the "window" in the clouds was meant as a metaphor for letting through the latter-rains (see note 278). With these rains the correct time was vital to agriculture and for that reason no one but Baˁlu could choose the right moment to open the "window".

"Baʿlu, you will come back to my word!"
Kotharu-and-Khasisu spoke a second time:
"Now listen, o Baʿlu Almighty!
Should I not put a window in the mansion,
a lattice in the middle of the palace?"
But Baʿlu the Almighty answered:
"Do not put a window in the mansion,
(not) a lattice in the middle of the palace,
lest Pidrayu, the girl of the honey-dew, flies away,[257]
lest Tallayu, the girl of the mist, be seen!
[*When I was with*] *Yammu,* [*Be*]*loved of Ilu,*[258]
[*Naharu*] *did revile me*
and spat [*on my daughters*]*!"*
And Kotharu-and-Khasisu said:
"Baʿlu, you will come back to my word!"
[*The two gods*][259] *(did build) his mansion,*
they did build the h[*ouse*],
they did set up his mansion.
They went to the Lebanon for its trees,
to the Shiryon[260] *for the choicest of its cedars*
yes, (to) the Lebanon for its trees,
(to) the Shiryon for the choicest of its cedars.[261]

[257] Cf. Isa. 16:2 and note 18. It is noteworthy that these two goddesses who represented certain types of dew of autumn were kept home during the episode corresponding to the summer.

[258] Baʿlu is referring to a destroyed episode between Baal III:iii and III:iv (KTU 1.2:III-IV). At the end of III:iii the sea-god Yammu asserted that he would obtain a wife somehow. At the beginning of column IV Baʿlu is still powerless. So it is certainly not too bold to assume that in between Yammu tried his luck with the wives and daughters of his defeated opponent. Cf. note 173. Note that in this passage Baʿlu still fears that Yammu might try something.

[259] *I.e.* the double god Kotharu-and-Khasisu.

[260] Probably the northern name of Mt. Hermon, cf. M. C. Astour, RSP II, viii.105; Y. Ideka, AJBI 4 (1978) 32-44.

[261] The Lebanon was still densely forested. Cf. AOAT 16,64, n. 8.

The mansion was set on fire,
the palace in flames.[262]
Look! For one day and a second
fire raged in the mansion,[263]
flames in the palace.
For a third (and) a fourth day
fire raged in the mansion,
flames in the palace.
For a fifth (and) a sixth day
fire raged in the mansion,
flames within the palace.
Then, on the seventh day,[264]
the fire was removed from the mansion,
the flames from the palace.
The silver had turned into[265] *sheets,*
the gold had been turned into bricks.[266]
Baʿlu the Almighty rejoiced:
"I have built[267] *my mansion of silver,*
my palace of gold!"

[262] Not to destroy it, as in Baal III (KTU 1.2):iii.13f., but to cover the walls with a coating of silver and gold. The miraculous process involved may have been inspired by the method used to purify the site of a temple with fire (cf. A. Falkenstein, Or 35 (1966) 230ff.).

[263] Cf. Lam. 4:11, to be understood in conjunction with the preceding note.

[264] The climactic seven-day pattern was used very frequently in Ugaritic literature (cf. UF 10 (1978) 190ff.; D. N. Freedman, JANES 3 (1970-71) 65-81; S. E. Loewenstamm, AOAT 204,192ff.). It is also attested in other ancient oriental texts (cf. Gen. 1; E. Ullendorff, BJRL 46 (1963-64) 245; J. van Dijk, RAI VII, Paris 1960, 69ff.).

[265] Cf. Zech. 14:10.

[266] Cf. Rev. 21:18.

[267] It was customary for the principal to claim all the credit for the building he commissioned. See *e.g.* 1 Ki. 3:13,27,43f.,48. For a close Sumerian parallel see H. Limet, Or 40 (1971) 21, line 49, with p. 27. According to Ex. 15:17 and Ps. 78:69 YHWH established his sanctuary Himself. According to Ps. 102:17 it was He who built Zion. See also 1 Sam. 2:35; Ps. 147:2.

Ba^{c}lu equipped his mansion with furnishings,
Haddu equipped his palace with furnishings.
He slaughtered oxen,
and small stock as well.
He slew bulls
and the fattest of rams,
yearling calves,
sheep, a multitude of lambkins.[268]
He invited his brothers to his mansion,[269]
his kin inside his palace,
he called the seventy[270] *sons of Athiratu.*
He supplied the ram gods with wine,
he supplied the ewe[271] *goddesses with wine.*
He supplied the ox gods with wine,
he supplied the cow goddesses with wine.

[268] For the seasonal background see the notes 226 and 271. Since the episode has its place in the part of the myth corresponding to the time around the spring equinox (see notes 269, 277, 288) it is admissible to compare the Passover lamb and the consecration of the firstborn males of the livestock which in Israel took place at exactly the same time of the year. In this case too a ''historical'' narrative had to provide the basis for the cultic practice. Cf. Ex. 12:21; 13:1,12f.,15; 34:19f.; Deut. 16:2. It is certain that the firstborn of the cattle were sacrificed in Ugarit, cf. Ritual III, note 19.

[269] The house-warming described here may be the mythological prototype of the dedication feast of the temple of Ba^{c}lu at Ugarit which could have taken place around the time of the vernal equinox, cf. AOAT 16,59-62 (add to the parallels cited there the date of the dedication of the temple of Bel at Palmyra: J. T. Milik, Recherches d'épigraphie proche-orientale, t.1, Paris 1972, 155). For the deification of the sacrificial animals and the furniture of the temple see UF 2 (1970) 199, 224f.; V. Haas — G. Wilhelm, AOATS 3 (1974) *passim*.

[270] Seventy is a significant round number, cf. F. C. Fensham, PEQ 109 (1977) 113ff. According to post-biblical tradition the number of the sons of El mentioned in the original text of Deut. 32:8 was seventy (the ''seventy angels'' of Targum Yerushalmi I).

[271] The Akkadian cognate usually adduced to explain this Ugaritic word denotes a female *spring* lamb. Cf. note 226.

He supplied the throne gods with wine,
he supplied the chair goddesses with wine.
He supplied the vase gods with wine,
he supplied the bowl goddesses with wine.
Again they ate, the gods drank,
and they were supplied with a suckling,[272]
with a salted knife they carved a fatling.
They drank beakers of wine,
from golden cups blood from the trees.[273]
(traces of 5 more lines, then broken off)

Just a few lines are missing between column VI and column VIII.

[ ] *of lap*[*is*]
[ ] *Baᶜlu the Almighty*
Then [*he poured*] *into Yammu, Beloved of Ilu,*[274]
[ ] *on his skull.*
The god [*Haddu*] *removed himself from the mountain*
while the gods were [*eating*] *on Sapanu.*
He marched from town to town,[275]
turned from city to city.
Sixty-six towns he seized,
seventy-seven cities,
Baᶜlu st[*ruck*] *eighty,*[276]
Baᶜlu expelled ninety.

[272] Cf. note 268.

[273] Cf. note 227.

[274] Apparently Baᶜlu pours a drugged potion into Yammu (the Sea) to keep him quiet during his absence. Cf. note 258.

[275] Cf. 2 Chron. 30:10. YHWH marches from place to place in Deut. 33:2; Judg. 5:4; Ps. 60:6ff.

[276] For the verb "to strike" with a geographic object see CAD (M)1, 77b and Num. 24:17.

(Then) he came [back] in the house,
Baᶜlu (back) inside the house.[277]
And Baᶜlu the Almighty said:
"*I will put (it in), Kotharu,* this very day,
(*I will put it in*), *Kotharu,* this very moment![278]
Let a window be opened in the mansion,
a lattice in the middle of the palace,
yes, let a rift be opened in the clouds,
according to your counsel, Kotharu-and-Khasisu!"
Kotharu-and-Khasisu laughed.
He raised his voice and cried:
"*Did I not tell you, o Baᶜlu Almighty,*
that you, Baᶜlu, would come back to my word?[279]

[277] This passage might commemorate the spreading of the cult of Baᶜlu after the founding of his sanctuary. While the sons of Ilu were dining on Mt. Sapanu Baᶜlu took over their territories. Since Baᶜlu re-enters his house soon afterwards it is possible that this episode was re-enacted in the form of a procession in the actual cult of Ugarit, cf. M. Dijkstra, Gods voorstelling, Kampen 1980, 208, n. 77. In Babylonia such processions were also held in connection with the New Year festival in spring (RAI XVII, 155ff., 160ff.). According to some scholars the Israelite Exodus and Conquest were re-enacted in a similar way during the festival of Passover/Mazzot, cf. *e.g.* J. B. Segal, The Hebrew Passover, London 1963, 137ff.; E. Otto, Das Mazzotfest in Gilgal, Stuttgart 1975. Cf. note 268.

The vernal equinox was the time when kings went to battle (cf. 2 Sam. 11:1; 1 Ki. 20:22,26; 2 Chr. 24:23; AOAT 16,157f.) and Baᶜlu was a "king", cf. column IV.43, VII.49f.

[278] The translation is somewhat uncertain. It is based mainly on the standard parallelism between "day" and "moment, time" in Jer. 46:21; 50:27,31; Ez. 7:7,12; 30:3. *bn* is interpreted as *b* + *hn*. Because the lattice is actually a rift in the clouds (lines 19,28) it is identical to the lattices through which the rain was poured according to Gen. 7:11; 8:2; 2 Ki. 7:2,19; Isa. 24:18; Mal. 3:10.

With the latter-rains of spring the correct time was of crucial importance. That may be the reason why Baᶜlu emphasizes the timing of his decision. See notes 240 and 256.

The opening of the window will have grave consequences. Soon afterwards Baᶜlu is threatened by the god of death Motu. According to an Anatolian myth the man Hupashiya was killed when he opened a window in his house, cf. V. Haas, Hethitische Berggötter, Mainz 1982, 110f. See also Jer. 9:20.

[279] Cf. col. V.58-VI.16.

Let a window be opened in the mansion,
a lattice in the middle of the palace!"
Baᶜlu opened a rift in the clouds.
Baᶜlu gave forth his holy voice,
Baᶜlu repeated the u[tterance of his li]ps.[280]
His holy voice made the earth [qu]ake,[281]
[the utterance of] his [lips] the mountains:
"I want to invade the inaccessible [ ],
[ ] the ancient [mountains]!"[282]
The heights of the earth[283] *rocked.*[284]
The foes of Baᶜlu[285] *seized the forests,*
the enemies of Haddu[286] *the slopes of the mountain.*
And Baᶜlu the Almighty said:
"Foes of Haddu, why do you invade?
Why do you invade, armour-bearers of the Place of Perdition?"[287]

280 Cf. Akkad. *ṣīt pî* and Num. 30:13; Deut. 23:24; Prov. 10:18. Also Aqhat III (KTU 1.19):iii.7 (par.).

281 Cf. Isa. 24:18; Joel 4:16; Ps. 18:8-14; 29:3-9, and for more parallels: M. Weinfeld, in: History, Historiography and Interpretation, Jerusalem/Leiden 1984, 121-147.

282 Cf. Num. 23:7; Deut. 33:15; Hab. 3:6.

283 Cf. Deut. 32:13; Isa. 58:14; Am. 4:13; Mic. 1:3.

284 Cf. Ps. 99:1.

285 Cf. 1 Sam. 30:26; 2 Sam. 12:24; Ps. 37:20, etc. The helpers of the god of death seized the forests and the slopes because they were thought to take the physical forms of violent east winds and flocks of migrating birds. See notes 288 and 301.

286 Cf. Ex. 20:5; 2 Chr. 19:2, etc.

287 Baᶜlu perceives beforehand that his attackers are the lackeys of Motu. He also foresees that he will be invited to descend into the gullet of the insatiable Death (lines 47ff., see Baal II:v [KTU 1.1:V] for a similar moment of "clairvoyance"). But even at the pinnacle of his power Baᶜlu is unable to stop the inexorable course of fate (see also note 300 below).

The basically cyclic concept of time underlying the nature myth of the Canaanites gave rise to a certain fatalism. Neither the good nor the bad forces in the realm of the gods could ever hope to win the final battle. Just as the mythopoet deliberately drops his metaphorical cover when he calls the window a "rift in the clouds", so he occasionally abandons the historical form of his story to indicate that the great gods,

Baʿlu watched the East,[288]
his hand verily shook,[289]
the cedar pole[290] *in his right hand.*
Then Baʿlu went back to his mansion.
"Should either king or commoner[291]
establish a territory of dominion for himself?
I must certainly send a scout
to Motu, the son of Ilu,
a courier[292] *to the Beloved of Ilu, the hero!*
Motu will invite (me) into his throat,
he will hide me in his gullet![293]

like man, knew perfectly well that they were subjected to the eternal cycle of the seasons. See OTS 24(1986) 1ff.

The "Place of Perdition" is a designation of the Nether World, comparable to Hebrew Abaddon, cf. Ps. 88:12; Job 26:6; 28:22; 31:12; Prov. 15:11; 27:20, with UF 17(1986)229.

[288] The description of the enemies, especially in the lines 55ff., makes it absolutely clear that they came with the sirocco, a very dry and hot east wind. Motu was held responsible for its blowing, see note 87 for the (less dangerous) sirocco of autumn. In Hos. 13:14f. death and the scorching east wind are paired. See also note 335 below.

The sirocco blows at intervals in spring from the end of March onwards. Traditionally it is expected to occur during the fifty days following the spring equinox (cf. notes 268, 269, 277). The dust from the Syrian desert obscures the sun during a spell of sirocco. The hot wind causes the annual flora to die. It is often noxious to fruit-trees and to the health of man. For details consult AOAT 16,173ff.

[289] Threatening the enemies, cf. Isa. 10:32; 11:15; 19:16; 49:22; Zech. 2:13; Job 31:21.

[290] The shaft of his spear-like thunderbolt, cf. A. Caquot-M. Sznycer, Ugaritic Religion, Leiden 1980, Pl. X.

[291] Cf. Baal III:iii.22 (KTU 1.2:III.22); KAI no. 10:10; 14:4. Note the unintroduced direct oration, cf. notes 337 and 399.

[292] Cf. KAI no. 202:A.12.

[293] Cf. Baal V: (KTU 1.5):i.6f.; ii.1ff.; Job 14:13. The word *gngn*, here translated by "gullet", actually means "pipe", also a "libation-pipe" (cf. notes 306 and 374). It serves as a metaphor for the esophagus (cf. note 312).

Libation-pipes were used in the cult of the dead at Ugarit and "the Great Libation-pipe" was a name for the entrance of the Nether World in Sumerian literature. Cf.

I alone am the one who can be king over the gods,[294]
who can fatten gods and men,
who can satisfy the multitudes of the earth!''[295]
Baᶜlu cried aloud to his lads:
''Look, Gupanu-and-Ugaru![296]
The sons of darkness[297] *obscure the day,*[298]
the sons of deep darkness (obscure) the Exalted Princess![299]
The wings of Fate[300] *are dust-coloured,*
flocks (of birds) are circling round in the clouds,
birds are circling round in the sky![301]
I am sure I must bind the snow in [the storehouses],
the lightning [in] its [storehouses]![302]

AOAT 16,170f. (to be corrected with regard to *ḫlb gngnt* which is a place name). All this offers the oriental background for Rev. 9:1f. where the entrance to the Abyss is likewise a shaft or chimney.

[294] Cf. Ps. 95:3. For Egyptian and Akkadian parallels as well as for the implications of this passage see J. C. de Moor, Uw God is mijn God. Over de oorsprong van het geloof in de ene God, Kampen 1983.

[295] Cf. Isa. 58:11; Ezek. 32:4; Ps. 103:5; 145:16; Job 38:27.

[296] Pair of servants of Baᶜlu. It is uncertain whether Ugaru has anything to do with the name of Ugarit.

[297] The helpers of Death. Cf. the ''sons of darkness'' in the Qumran literature.

[298] Cf. Am. 5:18,20; 8:9; Zeph. 1:15.

[299] Probably Lady Sun (Shapshu), cf. note 288.

[300] The word *mnt*, here translated by ''Fate'', actually means ''portion(s)'', just like the Greek μοῖρα and αἶσα. Sometimes the Moira are represented as winged goddesses, cf. S. Eitrem, PRE XV, Stuttgart 1932, 2472. Manat is also attested as a pre-islamic goddess, cf. T. Fahd, Le panthéon de l'Arabie Centrale à la veille de l'Hégire, Paris 1968, 123ff.

[301] A reference to the migration of birds in spring. Because the spirits of the dead could take the form of birds, the bird migration heralded both the revival of Baᶜlu in autumn and his journey to the Nether World in spring. See Aqhat, notes 170, 267, 268, 280.

[302] Cf. Job 38:22 (tautological parallelism!) and Baal I, fragment a, lines 3f. (KTU 1.101:3f.). Compare also Job 26:8 and Prov. 30:4, as well as Baᶜlu's ''ship'' with snow in Baal IV (KTU 1.4):v.7. Towards the end of April snow disappears even from the highest mountains. Cf. AOAT 16,176. Thunderstorms are a rarity in the Syrian summer.

[ ] will die [ ]
lift up [ ].''
(broken)

Here about six lines are missing. At the beginning of column VIII Baˁlu is still speaking to his lads.

VIII.

''*Then you must head straight*
for the mountain Targhuzaz,
the mountain Sharrumag,[303]
the two mounds at the edge of the earth.
Lift up a mountain with your hands,
a forested hill with your palms
and descend into the House of Freedom[304] *of the earth,*
be counted among those who went down into the earth.[305]
Then you must head straight
for his city Humurayu.[306]

[303] The vocalisation of these names is uncertain. Probably they are Hurrian names of the two mountains marking the entrance of the Nether World (cf. AOAT 16,171). The name ''Tharrumag'' might be connected with the Anatolian mountain god Sharruma whereas ''Targhuzaz'' resembles the name of the weather god Tarkunzai who throned on a majestic mountain, cf. Haas, *op. cit.* (note 278), 23, 67, 78ff. Differently M. Tsevat, JNSL 3 (1974) 71-75.

[304] Euphemism for the Nether World which in reality was a ''land of no return'' (cf. 2 Sam. 22:5f.; Ps. 116:3; Job 10:21; 16:22 and for more parallels AOAT 16,185f.). In 2 Ki. 15:5 ''house of freedom'' is a euphemism for a place of total confinement,a leper house. In Ps. 88:6 we read ''among the dead I am 'free' ''. Cf. RSP I, 27f.; RSP II, iii.29; O. Loretz, UF 8 (1976) 129ff.; also V. Haas, Or 45 (1976) 197ff. and O. R. Gurney, Some Aspects of Hittite Religion, Oxford 1977, 59ff. for some Hittite parallels.

[305] Cf. Ps. 88:5, with RSP I, i.21 and BiOr 31 (1974) 5.

[306] Vocalization uncertain. The name means ''deep pit, tunnel''. Cf. note 293.

The throne he sits on is a pit,[307]
the land of his inheritance[308] *is filth.*[309]
But watch out,[310] *attendants of the gods,*
do not come near[311] *to Motu, the son of Ilu,*
lest he make you like a lamb in his mouth,
lest you disappear *like a kid in the jaws of his gullet!*[312]
The Lamp of the gods, Shapshu, has a dusty colour,
the heavens are soiled by Motu, the son of Ilu.[313]
Over a thousand acres,
ten thousand square miles,[314]
bow down at the feet of Motu and fall down,
prostrate yourselves and honour him.
And say to Motu, the son of Ilu,
repeat to the Beloved of Ilu, the hero:
'A message from Baᶜlu the Almighty,
a word from the Mightiest of heroes:
I have built my mansion of silver,
[I have erected my palace of gold].
[And I have invited][315] *my brothers [and my kin],*

[307] The O.T. uses *bōr* or *šaḥat*. Because the former is identical to *beʾēr* "cistern, spring" it is definitely a watery place. Cf. Isa. 14:15; 38:18; Ez. 26:20; 32:23; Ps. 28:1; 55:24; 69:16, etc.

[308] See note 101.

[309] Others translate "pit" or "hole". However, this translation does not fit all the passages where the word *ḫḫ* occurs. The Nether World was a miry pit, cf. Ps. 40:2; T. H. Gaster, JRAS 1944, 35; N. H. Ridderbos, OTS 5 (1948) 174ff.; J. Bottéro, RAI XXVI, Copenhagen 1980, 33, 48. Especially interesting is KAR 22:Rev.10 where the chtonic deity Sumuqan is described as "the one who desires filth (*ḫaḫḫu*)".

[310] Cf. Prov. 3:21.

[311] Cf. Josh. 3:4.

[312] Lit. "in the molars of his cane", cf. note 134. In Jewish Aramaic and Syriac "cane" is likewise a metaphor for the esophagus or the wind-pipe. Cf. note 293. The verb *ḫtʾ* "to disappear" was misunderstood by the Masoretes in Hab.3:6f.: "for Him the ways of old disappeared".

[313] See the notes 87 and 288.

[314] Cf. note 68.

[315] Cf. Baal V(KTU 1.5):i.22ff.

I have called my brothers to my mansion,
my kin inside my palace.
I [*also*] *call Motu,* [*the son of Ilu*]:
[*let Motu, the son*] *of Ilu,* [*be sated*],
[*let*] *the Belov*[*ed of Ilu, the he*]*ro* [*be fa*]*ttened!*'"[316]
[*Gupanu*]*-and Ugaru* [*departed*].

[317]

[*And Mo*]*tu* [*answered:*]
["*Well, a lion's appetite craves live prey*]
[*(even) if the sperm-whales' pleasure is in the sea,*]
[*if it is the pool that attracts the wild oxen,*]
[*the spring the herd of does.*][318]
[*If I have an appetite, indeed, indeed,*][319]
[*to devour clay,*][320]
[*then, indeed, I shall eat (it) with both my hands,*]
[*if my seven portions are in the bowl,*]
[*if Naharu*[321] *mixes the cup!*]
[*Because Baʿlu did not invite me with my brothers,*]
[*Haddu did (not) call me with my kin,*]

[316] Cf. col. VII.50f.

[317] The scribe deliberately omits the episode describing the journey of the messengers, their encounter with Motu and the delivery of their message. See note 251.

[318] Cf. Ps. 42:2. Motu adduces these examples to prove that his own desires are just as natural as the instincts of animals.

[319] Cf. Num. 5:22; Deut. 27:15; Ps. 41:14; 72:19; 89:53; Neh. 8:6.

[320] Cf. Ex. 15:12; Isa. 5:14; Hab. 2:5; Ps. 49:15; 141:7; Prov. 1:12. "Clay" is the food in the Nether World, cf. *e.g.* Gilg.Ep. VII:iv.37 (cf. UF 1 (1969) 187, n. 149). It is also, however, the substance of mortal bodies, cf. Job 4:19; 33:6 and for more parallels: The Bible World. Essays ... C. H. Gordon, New York 1980, 180ff.). Motu eats this "clay", just like his Babylonian counterpart Ereshkigal, cf. Descent of Ishtar, 33.

[321] Cf. note 127.

[but did eat bread with my brothers]
[and did drink wine with my kin,]
[while I, (o) Ba^{c}lu, was forgotten —][322]
[(therefore) I shall certainly pierce you,]
[... you!"]

Edge:
[Scribe: Ilimilku, offi]ciant of Niqmaddu, king of Ugarit.

Nothing is missing between the restored end of column VIII of tablet IV and column I of tablet V.

Baal V

KTU 1.5

"Although you defeated Lotanu, [323] *the fleeing serpent,* [324]
destroyed the coiling serpent, [325]
the Tyrant with the seven heads,

[322] Just like his Babylonian colleague Ereshkigal the Ugaritic god of death had been excluded from the festive meal. Cf. ANET, 507f. As far as we know the god of death did not receive offerings in the regular cult of Ugarit.

[323] Identical to the Hebrew Leviathan, cf. Isa. 27:1. The name means "the wreath-like, the circular" because the primeval sea-serpent was thought to surround the earth. Cf. BiOr 31 (1974) 5.

[324] Cf. Isa. 27:1; Job 26:13. The great sea-serpent is called "the fleeing one" because it perpetually tries to catch up with its own tail. Cf. note 323.

[325] Cf. Baal I (KTU 1.3):iii.41. On the basis of Isa. 27:1 it has to be assumed that the coiling serpent is identical to the Leviathan. In Incantation II (KTU 1.83) these marine monsters seem to be identified with the sea-god Yammu himself. See also the notes 57-64 above.

The struggle between a god and a serpent-like dragon is a very popular theme in the ancient Near East, see *e.g.* Gudea, Cyl.A, XXV-XXVI; Lugal-e, 133; MIO 1 (1953) 80, line 3; En.el. IV, cf. I.121; II.27; III.31, 89; Ps. 74:14; Rev. 12-13. Compare also the many-headed Hydra of the Greeks. The struggle is also depicted on

you were uncovered, the heaven came loose[326]
like the girdle of your cloak![327]
I, however, will eat (you) in red lumps of two spans,
you will go down in two cubit chunks
into the throat[328] *of Motu, the son of Ilu,*
into the gullet[329] *of the Beloved of Ilu, the hero!"*
The two gods departed, they did not tarry.
Then they headed straight
for Baˁlu in the heights of Sapanu.
And Gupanu-and-Ugaru[330] *said:*
"A message from Motu, the son of Ilu,
a word from the Beloved, son of Ilu, the hero:[331]
'Well, a lion's appetite craves live prey,
(even) if the sperm-whales' pleasure is in the sea,
if it is the pool that attracts the wild oxen,
the spring the herd of does.
If I have an appetite, indeed, indeed,
to devour clay,

several Mesopotamian and Syrian seals, cf. E. Douglas van Buuren, Or 15 (1946) 19f., Pl.IV; L. J. Delaporte, Catalogue des cylindres orientaux du Musée du Louvre, t.2, Paris 1910, Pl.96(16) A.918; G. A. Eisen, Ancient Oriental Cylinder and Other Seals, Chicago 1940, No. 158-159; ANEP, No. 670-671; L. Gorelick-E. Williams-Forte, Ancient Seals and the Bible, Malibu 1983, No. 3. On the Syrian seals ˁAnatu seems to witness the killing of the dragon.

326 To be uncovered unwillingly was a humiliation, see *e.g.* 2 Sam. 10:4; Isa. 20:4; Am. 2:16. So Baˁlu's victory over the sea-monster was only a Pyrrhic one, as indeed it was (cf. UF 11 (1979) 641, nn.13-14; OTS 24 (1986) 1ff.; notes 186, 258). The heavens are viewed here as the mantle of Baˁlu, cf. Akkad. *nalbaš šamê* ("garb of the sky" = clouds); Isa. 40:22; Ps. 18:12; 97:2; 102:26-28; Rev. 6:14.

327 Reading *kr⟨k⟩s*. The loosening of the girdle was an ignominious act, cf. Gilg. VII:iv.5; En.el. I.67; Erra IV.2 and note 326.

328 Cf. Isa. 5:14; Hab. 2:5; Prov. 1:12.

329 Actually a place into which liquids were poured. See note 293 and col. II below.

330 See note 296.

331 See with this message the notes 318-322.

then, indeed, I shall eat (it) with both my hands,
if my seven portions are in the bowl,
if Naharu mixes the cup!
Because Baʿlu did not invite me with my brothers,
Haddu did (not) call me with my kin,
but did eat bread with my brothers
and did drink wine with my kin,
while I, (o) Baʿlu, was forgotten —
(therefore) I shall certainly pierce you,
[....] *you!*
Although you defeated Lotanu, the fleeing serpent,
destroyed the coiling serpent,
the Tyrant with the seven heads,
you were uncovered, the heaven came loose
like the girdle of your cloak!
I, however, will eat (you) in red lumps of two spans,
you will go down in two cubit chunks
into the throat of Motu, the son of Ilu,
into the gullet of the Beloved of Ilu, the hero!'"
(broken)

Between the end of column I and the beginning of column II about 40 lines describing Baʿlu's reaction are missing. When the tablet becomes readable again an unknown speaker is describing the gaping jaws of Motu, the god of death.

"[ ]*s.*
[*One lip* (*is*) *to the e*]*arth,*
one lip to the sky,
[*he sets*] (*his*) *tongue against the stars.*[332]

[332] Cf. Ps. 73:9 and Incantation II (KTU 1.83).

Baʿlu will enter his belly,
will go down in his mouth.''[333]
Because he[334] *was scorching*[335] *the olives,*
the produce of the earth
and the fruit of the trees,[336]
Baʿlu the Almighty feared him,
the Rider on the Clouds dreaded him.
''Depart![337] *Say to Motu, the son of Ilu,*
repeat to the Beloved of Ilu, the hero:
'A message from Baʿlu the Almighty,
a word from the Mightiest of heroes:
Hurry to meet me, o Motu, son of Ilu!
I am your slave,[338]
yes, yours for ever!' ''[339]
The two gods departed, they did not tarry.

333 Cf. note 293 and Ugaritica V, 268:40; Isa. 5:14; Ps. 141:7; 1 Petr. 5:8. For Egypt: J. Zandee, Death as an Enemy According to Ancient Egyptian Conceptions, Leiden 1960, 16f., 147ff.; H. te Velde, Seth, God of Confusion, Leiden 1967, 91ff.

334 *Scil.* Motu.

335 The poet is still relating the mythical events that according to him formed the prototype of the spring time, cf. notes 226, 268, 271, 277, 278, 288, 301, 302. In spring the sirocco which in Ugarit was thought to be caused by the god of death Motu threatened the future crops, especially the fruit trees (cf. Ez. 17:10; 19:12; AOAT 16,175,180). Here this circumstance provides a *rationale* for the death of the rain-god Baʿlu. His self-sacrifice will save the crops.

It is important to note that the Ugaritic verb *ḥrr* ''to scorch'' is related to one of the Arabic names for the sirocco (*ḥrwr*). The Dictionnaire arabe-français-anglais, t.4, Paris 1978, 2389 has the following highly interesting quotation: ''any burning heat or torrid wind (sirocco) you feel is but the breath of Hell''.

336 Cf. Judg. 6:4; Hab. 3:17.

337 Unintroduced direct oration. Cf. note 291. Baʿlu is addressing his servants Gupanu-and-Ugaru.

338 Cf. KAV 159:6; Nbn. 1113:24; BMS 2:26, Ps. 116:16.

339 Cf. Kirtu I (KTU 1.14):i.49;iii.35, etc.; Deut. 15:17; 1 Sam. 27:12; Job 40:28.

Then they headed straight
for Motu, the son of Ilu,
in his city Humurayu.[340]
The throne he sits on is a pit,
the land of his inheritance is filth.
They raised their voices and cried:
"*A message from the Almighty,*
an announcement from Baʿlu,
a word from the Mightiest of heroes:
'*Hurry to meet me, o Motu, son of Ilu!*
I am your slave,
yes, yours for ever!'"
Motu, the son of Ilu rejoiced.
[*He gave forth*] *his voice and cried:*
"*How can* [*Baʿlu*] *provide moisture* (*now*)?[341]
How can [*Haddu*] *sprinkle?*
[*My hand shattered*] *the strength of Haddu,*[342]
my war-hand [ ]!
[*I b*]*egot the Sting,*[343]
[ ]!"
He made wipe [ ]
[ ].
They departed [ ]
[ ]
fishes [ ]
(broken)

[340] See with this passage notes 306-309.
[341] Cf. Baal VI (KTU 1.6):i.48.
[342] Cf. Baal VI (KTU 1.6):i.50 and Job 20:10.
[343] An evil demon according to Deut. 32:24; Ps. 91:6 and especially Hos. 13:14. Cf. J. Trachtenberg, Jewish Magic and Superstition, repr. Philadelphia 1961, 36, as well as Job 18:13.

About 37 lines are missing between column II and the poor remnants of column III. Someone (the Sun goddess?) seems to be instructing Baʿlu about a safe journey through the Nether World which is euphemistically called a "dwelling/land of bliss".

III.

[ ]
"[*W*]*ide*[344] *is the dwelling you* [will enter],
great is the dwelling of blis[*s*][345]
[*and Happi*]*ness*[346] *is the land of bliss.*
[ ] *you must make ready,*
you must complete [ ].
Let [your clothes] *be white*,[347]
your white garb [*like the Moon*],[348]
pure like the star[*s*[349] your cloak].[350]
Then you must call Motu [*from his mansion*],
the Beloved from the mid[*st of his palace*].
Surely I shall make ... into [*a heifer*],[351]
I shall turn you into a bu[*ll-calf of the steppe*].[352]

[344] Cf. Ex. 34:24; Deut. 12:20; 19:8; Am. 1:13; Isa. 30:23; 54:2. With regard to the Hereafter, cf. John 14:2.

[345] The related Arabic word *ḥasanah* "beauty, delight" sometimes describes the bliss of the Hereafter.

[346] See for this euphemistic name col. VI.6 and AOAT 16,191.

[347] Cf. E. Hornung, Tal der Könige, Darmstadt 1983, 140; Ägyptische Unterweltsbücher, 2.Aufl., Zürich 1984, 264; Eccl. 9:8; Matth. 28:3; Rev. 3:18; etc., also Matth. 22:11f.; Ps.-Philo, Lib.Ant.Bibl., 64:6.

[348] Cf. Isa. 24:23; 30:26; Song of Songs 6:10.

[349] Cf. Job 25:5.

[350] Cf. col. V.24.

[351] For this meaning of *šyt b* see Isa. 5:6 ("make into a wildernis", *b^{e}tōhū*) and Ps. 12:6.

[352] This seems to be part of a plot to spare Baʿlu the horror of being crushed to death between the jaws of Motu. The trick is that Motu will be unable to distinguish Baʿlu from the other animals of the herd and will have eaten his fill before he discovers his opponent. For the guise see col. V.18ff. and Loves II, note 31.

Be horrified, but go[353], [*o Ba*ˁ*lu*]!
[Be horrified], *but go, o god*!
[Be horrified, *but go*], *o Most Graceful among the gods*!
[And say to Motu:]
'*Plenty offspring of cattle* [*I bring you*],[354]
plenty offspring of cattle [*I*].
So I ca[*ll Motu from his mansion*],
the Beloved from the midst [*of his palace*]!'
[Be horrified], *but go, o god*!
[Be horrified, but go!]
And say to [*Motu*], *the s*[*on of Ilu*]:
'*With plenty small stock* [*I have come*],
with plenty small stock a[*nd offspring of cattle*],
[I bring you] *many firm-fleshed animals.*
So I call Motu [*from his mansion*],
the Beloved from the midst [*of his palace*]!'
Be horrified, but go, [o Baˁlu]!
[Be horrified, but g]*o, o g*[*od*]!
[Be horrified, but go, o Most Graceful among the gods!]'''
(broken)

About 50 lines are missing between the end of column III and the beginning of column IV. Probably they contained more secret instructions for Baˁlu. Meanwhile a banquet is going on in the houses of Ilu and Baˁlu (line 21) and someone, probably Ilu, notices the absence of Baˁlu.[355]

----- [ ]
and to seek [ ].

[353] For this kind of pairing of imperatives see Gen 12:19; 24:51; 1 Sam. 23:27. For the epithet "Most Graceful", cf. note 40.
[354] Cf. Hos. 5:6.
[355] Cf. 1 Sam. 20:27.

A hundred spirit[*s* he sent out][356]
(*who*) *had to search* [the steppe-land].
He raised his voice and cried:
"*Where - o* (*where*) *is Baᶜ*[*lu*, our king]?
Where is Haddu who [fattens the gods]?[357]
Let Baᶜ[*lu*] *appear* [*in my chambers*],
in the eight en[*trances of* (*my*) *lockable rooms*]![358]
Let him come near [ ],
[*let him eat*] *the bread of* [*my banquet*]!"
Again they ate, the gods drank,
and they were supplied with a suckling,[359]
with a knife they carved a fatling.
They drank beakers of wine,
from golden cups blood from the trees.[360]
[They filled] *the cups of silver*,
beaker [*after beaker*].
And the cup-bearers came again,
they brought up must [*to the house of Baᶜlu*],
to the house of Ilu until no ready-made wine was left,[361]
on the carrying-net [ ].
"*Who is sending to* [ ]?
(*Who*) *is sending the* [ ]?"
They recounted him [ ],
the reviler of [ ].[362]
(broken)

[356] Cf. Judg. 9:23; Ps. 104:30; also 1 Ki. 22:21ff.; Isa. 6:8.

[357] Cf. Baal IV (KTU 1.4):vii.50f. with notes 294-295. The call "Where is Baᶜlu?" is a kind of prelude to Baal VI (KTU 1.6):iv.4f., 15f. In April there falls only *ca.* 80 millimetres of rain, half as much as in March and only a third of the amount of February.

[358] See note 85.

[359] See note 226. Here the formulaic verse has been shortened.

[360] See note 227.

[361] Cf. Num. 6:4; 1 Sam. 25:18; Ezra 9:14; 2 Chron. 14:12; 20:25.

[362] Baᶜlu had also been accused of having "reviled" the family of Ilu before he had to succumb to Yammu, cf. Baal II (KTU 1.1):iv.23.

About 40 lines are lost between the end of column IV and the beginning of column V. Again an unknown speaker, probably the Sun-goddess, instructs Baʿlu about his journey to the Nether World, providing him with a ruse to escape real death.

"[ ],
[*o Baʿlu*] *Almighty*!
[*You shall clothe him*] *with the cloak of your* sovereignty,[363]
[*with your strength*,[364] *the gift*] *of your right hand*,[365]
with the chains [*from your breast*].[366]
Your s[*on will hav*]*e the soul of a bull-calf*,[367]
him I will put into a grave of the earth-gods.[368]
And you, take[369] *your clouds*,
your winds, your thunderbolts,[370] *your rains*,[371]
(*take*) *with you your seven lads*,
your eight 'boars',[372]

363 Baʿlu did not need his own robe in the Nether World, cf. col. III.5-12 and the lines 18-26 below. For the transfer of power by means of a mantle, see *e.g.* Ex. 29:5; Num. 20:26; 1 Ki. 14:8; 19:19; Isa. 22:21.

364 Reading ʾu*lh* in line 24. Cf. Isa. 51:9; 52:1; note 376.

365 The strongest hand.

366 Cf. Ex. 28:14,22.

367 Cf. below lines 18ff. as well as col. III.11f., with note 352.

368 A standard formula for a decent burial with the deified ancestors. For "earth" in the meaning of Nether World, cf. Akkad. *erṣetu*, Hebr. *ʾrṣ*, Isa. 29:4; Jer. 17:13, etc.

369 Cf. Ez. 4:9, also Gen. 6:21; Ex. 30:23; 2 Sam. 20:6; Ez. 4:3.

370 Cf. Baal I (KTU 1.3):iv.26.

371 A very clear reference to the seasonal background of the myth. During a spell of vernal sirocco (cf. note 335) rain-clouds, rain-bringing west winds, lightning and rain disappear, not to recur in summer (about May-September), cf. AOAT 16,187-189.

372 An obscure metaphor, perhaps a reference to the seven or eight Pleiades. The disappearance of this constellation from the night sky was connected with the beginning of the dry season, cf. AOAT 16,187f.

(take) with you Pidrayu, the girl of the honey-dew,
with you Tallayu, the girl of the mist.[373]
Then you shall head straight
for the two mountains of my tunnel.[374]
Lift up a mountain with your hands,
a forested hill with your palms
and descend into the House of Freedom[375] *of the earth,*
be counted among those who went down into the earth,
and experience a weakness like the state of death!''[376]
Baʿlu the Almighty obeyed.
He loved a heifer in the steppe,[377]
a young cow on the field of the stream[378] *of the place of death,*[379]
He copulated with her seven and seventy times,
she made him mount eight and eighty times.[380]
She conceived and gave birth
to a twin-brother, an o[x].

[373] Note the absence of Arsayu, the goddess who had to stay on earth to provide the heavy dew of the Syrian summer. See note 18.

[374] The two mountains marking the tunnel in the west where the sun descended into the earth. Cf. notes 293 and 303. Also Gilg. IX:iv.46 and M. Tsevat, JNSL 3 (1974) 71-75.

[375] See notes 304-305 with these lines.

[376] Cf. Isa. 14:10; Ps. 88:4; Job 14:10; BiOr 26 (1969) 107, n. 20; 31 (1974) 18. See also Baal III (KTU 1.2):iv.1; V (KTU 1.5):ii.22f.; v.4,24.

[377] The immediate surroundings of the entrance of the Nether World are often depicted as a steppe or desert, cf. A. Haldar, The Notion of the Desert in Sumero-Accadian and West-Semitic Religions, Uppsala 1950, 14ff.; J. Bottéro, in: B. Alster (ed.), Death in Mesopotamia, Copenhagen 1980, 31. With regard to the theriomorphic intercourse see note 352.

[378] The river of death has many parallels, *e.g.* in Mesopotamia (Bottéro, *loc.cit.*), Greece (the river Styx) and Israel, cf. Job 33:18. See also col. I.21f. and Keret I (KTU 1.14), notes 8-9.

[379] Cf. Job 33:22 *mmt ym* ''the place of death of the sea'', and compare 33:18. See notes 129 and 169.

[380] Mythological exaggeration of the potency of Baʿlu. The picture of a heifer being mounted in the pasturage or on the shore was a familiar one about this time of the year, cf. AOAT 16,187,189.

*Ba*ʿ*lu clothed him with the cloa*[*k of his* sovereignty],
with his strength, the gift [*of his right hand*],
[*with the chai*]*ns from his breast.*
(broken)

About 41 lines are missing between the end of column V and the restored beginning of column VI. Two messengers[381] report to Ilu that they have found the dead body of Baʿlu. In reality it is probably the corpse of the twin-brother who meanwhile has been killed by Motu.

Then they headed straight
for Ilu at the fountain-head of the two Rivers,
in the middle of the bedding of the two Floods.[382]
They appeared in the encampment of Ilu
and entered the camp of the King, the Father of Years.
They raised their voices and cried:
"*We two went around to the fringes of the land,*
to the emmer[383] *of the lowland.*[384]
We reached Happiness,[385] *the steppe-land,*
Delightfulness, the field of the stream of the place of death.

381 Perhaps they belonged to the spirits that had been sent out to seek Baʿlu, col. IV.3. Because messengers used to travel in pairs there is no specific reason to think of Gupanu-and-Ugaru.

382 See with these lines notes 81-83.

383 The time of this episode is fixed between the middle of April and the middle of May by the circumstance that the emmer-corn is still ripening on the fields while Ilu strews ears of barley (*ʿmr*) on his head (lines 14f.). Cf. AOAT 16,195. Also below, Keret, note 93.

384 Cf. Keret III (KTU 1.16):iii.3f., with the pertinent note.

385 This euphemistic designation of the realm of death (cf. note 346, also note 304) is alluded to in Ps. 16:6, cf. 10f. See for the "place of death" note 129.

We came upon Ba^clu,
he had fallen to the ground!
Ba^clu the Almighty is dead,[386]
his Highness, the Lord of earth, has perished!"
The Benevolent, Ilu the good-natured,
descended from his chair,[387]
sat down on the foot-stool,
and from the foot-stool, he sat down on the ground.[388]
He scattered a sheaf of mourning on his head,[389]
the dust in which he rolled on his skull,
for clothing he covered himself with a loin-cloth.[390]
He scratched (his) skin with a stone,[391]
using a flint blade as a razor,
he gashed (his) cheeks and chin.[392]

[386] According to many scholars this would have been a cult cry. For mockery about the death of gods, cf. Ps. 82:7.

[387] Descending from the throne was a token of mourning, cf. Isa. 47:1; Ez. 26:16; Jonah 3:6.

[388] Sitting or wallowing in the dust is likewise a rite of mourning, cf. Isa. 58:5; Jer. 6:26; Ez. 27:30; Mic. 1:10; Job 16:15. It is doubtlessly a sympathetic rite, imitating the descent of the deceased into the dusty Nether World. Cf. note 396.

[389] It is unknown whether or not the "sheaf of mourning" was the Canaanite equivalent of the Israelite waving of the first sheaf of barley about this time of the year (April, cf. Lev. 23:10-14).

[390] A very simple garment was the appropriate wear of the mourner, cf. AOAT 16,192; Descent of Ishtar, 82.

[391] Knives of stone were used only for cultic purposes, especially for making incisions, cf. Josh. 5:2f.

[392] Cf. S. E. Loewenstamm, UF 14 (1982) 119-123. Lacerating one's own body was another sign of utter distress, see *e.g.* Aqhat III (KTU 1.19):iv.173,184; Jer. 16:6; 41:5; [illegible] and with regard to Baal Hos. 7:14; 1 Ki. 18:28. For other ancient oriental parallels cf. AOAT 16,194. Laceration of the body was forbidden in Israel (Lev. 19:28; 21:5; Deut. 14:1), probably not simply because it was a Canaanite rite of mourning, but because the Canaanites practised this rite in connection with the cult of Ba^clu.

The mourning for *ʾadn* Ba^clu lived on in the rites for Adonis in Byblos, see Lucian, De Dea Syria, par.6. It is also alluded to in Hos. 10:5 and Zech. 12:11.

Three times he treated[393] *his collar-bones,*[394]
he ploughed his breast, like a garden,
three times he treated his chest, like a valley.
He raised his voice and cried:
"*Baˁlu is dead!*
What about the people of the son of Daganu?
What about the multitude of the followers of Baˁlu?[395]
I will descend into the earth!"[396]
ˁAnatu also wandered about and scoured
every mountain to the middle of the earth,
every hill to the middle of the fields.
She reached Happiness, the steppe-land,
Delightfulness, the field of the stream of the place of death.
She came upon Baˁlu,
he had fallen to the ground,
For clothing she covered herself with a loin-cloth.

Nothing is missing between tablet V and tablet VI.

[393] The rather laboured metaphor may have been chosen because in this time of the year the third ploughing of the fruit-gardens took place (April, cf. AOAT 16,196). Because the precise meaning of the verb *ṯlṯ* "to do for the third time" is determined by the synonymous parallelism ("to plough like a garden") the severe criticism of L. L. Grabbe, UF 8 (1976) 63; 14 (1982) 89-92 would seem to be unjustified. See also Ps. 129:3.

[394] Cf. Job 31:22.

[395] The multitudes dependent on Baˁlu, cf. Baal IV (KTU 1.4):vii.52. On the basis of KTU 1.161:20 one might consider an alternative translation: "Baˁlu is dead—what of the people? / The son of Daganu (is dead)—what of the multitude? / After Baˁlu I descend into the earth". On the other hand the short colon "Baˁlu is dead" nicely balances the equally short "I will descend into the earth".

[396] Cf. Gen. 37:35. The descending was symbolical of course, cf. VI.11ff.

Baal VI

KTU 1.6

I.

Of Baʿlu.[397]

She scratched (her) skin with a stone,
using a flint blade as a razor,
she gashed (her) cheeks and chin.[398]
Three times she treated her collar-bones,
she ploughed her breast, like a garden,
three times she treated her chest, like a valley.
"Baʿlu is dead![399]
What about the people of the son of Daganu?
What about the multitude of the followers of Baʿlu?
Let us descend into the earth!"

[397] Heading for library purposes.

[398] See with this episode the notes 391-396. It is likely that ʿAnatu's roaming in the fields (Baal V (KTU 1.5):vi.25ff.) was represented in the form of a procession with the image of ʿAnatu/ʿAthtartu. It has been established that such a procession took place in Ugarit at the end of April, cf. AOAT 16,201. It is also significant that Lucian and Apuleius, recording a procession of the Syrian goddess Atargatis (= ʿAthtart-ʿAnat), expressly mention the fact that the priests accompanying the image of the goddess used to lacerate themselves, cf. P.-L. van Berg, Corpus Cultus Deae Syriae, vol. 1/1, Leiden 1972, 61-77. If the "appointed days" mentioned by Lucian, De Dea Syria, 50 fell during the great spring festival he describes in 49, the lacerating took place in the course of that festival.

According to Lucian, De Dea Syria, 6, the women of Byblos imitated the funeral of Adonis (= Adon or Adoni, a title of Baal, see note 435). They wept, beat their breasts, shaved off their hair, and sacrificed to Adonis as if he were a dead person. The date of this ceremonial funeral was determined by the arrival of the vernal sirocco, cf. note 335 and AOAT 16,201. Am. 8:11-14 might have been inspired by this.

[399] In contrast to Baal V (KTU 1.5):vi.22 the direct oration is not introduced by one of the standard formulae. Cf. notes 291 and 337.

With her descended
Shapshu,[400] *the Lamp of the gods.*
Until she was sated with weeping
she drank tears like wine.[401]
Aloud she cried
to Shapshu, the Lamp of the gods:
"Hoist, I pray,
Baᶜlu the Almighty on to me!"
Shapshu the Lamp of the gods obeyed.
She lifted up Baᶜlu the Almighty,
on the shoulders of ᶜAnatu she put him.
They brought him up to the heights of Sapanu.
They bewailed him and buried him,[402]
put him into a grave of the earth-gods.[403]
She [404] *slaughtered seventy wild oxen,*
because Baᶜlu the Almighty had been defiled,[405]
she slaughtered seventy oxen,
because Baᶜlu the Almighty had been defiled,
she slaughtered seventy sheep,
because Baᶜlu the Almighty had been defiled,
she slaughtered seventy harts,

[400] Cf. note 164. The more or less prosaic wording as well as the unbalanced verses and strophes of this episode express grief.

[401] Cf. ASKT 117:21f.; Ps. 80:6; Job 9:18; Lam. 3:15.

[402] Cf. note 398 and Zech. 12:11. The theme of the two women mourners may be significant, cf. Mar. 15:47 (par.).

[403] Cf. note 368. Although the two goddesses do not seem to know this, it is of course the "twin-brother" they are burying.

Graves of deities were no rarity in Canaan, cf. Pseudo-Clemens, Recognitiones, 10:24. The Phoenician Pyrgi-inscription, 7-9, mentions a "day of the burial of the god" in the month Kirari.

[404] *Viz.* ᶜAnatu.

[405] Death defiled, cf. Lev. 21:1; Num. 5:2; 6:9ff.; 9:10; 19:11ff.; Hag. 2:13 (in the Ethiopic Bible the root *gmn* corresponds to Hebr. *ṭmʾ* "be ritually unclean"); K. van der Toorn, Sin and Sanction in Israel and Mesopotamia, Assen 1985, 36f.

because Baᶜlu the Almighty had been defiled,
she slaughtered seventy mountain-goats,
because Baᶜlu the Almighty had been defiled,
she slaughtered seventy roebucks,[406]
because Baᶜlu the Almighty had been defiled.[407]
[*In*] *his* [*c*]*lan ᶜA*[*natu*] *proclaimed herself a nubile widow,*
[*so that*] *his* [*fe*]*llows would fulfil the nuptial duty for the gods.*[408]
Then she headed straight
for Ilu at the fountain-head of the two Rivers,
in the middle of the bedding of the two Floods.[409]
She appeared in the encampment of Ilu
and entered the camp of the King, the Father of Years.
At the feet of Ilu she bowed and fell down,
prostrated herself and honoured him.
She raised her voice and cried:
"*Let Athiratu and her sons rejoice now,*
the Goddess and the troop of her kin![410]
For Baᶜlu the Almighty is dead,
his Highness, the Lord of earth, has perished!"
Ilu cried aloud
to Lady Athiratu of the Sea:
"*Listen, o Lady Athiratu of the Sea!*

[406] Cf. H. L. Ginsberg, JANES 5 (1973) 131f.

[407] This episode reflects an actual sacrifice on Mt. Sapanu (for this mountain see note 4). The exact date of this festival is known from ancient sources: the 23rd of April. Of course the macrocosmic size of the sacrifices mentioned in the myth could not be matched in reality, but the correspondence with the actual numbers is arresting: seven bulls, seven rams and again seven bulls for Baᶜlu. Cf. KTU 1.148:2-4,10f. with AOAT 16,201.

[408] A custom comparable to the biblical levirate marriage (cf. Gen. 38; Num. 35:19ff.; Deut. 25:5-10; Ruth 4; Matt. 22:23f.). For ᶜAnatu as a nubile/wanton Widow see the notes 33 and 70.

[409] See notes 81-83.

[410] A clear example of the animosity that existed between the family of Ilu and the newcomer, his son-in-law Baᶜlu. See note 88.

Give one of your sons,
that I make him king!''[411]
And Lady Athiratu of the Sea answered:
''Shouldn't we make king one who is able to moisten?''[412]
And the Benevolent, Ilu the good-natured answered:
''One of feeble strength cannot run like Baᶜlu,[413]
one who knuckles under cannot poise the lance[414] *like the son of Daganu!''*
And Lady Athiratu of the Sea answered:
''Shouldn't we make king ᶜAthtaru the Rich?[415]
Let ᶜAthtaru the Rich be made king!''
Then ᶜAthtaru the Rich
went up into the highlands of Sapanu,[416]
he sat down on the throne of Baᶜlu the Almighty.
His feet did not touch the foot-stool,
his head did not touch the top of the back.
And ᶜAthtaru the Rich said:

[411] Ilu did not exercise the kingship himself, he always appointed a viceroy. In Baal I (KTU 1.3) it is Baᶜlu who is king. In Baal II-III (KTU 1.1-2) Ilu's son Yammu temporarily takes over. In Baal IV (KTU 1.4) Baᶜlu is king again (cf. note 294). In Baal V he has to surrender to Ilu's son Motu who for obvious reasons could not be allowed to reign on earth (contrast Rom. 5:14,17). At the end of Baal VI (KTU 1.6) Baᶜlu will soon be restored to power.

[412] One of the major functions of Baᶜlu as a rain-god. Cf. Baal V (KTU 1.5):ii.20 as well as Keret II (KTU 1.15):iv.12.

[413] Cf. CCT (4) no. 1a:3 ''Adad the Runner'', with AOAT 16,118. Also Ps. 19:6; Job 16:14.

[414] The thunderbolt-lance of Baᶜlu, cf. note 290.

[415] As a claimant to the throne the god ᶜAthtaru is portrayed as a slightly ridiculous figure next to the two gods who govern great bodies of water, Yammu/Naharu (sea/river) and Baᶜlu (rain). The reason for this is that this god was responsible for artificial irrigation, as in ancient South Arabia (cf. II.48,66f.; III.3f.).

From May through September the water-balance of Syria shows a deficit and vegetable gardens have to be watered constantly. Irrigation never became popular in Palestine, cf. AOAT 16,205f. and Deut. 11:10. ᶜAthtaru's epithet ''The Rich'' contains a pun on the Ugaritic verb ''to run'' used by Ilu in line 50. Cf. Prov. 11:16; Myth and Ritual II (KTU 1.12), note 29.

[416] See note 4.

"I cannot be king in the highlands of Sapanu!"[417]
ᶜAthtaru the Rich descended,
he descended from the throne of Baᶜlu the Almighty
and became king on all the divine earth.
[*did*] *draw water in basins,*
[*did*] *draw water in buckets.*

The first 30 lines of column II are missing. Judging from II.3f. they contained an extensive account of the hard labour imposed by the god of water-drawing during the rainless summer.

II.
To [ ]
and to [ ]
The jug was [shattered by the fountain,]
the jug fell [into the cistern].[418]
One day, two days passed,
and the Damsel[419] *ᶜAnatu sought him.*[420]
Like the heart of a cow for her calf,
like the heart of a ewe for her lamb,
so was the heart of ᶜAnatu after Baᶜlu.[421]

[417] Significantly Baᶜlu's earlier opponent Yammu also seems to have been unable to occupy the throne on Mt. Sapanu, not because he was too small, but because he was too big.

[418] Cf. Eccl. 12:6 and Keret III (KTU 1.16):i.54.

[419] Actually the title means "womb", then also "available woman", cf. Judg. 5:30. It is a special title of the goddess of love who is also called "the breast". Cf. Myth and Ritual I (KTU 1.23):13 and IV (KTU 1.13):2, with UF 12 (1980) 306, 308f. and note 34 above.

[420] The theme of the looking for Baᶜlu recurs time and again in this part of the myth. See line 27, IV.4f., 20. It is possible that it corresponded to a cultic ceremony like the ritual seeking of Dumuzi in Babylonia, cf. M. Dijkstra, Gods voorstelling, Kampen 1980, 126-128.

[421] Parallels to this simile have been collected by T. H. Gaster, Myth, Legend, and Custom in the Old Testament, London 1969, 605f. (with an alternative interpretation of Jer. 31:15). ᶜAnatu is often called "cow" in the texts of Ugarit.

She seized Motu by the hem of his garment,
she restrained him by the edge of his mantle.[422]
She raised her voice and cried:
"*You, Motu! Give up my brother!*"[423]
And Motu, the son of Ilu, answered:
"*What do you demand from me, o Virgin ʿAnatu?*
I was wandering about and scouring
every mountain to the middle of the earth,
every hill to the middle of the fields.
My throat was lacking humans,[424]
my throat the multitudes of the earth.[425]
(*Then*) *I reached Happiness, the steppe-land,*
Delightfulness, the field of the stream of the place of death.[426]
I approached Baʿlu the Almighty.
I made him like a lamb in my mouth,
like a kid he disappeared *in the jaws of my gullet.*"[427]

[422] A gesture of supplication, cf. 1 Sam. 15:27 with R. A. Brenner, JANES 6 (1974) 35-38; E. L. Greenstein, VT 32 (1982) 217f. for ancient Oriental parallels.
Because Motu is treated like the grain in lines 30ff., it is possible that at the same time this passage symbolizes the ingathering of the reaped grain which was a task of women (Ruth 2:2,6-8, etc.). The grain harvest fell between the middle of April (barley) and the middle of June (wheat). This symbolic interpretation tallies with the fact that later on Motu refers to this part of ʿAnatu's treatment not as seizing (*ʾḫd*) but as falling (*ql*), *i.e.* falling like the harvested grain (V.11f.): "because of you I suffered falling". This closely resembles a dictum of the Egyptian ruler of the Nether World, Osiris-the-barley: "I have fallen on my side" (J. Gwyn Griffiths, The Origins of Osiris and his Cult, Leiden 1980, 165). See also below notes 430-436.

[423] Remarkably enough ʿAnatu does not seem to view Baʿlu's death and burial as in any way definitive.

[424] Cf. Baal IV (KTU 1.4):vii.47-49; viii.19f.; Baal V (KTU 1.5):i.19; ii.1-4, with the notes 293 and 333. Cf. Hab. 2:5.

[425] Because Baʿlu had kept them alive and healthy, cf. Baal IV (KTU 1.4):vii.49-52.

[426] Cf. notes 385 and 378-379.

[427] Cf. Baal IV (KTU 1.4):viii.19f. with note 293.

The Lamp of the gods, Shapshu, had a dusty colour,
the heavens were soiled by Motu, the son of Ilu.[428]
One day, two days passed,
days became months,[429]
the Damsel ʿAnatu sought him.
Like the heart of a cow for her calf,
like the heart of a ewe to her lamb,
so was the heart of ʿAnatu after Baʿlu.
She seized Motu, the son of Ilu.[430]

[428] Again a reference to a spell of sirocco, cf. notes 87, 288, 312 and 335. According to the time-table underlying the myth it blows at the end of May or early in June. Cf. AOAT 16,207.

[429] For the construction see 1 Chron. 9:27, with D. G. Pardee, UF 8 (1976) 219, 243. Of course we are dealing with mythological time-reckoning here. In reality only days or weeks went by. Cf. note 122.

[430] For details concerning the seasonal interpretation of the following passage see AOAT 16,208-215 and N. Robertson, HTR 75 (1982) 346ff. According to others the passage would merely describe the utter destruction of Motu. See in addition to the literature discussed in AOAT 16,212f.: P. L. Watson, JAOS 92 (1972) 60ff.; S. E. Loewenstamm, AOAT 204 (1980) 426ff.,503ff. (criticized by L. G. Perdue, Bibl 54 (1973) 237ff.).

Two remarks of a general nature have to be made here:

1) Of course Motu is not simply identified with the grain ("his flesh" in line 37—no other translation is possible). And of course the surface meaning of the passage describes nothing but his utter destruction. Next to Ex. 32:20 one may cite Deut. 9:21, Jer. 15:7, Ez. 5:1-4, Am. 1:3f., Mic. 4:12f., Matth. 3:12 in support of this view. Another, most interesting, parallel may be found in N. Oettinger, Die Militärischen Eide der Hethiter, Wiesbaden 1976, 10f.

2) In a myth, however, such a passage usually has an underlying symbolic meaning and the simple circumstance that so many of ʿAnatu's actions are connected with the normal treatment of the grain in June strongly suggests that this is the case here (see also n. 422). The best proof that such an interpretation is by no means as far-fetched as some seem to think comes from Egypt where the scattering of the parts of the body of Osiris was represented in the cult by a ceremonial threshing of the grain (K. Sethe, UGAÄ 10 (1928) 83ff.,134; cf. W. Helck, Or 23 (1954) 386; J. Gwyn Griffiths, op.cit. (n. 422), 163ff.). Like Motu, Osiris was lord of the Nether World. Especially illuminating is the following equation: *beating Osiris: hacking the god to pieces: barley*. It should also be observed that the association of sheaves with death is a well-known phenomenon in the history of religion. It is even attested in Jer. 9:20f. and Job 5:26. See for further evidence the following notes.

With a knife she split him,[431]
with a sieve she scattered him,[432]
with fire she burnt him,[433]
with a mill she ground him,[434]
in the field she sowed him.[435]

431 The variant version in col. V.13 has "*scattering* with a knife", which should not be "emended" arbitrarily. This variant is understandable if we take the metaphorical background into account. In Hebrew the same verb "to scatter" is used in connection with the threshing-sledge in Isa. 41:16 and Prov. 20:26. Then the "knife" stands for the cutting blades of the Oriental threshing sledge. The edges of such blades could be denoted by the same word used in connection with the edges of swords (Isa. 41:15; Ps. 149:6). In Palestinian Arabic the word *sekākīn* "knives" designates the cutting blades under the threshing sledge (Dalman, AuS, III, 82). Interestingly enough the same Arabic word is used for the ploughshare (Barthélemy, 349), like Akkad. *ḫarbu*, M.Hebr. *ḥrb* and Syriac *ḥrbʾ*.

432 The addition "with a sieve" (in the variant V.16 "with a riddle") renders the metaphor too laboured to ignore the fact that Motu symbolizes the grain here. Winnowing followed the threshing-process.

433 Burning was doubtlessly one of the many cruel ways to dispose of enemies. On a secondary level, however, this too may symbolize the treatment of the grain. Three possibilities exist: the burning of the chaff (AOAT 16,210), the burning of the last sheaf (see T. Canaan, BASOR 167 (1962) 38) or the burning of the grain itself in order to render the husks brittle (J. F. Healey, Or 52 (1983) 248-251).

434 It has rightly been stressed that grinding in a mill may be interpreted as a metaphor for destruction. Cf. note 430. It is obvious, however, that within this context of agrarian imagery it also reflects the production of the first flour.

435 It may be that this too has to be understood as a metaphor for the scattering of the flesh of Motu (cf. Zech. 10:9). However, not a single instance of "to sow in a field" as a metaphorical expression for destruction has been produced by the protagonists of this type of interpretation. It is more likely therefore that the underlying symbolism surfaces here and that "to sow in a field" has a meaning close to the normal literal meaning which is attested in Ex. 23:16; cf. Gen. 26:12; Lev. 25:3f.; Hos. 2:25; Ps. 107:37.

Sowing in summertime would have been madness because of the heat and the total absence of rain. With Plato we have to conclude that sowing in summer must mean a rite like the sowing of the gardens of Adonis (cf. AOAT 16,214 for references; add M. Delcor, Syria 55 (1978) 371-394; N. Robertson, HTR 75 (1982) 346) or the sowing of the gardens of Osiris (see note 430 as well as Ch. Seeber, LÄ, III, 744ff.; J. G. Griffiths, op.cit. (n. 422). 167ff.; LÄ, IV, 630). Note the similarity of the designations employed: "garden", "bed", "field", in spite of the fact that mostly only pots or lumps of earth were used. Such gardens were sown in summer to demon-

The birds did eat his flesh,[436]
  the fowl did consume his limbs.
Flesh called to flesh,[437]

(broken)

About 40 lines of column III are missing. Probably it is ʿAnatu who is speaking when the text becomes readable again. She proposes a dream-oracle: if Ilu will have a particular dream (perhaps about a prolonged period of drought) she will know definitely that her husband Baʿlu is dead. However, if Ilu dreams about rivers of oil and honey, she will know that Baʿlu is still alive somewhere.

III.

1* "[*and I will know that Baʿlu the Almighty is dead,*]
1   *that his Highness, the Lord of earth, has perished.*

strate the vitality of the seed which held the promise of life after death (cf. 1 Cor. 15:36,42-44). After a few days the sprouts withered and the "gardens" were thrown away into the sea or into rivers. This tallies with the fact that the variant reading in V.19 speaks not of "sowing in the field" but of "wilting in the fields" and "throwing into the sea".

Possibly the ritual KTU 1.112:4 contains a reference to such a "field" of ʿAnatu: a "pot of lumps of earth" is offered to her there. In any case the practice of the sowing of the "gardens" for the fertility god of Canaan was probably known to the author of Isa. 17:9-11. The "plantations of the Most Graceful" are plantations for the Baals. Finally it should be noted in this connection that *ʾadn* (Adonis) was actually a name of Baʿlu (cf. O. Loretz, UF 12 (1980) 286-292; K. Spronk, Beatific Afterlife, Neukirchen 1986, 194) and that *nʿmn* "gracious one" is an epithet of Baʿlu (notes 40, 353, 398).

436 "Flesh" in accordance with the primary level of the narrative, cf. note 430 and Deut. 28:26; 1 Ki. 14:11; Ez. 29:5; Ps. 79:2. However, this "flesh" symbolizes the seed some of which is consumed by the birds (cf. Matt. 13:4, par.). The same ambiguity (scattering of flesh/seed) is attested with regard to Osiris, cf. note 430.

437 Compare the myth of Zu, ANET, 516, line 110 and Ez. 37:7f. With regard to the reciprocity of the calling cf. Ps. 42:8 and with regard to the calling out of the remains of someone who had been slain, cf. Gen. 4:10.

But if Baʿlu the Almighty is alive,
and if his Highness, the Lord of earth, exists,[438]
(*then*) *in a dream of the Benevolent, Ilu the good-natured,*
in a vision of the Creator of creatures,[439]
the heavens will rain oil,[440]
the wadis will run with honey,[441]
and I will know that Baʿlu the Almighty is alive,[442]
that his Highness, the Lord of earth, exists."
In a dream of the Benevolent, Ilu the good-natured,
in a vision of the Creator of creatures,
the heavens rained oil,
the wadis ran with honey.
The Benevolent, Ilu the good-natured, rejoiced.
He placed his foot on the foot-stool,
and his frown disappeared, and he laughed.
He raised his voice and cried:
"*I can sit down now and rest,*
and my soul can rest in my breast,[443]
for Baʿlu the Almighty is alive,
for his Highness, the Lord of earth, exists!"
Ilu cried aloud to the Virgin ʿAnatu:
"*Listen, o Virgin ʿAnatu!*
Say to Shapshu, the Lamp of the gods:

438 This line and line 21 may have given rise to a number of Canaanite personal names of the type "Baal exists".

439 Cf. note 209.

440 Cf. note 36. See for *šmn* "oil" in the sense of well-watered (soil): Gen. 27:28; 49:25; Num. 13:20; Isa. 5:1; 28:1, 4; Ez. 34:14; Neh. 9-25; 1 Chron. 4:40. Also Ps. 65:11f.

441 Compare the biblical expression "a land flowing with milk and honey" as a metaphorical description of the fertile, well-watered land of Israel, Ex. 3:8; Jer. 11:5; Ez. 20:6, etc.

442 Cf. Job 19:25.

443 Cf. KAI no. 26:A.II.7-8; Isa. 30:15 (with M. Dahood, CBQ 20 (1958) 41-45); Ps. 116:7.

IV.

'The furrows of the fields are cracked, o Shapshu,
the furrows of the fields of Ilu are cracked,[444]
Baᶜlu must harrow the furrows of the plough-land![445]
Where is Baᶜlu the Almighty?
Where is his Highness, the Lord of earth?' "[446]
The Virgin ᶜAnatu departed.
Then she headed straight
for Shapshu, the Lamp of the gods.
She raised her voice and cried:
"A message from the Bull Ilu, your Father,
a word from the Benevolent, your sire:
The furrows of the fields are cracked, o Shapshu,
the furrows of the fields of Ilu are cracked,
Baᶜlu must harrow the furrows of the plough-land!
Where is Baᶜlu the Almighty?
Where is his Highness, the Lord of earth?"
And Shapshu, the Lamp of the gods, answered:
"Pour sparkling wine[447] *into the wine-sink,*
let your kinsfolk bring wreaths,[448]

[444] During the hot Syrian summer the soil becomes so hard and dry that cracks and fissures rend the surface. It is impossible to plough and the farmer has to wait until the rains of autumn soften the ground. Cf. AOAT 16,222.

[445] The verb translated by "harrow" actually indicates the first ploughing, cf. Dalman, AuS II, 135, 179f.; A. Salonen, AASF 149 (1956) 234-238, 451f.

[446] This line may have inspired the name of Jezebel, the daughter of a Phoenician king who continued to worship Baal, cf. 1 Ki. 16:31; 18:19, 27. See also note 357.

[447] Cf. Prov. 23:31.

[448] Apparently this is the mythological prototype of a rite in preparation of the autumnal New Year and Wine-festival. See Baal I, fragm.a (KTU 1.101:9f.) and Baal I (KTU 1.3):i.9-21, with note 15.

The participants in wine-festivals used to wear wreaths, cf. Isa. 28:1,3f. and AOAT 16,225 for Egyptian and Greek evidence. It is highly important that according to Jub. 16:30 the participants in the Feast of Tabernacles also had to wear wreaths, because this festival was the Israelite continuation of the ancient autumnal festival of the Canaanites, cf. note 1.

and I will seek Baʿlu the Almighty!''[449]
And the Virgin ʿAnatu answered:
''*Whatever the outcome*[450], *o Shapshu*,
whatever the outcome, may Ilu protect you,
may [*the gods*] *protect you in p*[*eace*]![451]
[*Sparkling wine*] *will be poured* [*into the wine-sink*],
the family [*of Ilu will bring wreaths*],
and [*you seek Baʿlu the Almighty*!'']
(broken)

About 38 lines are missing from column IV. Possibly the poet described the period of suspense, waiting for the outcome of the Sun-goddess' quest. In the first lines of column V an unknown

The date of the preparatory festival can be established with a certain degree of confidence. The Sabians of Harran (cf. note 15) celebrated a festival of the treading of the new wine on the 8th of the month of Ab (al-Nadim, Fihrist, IX.1). According to the Mishna a vineyard-festival was celebrated in ancient Israel on the 15th of Ab (mTaan. IV.8). We may assume therefore that the libations of wine into the wine-sinks took place in Ugarit about the same time of the year, *i.e.* in the first half of August. See also the following note.

[449] According to Jewish tradition the power of the sun weakened from the 15th of Ab onwards (bBaba B., 121b; bTaan., 31a). The preparatory rite described in the preceding note may have been important to establish the correct date of the New Year festival which, as an agrarian festival, was largely dependent on the solar year whereas the normal calendar was based on the shorter lunar year. If it proved to be too early for the grapes to ripen in time for the production of the first new wine on the festival (note 15) a leap month had to be inserted into the lunar calendar. In view of the Jewish tradition mentioned above it is possible that the increasing duration of the sun's stay in the Nether World was believed to be caused by her ''seeking'' for Baʿlu. See Myth and Ritual I, note 25; Ritual I, note 56.

[450] Cf. the Akkadian expression *anniam lā anniam / annītam lā annītam* which should also be adduced to explain Hebrew *zʾt lʾ zʾt* in Ez. 21:31. The phrase expresses the anxiety of those waiting on earth.

Others translate ''(from) strength to strength'', referring to Ps. 84:8, or ''where (and) whither'', quoting 1 Ki. 2:36,42, etc.

[451] This echoes a greeting formula found in the Ugaritic letters, cf. B. Margalit, AOAT 206 (1980) 170.

speaker is predicting[452] Baʿlu's victory over the monsters inhabiting the Nether World.

V.

"[the gods],
Baʿlu will seize the sons of Athiratu.[453]
The big ones[454] *he will slay with an axe-blade,*
those who are like Yammu[455] *he will slay with an axe,*
the small ones[456] *he will pull to the ground.*[457]
Baʿlu [will sit down] on the chair of his kingship,
on the seat of the throne of his dominion."[458]
Days became months,
months became years.[459]

[452] Because according to col. VI.33ff. Baʿlu has yet to return to his throne it is impossible to translate these lines in the past tense. Cf. AOAT 16,226 and for other instances of predictions and clairvoyance in the myth of Baʿlu, OTS 24 (1986) 1ff.

[453] The sons of Athiratu had rejoiced over Baʿlu's death, cf. I.40f. Motu and Yammu were sons of Ilu and Athiratu. Ilu was also the father of other monstrous deities, cf. notes 61-64, Myth and Ritual II (KTU 1.12):i; also I (KTU 1.23):30ff.

[454] Cf. note 58.

[455] Cf. G. del Olmo Lete, UF 14 (1982) 68f. and for the construction also Gen. 44:15; Jer. 5:9,29; 9:8; Von Soden GAG § 114g.

The form *dkym* in Ps. 93:3 (// *rbym*, 93:4) may have had the same meaning in the original Canaanite hymn the Hebrew poet was adapting. He misunderstood it, however, as a parallel of *qwlm* "their voice".

Yammu had earlier been defeated with the same weapon made by Kotharu, cf. Baal III (KTU 1.2):iv.23ff. At this stage of the myth Yammu is a helper of the god of death Motu (cf. Baal V (KTU 1.5):i.21f.). To bring Baʿlu back to life on earth Kotharu will have to defeat Yammu's marine monsters again, cf. Baal VI (KTU 1.6):vi.51ff., see below. As in the O.T. the deep sea and the Nether World are closely related, cf. notes 127 and 379 as well as Ez. 26:19f.; Jonah 2:6; Ps. 18:16.; 88:6f.

[456] In Akkadian and Hebrew the same word may denote various small animals, cf. Jer. 49:20. Here it may denote the deities representing the innumerable small creatures inhabiting the sea, cf. Baal III (KTU 1.2):iv.3f.

[457] Like lambs to be slaughtered, cf. note 78.

[458] Predicting VI.33-35.

[459] See note 429.

Then, in the seventh year,
Motu, the son of Ilu, relented[460]
with Baʿlu the Almighty.
He raised his voice and cried:
"*Because of you,*[461] *o Baʿlu, I have suffered falling down,*[462]
because of you I have suffered scattering with a knife,
because of you I have suffered burning with fire,
because of you I have suffered grinding with a mill,
because of you I have suffered scattering with a riddle,
because of you I have suffered wilting in the fields,
because of you I have suffered sowing in the sea!
Give one of your brothers,[463]
that I may eat, so that the anger I harbour will turn away![464]
If you do not give one of your brothers,
look! I will make the dead visit the earth,[465]
I will consume mankind,
I will consume the multitudes of the earth!
So let on[e of your brothers] fall down,
put [ ],
bring [ ]
(broken)

[460] Cf. Zech. 1:12.

[461] Cf. Jer. 15:15; Ps. 44:23; 69:8; Job 34:16.

[462] See with this and the following lines notes 422, 430-437 above.

[463] Nobody could leave the Nether World without handing over a substitute, cf. B. Alster, Dumuzi's Dream, Copenhagen 1972, 13; S. N. Kramer, Anatolian Studies 30 (1980) 5-13.

[464] Cf. Gen. 27:45; Isa. 5:25; 9:11,16,20; 10:4; 12:1; Jer. 23:20; Hos. 14:5.

[465] Text and translation uncertain. However, a similar expression occurs in Arabic (AOAT 16,233) and the threat to bring up the dead who will devour the living is well-attested: Descent of Ishtar, 19; Nergal and Ereshkigal V.11, 26; Gilg. VI.iii.34f.; Erra I.175-177. The spirits of deceased persons were feared in Ugarit, cf. UF 16 (1984) 242. It is against this background that Isa. 26:14f. has to be read.

About 27 lines are missing. Probably Baʿlu pretends to comply with Motu's wish, but through a ruse[466] he succeeds in feeding him not his own brother, but brothers of Motu himself.

VI.

[ ],
[who had ex]pelled him [from the heights of Sapanu],
[who had] chased him [from his chair]
[like a bir]d from its [aerie].[467]
[He gave] his [own brothers into the hand of] Motu, [the son of Ilu],
[the sons of his own mother into the hand of the An]nihilator[468]*of the nations.*
Motu, the son of Ilu, [consumed them],
[he ate] his seven lads.
[Then] Motu, the son of Ilu, said:
"Look here! Baʿlu has given me my own brothers to eat,
the sons of my own mother to consume!"
He returned to Baʿlu of the highlands of Sapanu.[469]
He raised his voice and cried:
"You, Baʿlu, have given me my own brothers to eat,
the sons of my own mother to consume!"

[466] Cf. note 352. Possibly the ruse consisted in the offering of the seven "boars" accompanying Baʿlu (cf. Baal V (KTU 1.5):v.8f. and Baal VI (KTU 1.6):vi.8). In that case they must have been creatures begot by Ilu (cf. note 453).

If this episode corresponded to a sacrifice of swine in the actual cult of Ugarit, it is useful to note that swine used to be sacrificed to chtonic deities or deities responsible for death and diseases. Cf. AOAT 16,234; F. J. Stendebach, BZ 18 (1974) 263-371.

[467] Cf. Baal I (KTU 1.3):iv.1f.; Baal II (KTU 1.1):24ff.

[468] Both Baʿlu and Motu could be called *gmr* (cf. VI.16), Baʿlu in a positive way (Baal III (KTU 1.2):i.46), Motu in a negative way, in accordance with the ambiguous meaning of the verb in several Semitic languages.

[469] Not "*in* the highlands", cf. AOAT 16,234 and note 17 above.

They eyed each other like fighting-cocks,
Motu was strong, Baˁlu was strong.[470]
They gored like wild oxen,
Motu was strong, Baˁlu was strong.
They bit like serpents,
Motu was strong, Baˁlu was strong.
They tugged like sporting-dogs,
Motu fell, Baˁlu fell.
Shapshu cried to Motu from above:
"*Now listen, o Motu, son of Ilu!*
How can you fight
with Baˁlu the Almighty?
How can the Bull Ilu, your father,
fail to hear you?
He is sure to pull out the door-posts from your residence,
he is sure to overturn the chair of your kingship,
he is sure to break your judicial sceptre!"[471]
Motu, the son of Ilu, feared,
the Beloved of Ilu, the hero, dreaded (him),[472]
Motu was startled by her speech.
He raised his voice and cried:

[470] The ensuing fight is the mythological representation of the "fight" between hot dry east winds and moist west winds in September. This "fight" was vividly described by Dalman, AuS I,105. See also AOAT 16,238f. and on the strength of death: KTU 2.10:12f.; Song of Songs 8:6.

It is noteworthy that neither the god of death nor the god of life is strong enough to overpower his opponent. The struggle is only decided as a result of the intervention of the sun-goddess. Cf. in apparent contrast to this Isa. 25:8; 1 Cor. 15:54f.; 2 Tim. 1:10; Hebr. 2:14.

Baˁlu's victory over Death gives him the right to return to his throne on Mt. Sapanu where he is resting at the beginning of the whole myth (Baal I, fragm. a). Thus the beginning and the end of the myth have been linked up to each other. For an attempt to evaluate this cyclic world view see OTS 24 (1986) 1ff.

[471] Cf. note 165.

[472] Just as Baˁlu had feared Motu, cf. Baal V (KTU 1.5):ii.6f.

"Let them install Baᶜlu on the chair of his kingship,
on the seat of the throne of his dominion!
[Let him take his eternal kingship],[473]
[his] ev[erlasti]ng d[ominion]!
Look! [Let him count] the years [with Ilu],[474]
[the months with the Benevolent, Ilu] the good-natured!"
[ᶜAna]tu summoned [Kotharu and] the Friendly One:[475]
"[Please e]nter, please proceed,
[the me]at is fresh!
And please, eat the contribution-bread,[476]
please drink the presentation-wine![477]
Shapshu, you rule the Saviours,[478]
Shapshu, you rule the ghosts!

[473] Cf. Baᶜlu III (KTU 1.2):iv.10. Also 2 Sam. 7:16; 1 Chr. 28:7; Ps. 145:13; Dan. 3:33; 4:31; 7:14,18,27; Luke 1:32f.; Rev. 11:15; 20:4,6; 22:5. Baᶜlu is called "the Saviour, the Eternal King" in Incantation V (KTU 1.108):1.

[474] Cf. note 83 and Aqhat I (KTU 1.17):vi.28f. (with note 100). In the present context this is apparently a hint at the approaching New Year.

[475] Presumably the Sun-goddess Shapshu. The hymn spoken by ᶜAnatu is an invitation to the gods who had to guide Baᶜlu back home through the dangerous labyrinth of the Nether World.

[476] The specific term used points to the annual contribution to the cult at the end of the agricultural year, *i.e.* in connection with the autumnal New Year. Cf. Num. 18:27; Deut. 12:17; 16:13; Neh. 10:35-40; 13:5; Jub. 32. See furthermore AOAT 16,244; NYCI I, 9f.,10,12ff. and for an interesting Egyptian parallel: H. Bonnet, RÄR, 548a.

[477] Which is about to be presented on the New Year and wine festival, see note 15.

[478] Shapshu is prayed here to guide the "Healers" or "Saviours", *viz.* the deified spirits of dead kings and heroes, back to earth. They were thought to rise from the Nether World with Baᶜlu the Saviour (cf. Matt. 27:52f.) on the occasion of the New Year festival. Cf. K. Spronk, Beatific Afterlife, Neukirchen 1986, 145ff.

So we are probably dealing here with a prayer for the vigil on New Year's Eve. Night watches were far from uncommon (cf. *e.g.* Ex. 12:42) and several Psalms are thought to have been composed for such occasions (cf. J. W. McKay, ZAW 91 (1979) 229ff.). A vigil on New Year's Eve is also attested in Egypt, cf. P. Posener-Kriéger, Revue d'Égyptologie 22 (1976) 131-137.

Let the deities be your company,
look! let the dead be your company!
Let Kotharu be your friend,
and Khasisu your intimate.[479]
In the sea are Arishu and Tunnanu.[480]
Kotharu-and-Khasisu, please expel (them),
please startle (them), Kotharu-and-Khasisu!"

The scribe is Ilimilku, the Shubanite,
pupil of Attanu,[481] *majordomo,*
high priest, high shepherd,[482]
officiant of Niqmaddu,[483] *king of Ugarit,*

[479] As in the case of the earlier struggle with the sea-god Yammu (Baal III (KTU 1.2):iv) Kotharu has to assist Baᶜlu in vanquishing the marine monsters (cf. note 455). Just as the Sun-god and his companions had to defeat the Apophis-serpent according to Egyptian mythology (cf. AOAT 16,244), so Shapshu and her companions have to surmount considerable difficulties before they reappear triumphantly in the East on New Year's morning. Because New Year is a microcosmic reflection of the first day of creation this struggle may be regarded as a repetition of the conquering of the primordial chaos. Cf. Job 3:8. It is likely that originally it was Ilu who conquered the waters of chaos (note 81 above). The circumstance that Baᶜlu 'repeats' this victory in Baal III (KTU 1.2) and here points to his ambition to succeed the old creator-god. See also note 455.

[480] Cf. Isa. 27:1; Ez. 32:2; notes 59, 61 and 455.

[481] By expressly mentioning his teacher, Ilimilku apparently wants to claim the authority of Attanu for the correctness of his narrative. This may mean that hitherto the myth of Baᶜlu had been handed down orally. In itself it is significant that Ilimilku as a high priest was able to write down this extensive religious document. Because his title "officiant" (see note 483) is attested elsewhere it is impossible to regard Attanu as the high-priest, although it is likely that Ilimilku was his successor.

[482] Probably a metaphor for spiritual leadership. Cf. Am. 1:1, but also 7:14f.

[483] Niqmaddu II, king of Ugarit ca. 1365-1335 B.C. The king was the pivot of the Ugaritic ritual. Because the king was unable to attend every ceremony in person, the high-priest acted as his stand-in.

lord of Yaraggib, master of Tharrumannu.[484]

[484] Yaraggib and Tharrumannu were minor deities or spirits who were under the control of the medium Ilimilku (cf. 1 Sam. 28:7, *bʿlt ʾwb*). Tharrumannu is mentioned quite often in the cultic texts of Ugarit. Yaraggib is probably a hypocoristic name, like the divine name Ikshudum in Mari and like Yahweh (for Yahweh-El) in Israel. Possible candidates for the full name are the attested Ugaritic divine names *Yrgb-Hd*, *Yrgb-Bʿl* and *Yrgb-Lʾim*.

Spiritualistic sessions were held in connection with the royal ancestor cult of Ugarit and the ''officiant'' played an important role in them (cf. Ritual II [KTU 1.161]). As stated above (note 478) these spirits were conjured up especially in connection with the New Year festival.

If this interpretation of the colophon is correct, it is characteristic of the personality and theology of Ilimilku that in the end he wants himself to be known as master of gods. Cf. OTS 24 (1986) 1ff.

Passage	Summary	Seasonal Pattern	Note(s)	Approximate Date
I:i. 1-22	a) Baʿlu is served a suckling. b) Baʿlu has to taste the new wine.	a) Cult: Offering of new-born calves. b) Agriculture/Cult: During the New Year festival in autumn the new wine was produced.	10 15	September, 23-29
I:i.22-27	Baʿlu inspects his daughters, the goddesses of the dew.	Weather: Certain types of dew which are characteristic of autumn.	6,18	autumn
I:ii.2-3	ʿAnatu is adorned by her attendants with dye of the purple-snail.	Fishing: The fishing and processing of purple-snails in autumn.	24	autumn
I:ii.3-30	ʿAnatu performs a combat.	Army/Cult: A sham combat during four days of the New Year festival.	21,26, 28	September, 23-26
I:ii.30-41	a) ʿAnatu pours oil of pacification. b) She washes herself with dew and drizzle.	Cult: Pouring of oil, rain-charm. Cult: Rite of the Rain Bride. Weather: The first dew-like rain of autumn.	32, 36, 37	autumn
I:ii.42-43	ʿAnatu adorns herself with the purple-snail.	Fishing: The fishing and processing of purple-snails in autumn.	24	autumn

Passage	Summary	Seasonal Pattern	Note(s)	Approximate Date
I:iii.3a-3d	Pouring of rain and oil for ᶜAnatu.	See I:ii.30-41	31,36,37	autumn
I:iii.5-8	ᶜAnatu sings love-songs.	Domestic life: Love-songs are sung in connection with weddings in autumn.	42	autumn
I:iii.12-17 (cf. I:iv.7-10; I:iv.21-25; I:iv.28-32; II:ii.19-21)	a) ᶜAnatu has to oppose war on earth.	Army: Warfare stopped in autumn.	43	autumn
	b) She has to put love-fruit into the ground.	Agriculture/Cult: Rite in connection with plowing.	44	autumn
	c) She has to pour peace into the earth.	Cult: Pouring of oil of pacification.	32,36,45	autumn
I:iii.18-31 (cf. I:iv.11-20)	Baˁlu understands the lightning.	Weather: Thunderstorms.	49	autumn
I:iv.26-27	Baˁlu has to kindle the lightning.	Weather: Thunderstorms	49	autumn
I:iv.40-42	ᶜAnatu is served an ox.	Cult: Offering of new-born calves.	10	autumn
I:iv.42-46	ᶜAnatu washes herself with dew and drizzle.	See I:ii.30-41	18,36,37	autumn
I:iv-vi	Preparations for the building of a palace for Baˁlu.	See II:iii	108	autumn
I:v.17-18	Môtu obscures the sun with dust.	Weather: Autumnal sirocco.	87	autumn

Passage	Summary	Seasonal Pattern	Note(s)	Approximate Date
II:iii.26-29	Kotharu is commissioned with the building of the palace for Baʿlu.	Domestic life: Late autumn was a suitable time to lay the foundations for a house.	108	late autumn
II:iv.5-10	Baʿlu falls in disgrace because of his excessive rains, which are a nuisance.	Weather: The abundant rains of December. Domestic life: Building has to stop.	115	December
II:iv.30-32	Ilu slaughters young animals.	Cult: Sacrifice Agriculture: Many young animals were born in November-December.	121	November/ December
II:v.5-6 (cf. II:v.18-19)	Baʿlu prepares a deer.	Domestic life: The cold season was the preferred time for hunting.	122	winter
III:i	Baʿlu is handed over to Yammu.	Weather: Gales, torrential rains. Agriculture: The growth of the vegetation comes to a temporary halt because of the cold.	125, 150	winter
III:i.43-44	The terraces with vines will wither.	Agriculture: Vines may be damaged.	150	winter
III:iv	Yammu is defeated by Baʿlu, there is heat for the stalks sprouting in the fields.	Agriculture: Stalks of grain are sprouting again. Weather: Temperature rises, gales become less frequent.	191	end of winter

Passage	Summary	Seasonal Pattern	Note(s)	Approximate Date
IV:i.23-43	Kotharu at work in his smithy.	Domestic life: Men seek the warmth in the smithy.	206	winter
IV:ii.1-9	Athiratu washes her laundry in the sea.	Domestic life: Women clean their garments.	208	end of winter
IV:ii.28-36	Athiratu orders her fisherman to cast his net into the sea.	Fishing: Re-opening of the fishing-season.	214	first days of March
IV:iii.40-43	Sucklings are served.	Cult: Sacrifices. Agriculture: Young animals.	226	March/ April
IV:v.6-9	Athiratu stresses that Baʕlu has to give his rains and thunder in time.	Weather/Agriculture: Latter-rains of early spring have to come exactly in time for the crop.	240	First half of March
IV:v.13-14 (cf.IV:v.29-31; IV:v.36-37)	Baʕlu has to call caravans into his mansion.	Trade: Departing of caravans.	243	Early spring
IV:v.49-vi.8	a) Baʕlu instructs Kotharu to build his palace.	Weather: Neither too dry nor too hot. Domestic life: March and April provided ideal weather for building.	254	March
	b) The installation of an air-hole is postponed.	Weather/Agriculture: The latter-rains should be let through exactly on time.	240, 256, 278	March

Passage	Summary	Seasonal Pattern	Note(s)	Date
IV:vi.8-14	The dew-goddesses representing the dew of autumn are kept home.	Weather: Apparently these types of dew did not occur.	257	*not* autumn
IV:vi.40-59	Dedication feast for the palace of Baʿlu. Sucklings are served.	Cult: Dedication feast of the temple of Baʿlu around the time of the spring equinox. Agriculture/Cult: Sacrifice of the firstborn of the cattle.	226,268, 269, 271	March, 21
IV:vii.5-14	Baʿlu proceeds to capture many cities.	Army: Kings went to battle around the time of the spring equinox. Cult: Spring procession.	277	March, 21
IV:vii.14-34	Baʿlu opens an air-hole in his palace and thunders.	Weather: A rift in the clouds (for the latter-rains) and thunder.	240, 256, 278	March
IV:vii.34-60	a) The armies of Motu invade the country and veil the daylight with dust.	Weather: Sirocco	285, 287, 288	March/ April
	b) Birds are circling.	Nature: Migration of birds in spring.	301	Spring
	c) Baʿlu will have to bind the snow and the lightning in storehouses.	Weather: Snow disappears from the mountains, thunderstorms occur hardly ever in summer.	302	April
IV:viii.21-24	Motu obscures the sun with dust.	Weather: Sirocco in spring	288	March/ April

Passage	Summary	Seasonal Pattern	Note(s)	Approximate Date
V:ii.5-25	a) Because Motu is scorching the crops and the fruit-trees, Baˁlu accepts his invitation to descend into the Nether World. b) Motu rejoices: Baˁlu will be unable to give rain.	Weather/Agriculture: The sirocco threatens the future crops, especially the fruit-trees. Rain will soon disappear entirely.	335	March/ April
V:iii.16-24	Baˁlu brings Motu much offspring of cattle.	Agriculture: Young animals. Cult: Sacrifices.	226	March/ April
V:iv.1-11	Where is Baˁlu?	Weather: In April half as much rain as in March, one-third of the amount in February.	357	April
V:iv.12-14	The gods are supplied with a suckling.	Agriculture: Young animals. Cult: Sacrifices.	226	March/ April
V:v. a) v.6-8 b) v.8-9 c) v.10-11 d) v.17-26	a) Baˁlu disappears with his clouds, winds, thunderbolts and rains. b) He takes with him his seven lads. c) He takes Pidrayu and Tallayu with him. d) He mounts a heifer on the shore.	a) Weather: During the sirocco rain-clouds etc. disappear, they remain absent in summer. b) Nature: Disappearance of the Pleiades from the night sky. c) Weather: Disappearance of these types of dew in the dry season. d) Agriculture: Cows are in heat.	371 372 18, 373 380	March/ April
V:vi.4-5	Two messengers go around to the emmercorn.	Agriculture: The emmercorn is still ripening.	383	Middle of April -Middle of May

Passage	Summary	Seasonal Pattern	Note(s)	Approximate Date
V:vi.15-17	Ilu strews a sheaf of mourning on his head.	Cult: First sheaf of barley?	389	April
V:vi.20-22	Ilu "ploughs" his chest for the third time.	Agriculture: Third ploughing of fruit-gardens.	393	April
V:v.25-VI:i.17	ʿAnatu roams in the fields, finds Baʿlu, "ploughs" her chest for the third time, buries Baʿlu.	Cult: Procession with the image of ʿAnatu/ʿAthtartu. Mourning for Baʿlu, "burial". Agriculture: Third ploughing of fruit-gardens.	393, 398	end of April
VI:i.18-29	ʿAnatu sacrifices on Mt. Sapanu.	Cult: Sacrifices on Mt. Sapanu.	407	April, 23
VI:i.43-67	ʿAthtaru is appointed as an unsatisfactory successor to Baʿlu.	Agriculture: Artificial irrigation starts with the dry season.	415	May
VI:ii.9-11	ʿAnatu seizes Motu by the hem of his garment.	Agriculture: Grain harvest.	422	Middle of April -Middle of June
VI:ii.24-25	Motu obscures the sun with dust.	Weather: Sirocco.	428	End of May, early June
VI:ii.26-37 (cf. VI:v.8-19)	ʿAnatu splits Motu with a knife, scatters him with a sieve, burns him with fire, grounds him with a mill and sows him in the field.	Agriculture: Treatment of the grain. Cult: Sowing of gardens of Baʿlu.	422, 430-434 435	June

Passage	Summary	Seasonal Pattern	Note(s)	Approximate Date
VI:iii.22-iv.16	The furrows of the fields are cracked, ploughing is impossible.	Agriculture: The soil becomes hard and dry in summer. Farmers have to await the rain before they can plough.	444, 445	Summer
VI:iv.17-27	a) Shapshu is asked to seek Baʿlu who is the only one who can make the soil arable.	Nature: Weakening of the sun.	449	after the summer-solstice
	b) The gods have to libate wine and have to bring wreaths.	Cult: Preparations for the New Year festival.	448, 449	first half of August
VI:vi.5-37	Motu eats seven "brothers". Fight between Motu and Baʿlu, victory of Baʿlu.	Cult: Sacrifice of seven boars? Weather: "Fight" between hot dry sirocco and cool west winds, "victory" of the latter.	466, 470	September
VI:vi.37-40	Baʿlu has to count the years with Ilu.	Domestic life: Time-reckoning in connection with the approaching New Year.	474	September
VI:vi.40-53	ʿAnatu's hymn to Shapshu and Kotharu	Cult: a) Annual contributions to the cult in connection with the New Year festival. b) Impending return of spirits. c) Recounting of struggle with monsters in connection with the creation of the cosmos.	476-479	September, 23

MYTH: LOVES

The Loves of Baal and Anath I

KTU 1.96

Several Ugaritic tablets describe the love life of Baᶜlu and ᶜAnatu.[1] Some of these stories are quite explicit about the sexual activities of the pair, and may reflect a rather liberal attitude towards sexuality among the Canaanites. This would explain some of the scathing criticism of Baal worship in the Old Testament.[2]

ᶜAnatu went away
  and she left.[3]
The beauty of her brother[4]
  and the loveliness of her brother -
    how delightful they were!
She ate his flesh without a knife,
  she drank his blood without a cup.[5]
She turned to him the eye[6] *of a flatterer,*[7]
  the eye of a flatteress,

[1] See next to the texts selected for this rubric also Baal I (KTU 1.3):iii.5ff.; Baal V (KTU 1.5):v.17ff.; KTU 1.7:I.22f.; 1.101:17f.; Myth and Ritual IV (KTU 1.13):29ff.

For the loves of other gods see Baal IV (KTU 1.4):ii.5-11 (Athiratu and Ilu); iv.38f. (Ilu and Athiratu); Myth and Ritual I (KTU 1.23) and II (KTU 1.12):i (Ilu with two women); V (KTU 1.24, Yarikhu and Nikkalu).

[2] *E.g.* Num. 25:1-3,6-8; Jer. 2:23f.; Hos. 2:11f., probably also texts like Mic. 1:7; Isa. 57:3,5-8.

[3] Probably to visit her husband Baᶜlu, cf. Baal I (KTU 1.3):iv.32ff.

[4] "Brother" and "sister" mean lovers. Cf. Baal, note 69; Aqhat, note 128.

[5] Not a frenzied Bacchante. She only devours him with her eyes. Cf. A. Saarisalo, Songs of the Druzes, Helsinki 1932, 2f.: "Her eye slaughters her lover by turning".

[6] Cf. Gen. 39:7; Sir. 26:9.

[7] Cf. Job 32:21; 2 Peter 2:14.

she turned to him the eye of a rival,[8]
the eye of a potter,[9]
the eye of a gate-keeper.[10]
Let the eye of the gate-keeper return to the gate-keeper,
let the eye of the potter return to the potter,
let the eye of the rival return to the rival,
let the eye of the flatterer return to the flatterer,
let the eye of the flatteress return to the flatteress,[11]
[*but let the eye of*] *ʿAna*[*tu be on her brother*]
[*for ever and ever!*][12]

The Loves of Baal and Anath II

KTU 1.10

About 20 lines of the beginning of column I are missing. Since only one side of this tablet was inscribed it may be assumed to have contained a relatively short poem.

I.

The Virgin[1] *ʿAnatu* [*washed herself*].
[*ʿAnatu m*]*ade herself up with powder,*[2]

[8] Cf. Gen. 30:1.

[9] Cf. BWL 263:Rev. 4.

[10] What all these people have in common is a keen eye. The keenest eyes in the world, however, are the eyes of a girl in love. The whole passage may be compared to Ps. 123:1f.

[11] With regard to the masterful poetic structure of the poem see W. G. E. Watson, Classical Hebrew Poetry, Sheffield 1984, 277f. with reference to Isa. 28:10 and Jer. 15:2 for the repetitive pattern. See also Descent of Ishtar, 70ff.

[12] The hypothetical restorations rest on a combination of Deut. 11:12 and Aqhat III (KTU 1.19):iii.47f.

[1] Cf. Baal, note 33.

[2] Restorations according to Baal I (KTU 1.3):ii.38-iii.1.

[with sc]ent[3] *which the sons of Ilu*[4] *did not know,*
(which) the assembly of the stars[5] *[did not know],*
(which) the race of heaven[6] *did [not understand].*[7]
[She wanted to charm] Baʿlu the Almighty,
[wanted to please][8] *the Rider on the Clouds.*[9]
[If only Baʿlu would] *turn towards the nations,*
[if only the god Had]du[10] *would return to the earth!*[11]
[If only he would revive] *the dead,*[12]
[if only] *the hand of the warrior* [would collect] *the herb!*[13]
[Mo]tu, [the son of Ilu], *will show him favour*
[when Baʿlu] *has given the [g]ift.*[14]
The Virgin ʿAnatu [ ],
the Wanton Widow of the Nations[15] [ ]:
"[If only Baʿlu would incline himself] *to the nations,*
[if only the god Haddu would retur]n *to the earth!*
[ ] *to the flesh*[16]
[ ]
[ ] houses

[3] Cf. Baal I (KTU 1.3):ii.2.
[4] Father of the gods, head of the pantheon.
[5] Cf. Aqhat, note 242.
[6] Cf. Aqhat, note 241.
[7] For the restorations see Baal I (KTU 1.3):iii.26-28.
[8] Restorations after Baal IV (KTU 1.4):ii.10f.
[9] Cf. Baal, note 37.
[10] True name of Baʿlu, identical to Hadad/Adad. It is never used outside the myths and proper names. Cf. Baal, note 188.
[11] Cf. Baal, notes 470, 475, 478. An alternative translation is: "he sat/will sit down on the earth", cf. Baal V (KTU 1.5):vi.13f.
[12] Cf. Aqhat, notes 98-102, 269-270, 289.
[13] A reference to Aqhat III (KTU 1.19):ii.17,24? Or perhaps the herb of life (cf. Gilg., XI.274)?
[14] Cf. Baal VI (KTU 1.6):v.7ff.
[15] Cf. Baal, note 34.
[16] Cf. Baal VI (KTU 1.6):vi.43, in expectation of Baʿlu's return.

[ ] my hands
[ ] my [ ]
[h]arts,
[wi]ld oxen
[ ]
(broken)

About 34 lines describing ʿAnatu's journey to the mountain of Baʿlu[17] are lost.

II.

"[*Is Baʿlu the Almighty in his ma*]*n*[*sion*],
  [*is the god Haddu within*] *his palace*?"
And the lads of Baʿlu answered:
"*Baʿlu is not in his mansion*,
  the god Haddu (*is not*) *within his palace.*
He has taken his bow in his hand
  and his arrows in his right hand.
Then he headed straight
  for the shore of Shamku[18] *teeming with wild oxen.*"
The Virgin ʿAnatu raised her wings,
  she raised her wings and flew up,
    to the shore of Shamku teeming with wild oxen.
And Baʿlu the Almighty raised his eyes,
  yes, *he raised his eyes and saw*,
yes, *he saw the Virgin ʿAnatu*,
  the most graceful among Baʿlu's sisters.[19]
He stood up before her, *yes*, *he arose*,
  at her feet he kneeled and fell down.[20]

[17] Cf. Baal I (KTU 1.3):iv.32ff.

[18] Probably Lake Hule, cf. E. Lipiński, OLP 2 (1971) 16f.

[19] Cf. Loves I, note 4. Polygamy was accepted.

[20] An exceptional tribute to a beautiful woman. Baʿlu does not bow for ʿAnatu when she arrives in Baal I (KTU 1.3):iv.39ff.

He raised his voice and cried:
"*May you be revived, my sister, and let us shine upon you!*[21]
The horns[22] *of your head-dress, Virgin ˤAnatu,*
  Baˤlu will anoint the horns of your head-dress,[23]
    Baˤlu will anoint them while flying!
We shall pierce my foes into the earth,[24]
  the adversaries of your brother into the dust!"
And the Virgin ˤAnatu raised her eyes,
  yes, she raised her eyes and saw,
yes, she saw a cow and started to flow,[25]
  she started to flow and started to convulse
    [*with*] *happiness, with delight, the pangs*[26] *of the Kathiratu.*[27]
ˤAnatu addressed [*herself*] *to Baˤlu:*
"[*Look*] *at her, o Baˤlu who* [ ] *the drizzle,*
  [*god*] *Haddu who* [ ] *the clouds!*"
[*And*] *Baˤlu the Almighty* [*answered*]:
"[*Let*] *the Virgin ˤAnatu* [*open*] *her orifice*[28]
[ ]..[ ]..
[ ] my [ ]
[ ]
[ ]"
[*the pa*]*ngs of the Kathiratu*

[21] Cf. Ps. 80:19f., also Num. 6:25; Ps. 67:2; 118:27; Myth and Ritual V, note 32.

[22] Either a metaphor for curls of hair, as would be possible in Akkadian and Arabic, or the horns ˤAnatu is shown wearing on seals (so J. Sanmartín, UF 12 (1980) 341-344).

[23] The anointing of the beloved, cf. K. R. Veenhof, BiOr 23 (1966) 311; D. Pardee, BiOr 34 (1977) 14ff. See also S. Schott, Altägyptische Liebeslieder, 2. Aufl., Zürich 1950, 58; J.&A. Westenholz, Or 46 (1977) 203.

[24] Cf. Isa. 14:19; 51:9; Job 26:13.

[25] From sexual excitement, cf. CAD (A)1, 306. In III.17 the amniotic fluid.

[26] Cf. Isa. 26:17f.

[27] Goddesses overseeing conception and childbirth.

[28] Euphemism for the vagina, as in Akkadian and M. Hebrew. Cf. III.9f.

About 20 lines are missing. Apparently ᶜAnatu proposes that she should enter into the cow so that the cow would be able to bear offspring for her. The "Virgin" ᶜAnatu herself was unable to bear offspring.[29]

III.

"[*The wom*]*b of the cow can bear* [*for me*],
the ox[30] *for the Virgin ᶜAnatu,*
yes, the beautiful (beast) for the Wanton Widow of the Nations!"
And Baᶜlu the Almighty answered:
"*Surely I can mount* [*you*] *like our Creator,*[31]
like the old generation that created [*us*]!"[32]
Baᶜlu strode forward with a filled 'hand',[33]
the god Haddu filled his 'finger'.[34]
The orifice of the Virgin ᶜAnatu was deflowered,
yes, the orifice of the most graceful of the sisters of Baᶜlu.

[29] Cf. Myth and Ritual IV (KTU 1.13):29ff., which may have been part of the section missing between column II and III.

[30] The word *ʾalp* is a general term like "ox" and includes female animals, cf. lines 15ff. See also CAD (A)1, 370f.; Deut. 7:13; 28:4,18,51.

[31] *Scil.* the Bull Ilu, the procreator of the gods. Cf. Baal, note 77. It is obvious that such a statement reflects Baᶜlu's ambition to replace his old father-in-law. Cf. OTS 24 (1986) 1ff.

In several other passages Baᶜlu transforms himself into a young bull to mount a cow: Loves III (KTU 1.11):3; Baal V (KTU 1.5):v.18ff. This motif was also adopted in Egypt: R. Stadelmann, Syrisch-palästinensische Gottheiten in Ägypten, Leiden 1967, 132f. A similar Babylonian myth is "The Cow of Sin", KAR No. 196. See Myth and Ritual II, note 10. A Hurrian myth relates how the Sun impregnated a cow, KUB 24, No.7:II.46-IV.59.

All this explains why attempts to respresent YHWH as a young bull met vigorous opposition in Israel. Cf. Ex. 32; Deut 9:21; 1 Ki. 12:28-32; 2 Ki. 10:29; 17:16; Hos. 8:5f.; 10:5; 13:2; Ps. 106:19.

[32] Again a clear reference to Ilu, cf. The Bible World. Essays in Honor of C. H. Gordon, New York 1980, 172ff.

[33] "Hand" is a euphemism for the penis, cf. Myth and Ritual I, note 38; IV, note 47; V, note 15; Isa. 57:8.

[34] Euphemism, as in Middle Hebrew.

Baᶜlu ascended the moun[tain of Araru],[35]
yes, the son of Daganu the sum[mit of Sapanu].
Baᶜlu sat down on the chair of his kingship,
the son of Daganu on the throne of his dominion.
A fl[uttering of] *fell upon the ox,*
a trembling of [ ] *fell upon the ox.*
She flowed and started to convulse
[*with*] *happiness, with delight, the pangs* (*of birth*).[36]
The cow, the cow [*of the Virgin ᶜAnatu*],
bore a bull to Baᶜlu,
yes, a wild ox to the Rider on the Clouds.
The c[*ow*] *embraced* [*her son*],
the cow embraced [*her young*],
and covered him with her udder.
He sucked his navel-string[37] *and his beestings,*[38]
yes, the beestings of his infancy.
She ascended the mountain along the spur,
the mountain of victory[39] *along the stairs.*
Yes, she then ascended Araru,
Araru and Sapanu,
the lovely one, the mountain of victory.
She addressed herself to Baᶜlu:
"*Receive divinely good news, Baᶜlu,*
yes, receive good news, child of Daganu!

[35] Probably Araru is the name of a promontory of Sapanu (*pace* P. Bordreuil, Syria 61 (1984) 10). Cf. Baal, note 4, as well as Ps. 47:6,9.

[36] In the myth the period of pregnancy is usually skipped, cf. Baal V (KTU 1.5):v.22; Myth and Ritual I (KTU 1.23):51f.; II (KTU 1.12):i.17ff.

[37] On the sucking of the navel-string see H. Granqvist, Birth and Childhood among the Arabs, Helsinki 1947, 75.

[38] Cf. M. Sznycer, GLECS 17 (1972-73) 74; TO I, 288.

[39] Cf. Baal, note 52.

For a bull is born to Baᶜlu,[40]
yes, a wild ox to the Rider on the Clouds!"
Baᶜlu the Almighty rejoiced.

The Loves of Baal and Anath III

KTU 1.11

[*Baᶜ*]*lu stripped and grasped her abdomen.*[1]
ᶜAnatu stripped and grasped his testicles.
[*And*] *Baᶜlu transformed himself into an ox.*[2]
[*the V*]*irgin ᶜAnatu was* [*the cow*].
[*Through the kis*]*sing there was conception and childbirth,*
[*the happiness, the de*]*light, the pangs of the Kathiratu.*[3]
[*Vir*]*gin ᶜAnatu,*
[ ] *Baᶜlu the Almighty*
(traces, broken)

[40] Cf. Myth and Ritual I (KTU 1.23):52ff.; Isa. 9:6.

[1] Euphemism for the vagina, cf. Gen. 25:22. Naked lovers touching each other's private parts are represented in Sumerian literature and in the art of Mesopotamia, cf. UF 9 (1977) 277; 11 (1979) 641, n. 13.
[2] Cf. Loves II, note 31.
[3] Cf. Loves II, notes 26-27.

MYTH AND RITUAL

Myth and Ritual I

KTU 1.23

Among the tablets of Ugarit there are several that combine a mythological narrative with a ritual or an incantation. The connection between the myth and the ritual is usually very clear, lending support to the view that the myth served to explain the ritual and was recited or symbolically re-enacted in the cult.

The first text of this genre is very interesting because it describes some of the ceremonies of the New Year festival,[1] including the sacred marriage rite. As in the Sumerian *hieros gamos*,[2] the king represented the god, in this case Ilu, the head of the Ugaritic pantheon.[3] The queen represented Ilu's wife Athiratu, whereas a

[1] Cf. J. C. de Moor, New Year with Canaanites and Israelites, 1, Kampen 1972, 6-8. The main arguments for this dating are:
a) The drinking of foaming new wine (line 6), cf. Baal, note 15, and note 11 below.
b) The humiliating treatment of Motu (lines 8-11) whose defeat was celebrated on this festival. Cf. Baal, note 470.
c) The singing of the sweet-voiced boy (lines 14, 17), corresponding to Baal I (KTU 1.3):i.20.
d) The presence of booths of branches on the roof of the temple (line 19), cf. note 25 below.
e) The sacred marriage rite which in at least some of the Mesopotamian cases took place on the New Year festival, cf. the next note.

[2] On the sacred marriage in Mesopotamia see: W. H. P. Römer, Sumerische 'Königshymnen' der Isin-Zeit, Leiden 1965, 143ff.; S. N. Kramer, The Sacred Marriage Rite, Bloomington/London 1969, 64ff., 79; D. Reisman, JCS 25 (1973) 185ff.; F. R. Kraus, RAI XIX (1974) 243ff.; Th. Jacobsen, in: H. Goedicke, J. J. M. Roberts (eds.), Unity and Diversity, Baltimore/London 1975, 65ff. J. Renger, J. G. Cooper, RLA IV, 251ff., 259ff.; K. Oberhuber, in: Fs. L. R. Palmer, Innsbruck 1976, 261-272.

[3] The kings of Ugarit were deified officially only after their death when they

priestess, possibly a princess,[4] played the role of the goddess of love ᶜAnatu.

Just as in the Sumerian texts concerning the sacred marriage the king sometimes acts out of character in addressing Ilu.[5] So it may be assumed that the deities were present during the ceremonies in the form of cult images.[6]

"*Let me invoke*[7] *the gracious gods,*
[ ] *and delightful,*
the sons of the bare hill]*s*],
who placed a city on high,
[*established a sanctuary*][8] *in the desert of the bare hills,*
founded [*the houses of* Tadma]ru[9] *on their top.*"[10]

"joined Ilu", cf. Keret, note 63. However, already during his life-time a Canaanite king was glorified as a "son of Ilu", cf. Keret, note 74.

This royal ideology, of which KTU 1.23 is an important witness, was centered around the head of the pantheon, Ilu. Other texts, however, reflect a shift from the older pair Ilu-Athiratu to the younger and more popular pair Baᶜlu-ᶜAnatu. Cf. Incantation I, note 5 and below, note 58.

[4] Compare the case of princess Pughatu, cf. Aqhat, notes 249-251.

[5] Lines 52f., 60.

[6] See lines 19, 57.

[7] Cohortative, see Myth and Ritual V, note 3.

[8] Cf. line 65, a task they carried out only after their encounter with the watchman. Apparently the gracious gods decided to found their sanctuary with the watchman who gave them such a hearty reception, lines 70ff. For a vivid description of people coming in from the desert to establish a city for themselves in an oasis see Ps. 107:36, cf. 107: 4-9,33-38. For *ydy* as a verb denoting the founding of a building or a city see the related Akkad. verb *nadû*, CAD (N) 1, 82ff.

[9] In the opinion of the present writer the holy city in the desert might well be the oasis of Palmyra. Its ancient name Tadmar/Tadmor occurs in Old Assyrian and Old Babylonian documents. Under Tiglathpileser I (*ca.* 1115-1077 B.C.) it was part of Amurru and was inhabited by Aramaeans. Cf. J. Starcky, Palmyre, Paris 1952, 27f. The kingdom of Ugarit maintained very close ties with Amurru and it is certainly not too far-fetched to suppose that the cult-myth of Tadmor/Palmyra was known here. See note 13 for the reasons why it may have been recited on this particular occasion. According to the lines 73f. the location for the future city was ideal for caravan traffic (see note 68). It was a guarded oasis even before the founding of its temple (see note 66).

And the [ ] shall ra[ise th]eir [voices]:
"Eat of any bread,
and drink of any foaming wine![11]
Hail the king,
hail the queen,[12]
the bedouin-warriors[13] *and the life-guard!"*[14]

If this hypothesis proves to be tenable it might finally offer an explanation for the enigmatic name of Tadmor: **tadmāru* "guard-post" (cf. Ugar *tʿḏr, tʿdt*, etc.) which became *tadmōr* in Aramaic.

[10] Cf. 2 Chr. 25:12.

[11] It is certain that *ḫmr* was not a general term for wine. It indicated a foaming, freshly fermented wine. Cf. the grapes in line 26 below, the bunch of grapes in Ritual I (KTU 1.41):2 as well as Deut. 32:14 (an incomplete verse).

The first new wine was pressed ceremonially in the course of the festival. Everybody was allowed to drink his fill. The combination *ḥmr yn* is also attested in Phoenician whereas Ps. 75:9 reverses the hendiadys: *yyn ḥmr*. See also Aqhat, note 78 as well as Prov. 9:5. Kings are warned for the hazards of indulging in the consumption of wine in Prov. 31:4.

[12] The queen too played an important role in the cult of Ugarit. Cf. KTU 1.40:36; 1.115:8; 4.149:14f. The king and the other members of the royal family are greeted in a similar way in Ritual II (KTU 1.161):31-34. Compare also the opening lines of Iddin-Dagan's sacred marriage hymn (D. Reisman, *op.cit.* (n. 2), 186:1-9) as well as 1 Chr. 12:19.

[13] Next to the *ṯnnm* the *ʿrbm* are probably "Arabs", bedouin elite troops serving the king of Ugarit as mercenaries. Cf. the *ʿrbm* feeding Eliah (1 Ki. 17:4,6), the *urbi*-troops serving Hezekiah (OIP 2,33, III.39), Hebr. *ʿrbh* "desert", Arab. *ʿurb*, etc. Also H. Schmidt, P. Kahle, Volkserzählungen aus Palästina, Bd. 2, Göttingen 1930, 12*. Furthermore M. C. Astour, Fs E. Edel, Bamberg 1979, 29. Of course the recitation of this text, praising the divine founders of a sanctuary in the desert and exhibiting a rather bawdy character, may have been intended to captivate the attention of these soldiers. On the other hand it should be remembered that the Ugaritic dynasty traced its origins back to this particular region of Amurru, cf. B. Levine, J.-M. de Tarragon, JAOS 104 (1984) 654f.

[14] Military class belonging to the entourage of the king. In view of the ritual combat enacted during four days of the New Year festival (Baal, note 21) the presence of soldiers is not surprising. In the ceremonies for the Sumerian sacred marriage military men also played a part (Reisman, *op.cit.* (n. 2), 187).

"Motu-and-Sharru[15] *is sitting,*
with the staff of bereavement in one hand,
the staff of widowerhood in the other.
The pruners of the vine shall prune him,
the binders of the vine shall bind him,
they shall let him fall on the terrace like a vine!"

Seven times he[16] *shall recite (this) on the dais*
and the bedouin-warriors shall answer him.[17]

"And the field, the field of the two gods,
is the field of Athiratu and the Damsel."[18]
The sweet-voiced youth[19] *(shall sing this) before the fire.*

[15] The god of death Motu, here appearing as a dual god: "Death-and-Evil". Among the Arabs *al-šarr* is a name of the devil.

At the New Year festival the defeat of Motu was celebrated. Apparently the god of death was represented on this occasion as a kind of scarecrow constructed out of tendrils of picked vines, just as he was a sheaf of corn at the end of the grain harvest (Baal, notes 430-436). His ritual mutilation is an obvious hint at the vintage, cf. Isa. 47:8f.; Jer. 15:7f., with the same standard metaphors. The fruit of the vine was viewed with mixed feelings. It could make people "like dead" (Myth and Ritual III (KTU 1.114), see also Deut. 32:33 and 2 Ki 4:39f.).

[16] *I.e.* the king as the principal officiant. Cf. Ritual I (KTU 1.41):52f.

[17] A convincing example of responsion in the cult. Cf. Deut. 27:14f.; Ex. 32:18(?).

[18] Apparently the opening lines of a song. Cf. also lines 28f. Their enigma is solved by a parallel in a Sumerian hymn for the sacred marriage: "Lordly Queen, your breast is your field, Inanna, your breast is your field" (Kramer, *op.cit.* (n. 2), 81, cf. ANET, 206). So the song hints at the lines 24, 59 and 61 where Athiratu and ᶜAnatu act as wet-nurses for the two gods. See also notes 30 and 58 below.

"Damsel", literally "womb", is an epithet of ᶜAnatu, cf. Baal, note 419.

[19] See note 1.

(Put) coriander in the milk,[20]
mint in the butter.
And burn incense seven times over the fire-pan.[21]

''The Damsel[22] *went and scoured (the area).*
She wanted to gird him [by her eyelashes].''[23]
The gracious youth[24] *[shall sing this before them].*
And he shall call [out] the names of the bedouin-warriors.

Eight (and) ei[ght] dwellings for the gods [on the roof].[25]

[20] The parallelism with ''mint'' renders this interpretation more likely than the translation ''a kid in milk'' proposed by many scholars who refer to Ex. 23:19; 34:26; Deut. 14:21 for support. Cf. P. C. Craigie, Tyndale Bulletin 28 (1979) 155-169; O. Keel, Das Böcklein in der Milch seiner Mutter und Verwandtes, Freiburg/Göttingen 1980, 36ff.

[21] Cf. Aqhat, note 242.

[22] Here the feminine *rḥmy* is used. The formula ''go and scour'' is often applied to ʿAnatu.

[23] Cf. Keret I (KTU 1.14):iii.43f. and Loves I (KTU 1.96).

[24] The minstrel, cf. Baal, note 16. It is not to be excluded that the performer belonged to a group of homosexual cultic personnel (*qdšm*). In the Sumerian sacred marriage ceremonies homosexual actors played a part too (Reisman, *op.cit.* (n. 2), 187).

[25] Restored after Ritual I (KTU 1.41):50f. Both these texts as well as Myth and Ritual IV (KTU 1.13):11 prove that during this festival booths of branches and foliage were erected on the roof of the temple. Cf. Jer. 19:13; 32:29. This is one of the arguments in favour of the hypothesis that the Israelite Feast of Booths evolved out of the Canaanite New Year festival. It should be noted that during the Sumerian sacred marriage ceremony certain offerings took place on the roof of the temple (Reisman, *op.cit.* (n. 2), 190:143).

A further confirmation of this theory may be found in the ritual KTU 1.104:15-24: ''*And on the tenth day* [ ] *shall turn around the gear of her baldachin. And she shall stay out the renewal of the two* (halves of the day, cf. Arab.*ḥadaṯān* and Lam. 5:21). *And at the renewal she shall judge them* (compare their respective lengths) *and she shall fix* (cf.

[He shall invoke (the gods)][26] *seven times.*

Lapis-blue, gold-coloured, scarlet (are) the singers.[27]

"Let me invoke the gracious gods,
the ravenous[28] *sons of one day,*[29]
who suck the nipple of the breast of Athiratu,[30]
[the puppies] of Shapshu,[31]
the watch-dog at their door."[32]
[ ] *and grapes (are offered).*
"Hail the bedouin-warriors, the life-guard,
who came to the sacrifice of grace!"

"The field of the two gods,
is the field of Athiratu and the Damsel."
He shall [re]c[ite] (this) again.[33]

Job 14:13) *the two* (halves, *i.e.* establish that it is an equinox). *And eight (and) eight dwellings for the gods, eight (made of) branches with ripe fruit* (*gmlm*, cf. Num. 17:23; Isa. 18:5, also Lev. 23:40), *eight (made of) greenery, [on the roof]. And for Pi[rigalu he shall sacrifice]*". See also Ritual I, notes 56, 58.

[26] After Ritual I (KTU 1.41):52f., cf. line 12 above.

[27] Alternatively "*the leaders*".

[28] A comparison between lines 63f. and Isa. 9:19 would seem to impose this interpretation.

[29] *I.e.* twins marking the beginning and end of the same day. Cf. note 48.

[30] Cf. Keret, note 51.

[31] Sun-goddess.

[32] Cf. Keret I (KTU 1.14):iii.19 (par.).

[33] Cf. lines 13f.

(Myth:)

[And Ilu w]ent out[34] *to the shore of the sea,*
and strode along the shore of the Flood.
[And] Ilu [placed] two girl-acrobats,[35]
two girl-acrobats *over a fire-pan.*
Look! One was low,
Look! The other was high.
Look! One cried: "My father, my father!"[36]
And look! The other cried: "My mother, my mother!"[37]
"May the 'hand'[38] *of Ilu be as long*[39] *as the sea,*[40]
yes, the 'hand' of Ilu like the ocean!"

[34] Cf. Judge. 5:4; Hab. 3:12f.; Ps. 68:8.

[35] Many different translations have been proposed for this word. See the survey by Del Olmo Lete, MLC, 443f.; Aula Orientalis 1 (1983) 111ff.

Any interpretation making the *mštʿltm* inanimate objects such as "torches" has to face the difficulty that they are introduced as acting and speaking beings in lines 33ff. Because they seem to be identical to the two women Ilu will seduce presently (lines 39ff.) a personal interpretation is by far the most natural one. In that case, however, the circumstance that Ilu places the two *mštʿltm* over the fire-pan in line 31 forms an obstacle.

First of all it should be observed that a fire on the beach was not unusual (cf. Baal IV.ii.5-9; John 21:9). The form *mštʿlt* looks like a participle of the Št-stem of *ʿly* meaning "woman making herself rise, pushing herself up". It could be a female acrobat making a backward arch then. Such an acrobat is represented in Egyptian art (cf. J. Leclant, Ägypten, Bd. 2 (Universum der Kunst, 27), München 1979, No. 102). According to the Sumerian texts acrobats were partaking in the ceremonies for the sacred marriage. It is submitted here that the two women were arching over the fire-pan in a posture that was as dangerous as it was erotic, symbolizing their willingness to take the "heat" (Ugaritic *ḥmḥmt*) of Ilu's love. Ilu saves them from burning by taking them away from the fire-pan (lines 36ff.) and substituting a bird for them (lines 37ff.).

[36] Not Ilu's usual epithet *'ab* "Father" but the more formal *'ad*. Nevertheless 2 Ki. 2:12-14 may be compared.

[37] Ilu seems to be called "Mother" here, just like Amun-Re in Egypt, cf. J. Assmann, Re und Amun, Freiburg/Göttingen 1983, 119f., 166.

[38] Loves II, note 33.

[39] A long penis is an ancient ideal, cf. TCS (2) 33:11 "May your penis become as long as a cudgel"; BRM 4, 22:27 "if the penis is long and thick, that man will beget males".

[40] The sea is immeasurable, cf. Lam. 2:13.

The 'hand' of Ilu became as long as the sea,
yes, the 'hand' of Ilu like the ocean.
Ilu took the two girl-acrobats,
the two girl-acrobats *from over the fire-pan,*
he took (them), placed (them) in his house.
Ilu lowered his staff,[41]
Ilu aimed his walking-stick with his right hand,[42]
raised (it), shot heavenward,
shot a bird in heaven.
He plucked (it), put (it) on the coals.[43]
Surely Ilu wanted to seduce the two women![44]
If the two women would cry:
''O my husband, my husband,
lowering your staff,
aiming your walking-stick,
look! you are roasting a bird on the fire,
it is browning on the coals!''
- they would be wives, each one a wife of Ilu,
a wife of Ilu for ever.
But if the two women would cry:
''O my father, my father,
lowering your staff,
aiming your walking-stick,
look! you are roasting a bird on the fire,
and it is browning on the coals!''

[41] In spite of the obvious erotic symbolism a real staff which Ilu handles after the manner of a javelin-thrower.

[42] The forms *ymnn* and *mmnnm* are derived from the denominative L-stem of *ymn*. Cf. Ugar. *brkk*, *ṣḥrr*, etc., as well as 1 Chr. 12:2.

[43] Birds are used to cure a loss of potency in Babylonia, cf. TCS (2) 49ff. The underlying imagery is clear: the ''chick'' is a woman, cf. W. G. E. Watson, UF 9 (1977) 281.

[44] Cf. Exod. 22:15; Hos. 2:16 and for an easily seduced ''bird'': Hos. 7:11.

- they would be daughters, each one a daughter of Ilu,
a daughter of Ilu for ever.[45]
But look! The two women cried:
"O my husband, my husband,
lowering your staff,
aiming your walking-stick,
look! you are roasting a bird on the fire
and it is browning on the coals!"
They were wives, each one a wife of Ilu,
a wife of Ilu for ever.
He stooped, kissed their lips.
Look! Their lips were sweet,[46]
sweet as pomegranates.
While he was kissing, there was conception,
while he was embracing, there was heat.[47]
They travailed (and) gave birth
to Shaharu and Shalimu.[48]
Word was brought to Ilu:
"You, Ilu, made my[49] *two wives give birth!"*[50]
"What did I beget?"
"My two boys, Shaharu and Shalimu!"

[45] Probably the alternatives described in the lines 39-46 mean that the women playing this part in the actual cult could refuse to subject themselves to the erotic scenes by calling out "My father, my father".

[46] Cf. Song of Songs 4:11; 7:10.

[47] Cf. Aqhat, note 41.

[48] Shaharu is the deified dawn, Shalimu the deified dusk. The birth of the two gods is referred to in Myth and Ritual II (KTU 1.12):i.7f. It appears that Shalimu was also called Qadmu, the East.

No time is spared for pregnancy in the myth. Cf. Loves II, note 36.

[49] The king who is supposed to play Ilu's role (see the introduction) is speaking out of character.

[50] Against the widely accepted translation that makes the two wives the subject. This would require a form without *-y*. See also line 65 *ʾašld*.

"Arise![51] *Perform great works*[52] *for Shapshu,*[53]
and lasting works[54] *for the stars!"*

(Ritual:)
"He stooped, kissed their lips.
Look! Their lips were sweet.
While he was kissing, there was conception,
while he was embracing, there was heat."
He[55] *shall recite (this) again five times before the images,*
and the congregation shall sing (it).[56]

(Myth:)
Both of them laboured and gave birth,
they gave birth to the two gracious gods,
the ravenous sons of one day,[57]
who suck the nipple of the Breast.[58]
Word was brought to Ilu:
"You, Ilu, made my two wives give birth!"
"What did I beget?"
"The two gracious gods,
the ravenous sons of one day,
who suck the nipple of the breast of the Lady.

[51] Intransitive use of *nšʾ*, as in Ps. 89:10 and in Akkadian, cf. CAD (N)2, 103.
[52] The feminine plural is used for the abstract, cf. Ps. 71:19; 106:21; Job 37:5.
[53] Cf. note 31.
[54] Cf. Hos. 6:3.
[55] Cf. note 33.
[56] The soldiers (notes 13-14) must have loved to repeat these lines. The first time the minstrel has sung them alone. Then the song is repeated five times together. The seventh time the singer sings alone again because then he will elaborate and continue his story (lines 58ff.). So it is highly probable that the gracious gods are none other than Shaharu and Shalimu. See also the notes 8-9.
[57] Cf. notes 28-29.
[58] Cf. note 18. It is not necessary to emend the text here. "Breast" is an epithet of ʿAnatu, cf. Myth and Ritual IV, note 28.

One lip (is) to the earth,
one lip to the heavens,[59]
and they enter their mouth:
the birds of heaven
and the fish from the sea.[60]
And there they stand, ravenous lad with ravenous lad,
they put (food) into their mouths from the right and the left,
but they are not satisfied!"[61]
"*O wives whom I have married,*
o sons whom I have begotten!
Arise! Establish a sanctuary in the desert.[62]
There you shall drag along[63] *stones and trees,*[64]
for seven full years,
eight cycles of time."[65]
The gracious gods went out to the field,
they scoured the fringes of the desert.
And they came upon a watchman of sown land.[66]
And they cried to the watchman of the sown:
"*O watchman, watchman, open!*"
And he made an opening for them
and they entered.

[59] Description of their gaping mouths, cf. Baal, note 332.

[60] Cf. Zeph. 1:3.

[61] Clearly Isa. 9:19 was inspired by these lines.

[62] Cf. notes 8-9 as well as Gen. 21:8-21; 25:6.

[63] Syr. *gargar*, Syr. Arab. *ǧarǧara* "drag", *i.e.* building materials for the sanctuary.

[64] Cf. 1 Ki. 5:32; 1 Chr. 22:14, etc.

[65] A standard formula, cf. Myth and Ritual II, note 39. It is hardly a coincidence, however, that the building of the temple of Solomon also took seven years (1 Ki. 6:38).

[66] Irrigated land, as in Isa. 19:7, so the two gods happened to find an oasis. For that reason it was fenced in and guarded, cf. KTU 1.92:23; Song of Songs 1:6; 8:11f.

From this line on the poetical structure deteriorates. Apparently the scribe noticed he had only a few lines left.

"If [there is] bread [in your house],
give it, so that we can eat![67]
If there is [wine in your house],
give it, so that we can drink!"
And the watchman of the sown answered them:
"[There is bread that came from Ya]rti,
there is wine that came from Thuka[la].[68]
[ ]."
One of them came to the hin,[69]
the log[70] *of his wine* [ ]
[ ]
and his companion was full of wine.[71]
[ ]

Myth and Ritual II

KTU 1.12

This tablet was written by an inexperienced scribe. Many lines of column I flow over into the space intended for column II. The writing of column II is cramped, obviously because the scribe had not planned his work very well. This may mean that he has managed to complete this text within the two extant columns, so that columns III and IV (which are now lost) were used to inscribe another text.

[67] Cf. 1 Sam. 21:3.

[68] These cities are paired in PRU VI, No. 70:18f. The availability of food and wine from distant places indicates that the location was ideal for caravan trade.

[69] Measure for wine and other liquids, as in Hebrew.

[70] Also a liquid measure, about $\frac{1}{12}$ hin.

[71] Cf. Ps. 75:9; Acts 2:13. Unlike the Recabites (Jer. 35) these desert-dwellers were glad to sample the blessings of civilization. Comparable is the case of Enkidu who took seven cups of strong drink the very first time he tasted it, Gilg. II:ii.97f.

The anomalous spellings of the text should also be attributed to the lack of experience of the scribe, not to the antiquity of the document. The myth reflects the same tension between Ilu[1] and Baʿlu[2] that is characteristic of many other religious texts of Late Bronze Ugarit.[3]

About 10 lines are missing from the beginning of column I. Two minor goddesses are addressing Ilu:

"[ ]s
[ ]
[ ]s *of the earth.*
[*Please, will y*]*ou be* [*an ox*] *to us?*[4]
[*Then we*] *shall be the cattle!*
[*Please, make*] *us* [*pr*]*egnant,*
[*please, make*] *us* [*p*]*regnant, as with Shaharu,*[5]
[*please, make*] *us bear, as with Qadmu!*[6]
Our bosom, Ilu, our father,
(*our*) *bosom devours us like fire,*[7]
our breasts pinch us as with bitter pains!"[8]

[1] Head of the Ugaritic pantheon.

[2] God of rain and life, son-in-law of Ilu.

[3] Cf. OTS 24 (1986) 1ff.

[4] With regard to the construction cf. Judg. 10:15; Ps. 90:1, also Ex. 4:25; 18:19; Num. 11:29; Deut. 7:6; Jer. 51:20. For the theriomorphic intercourse see Loves II, note 31.

[5] The two goddesses refer to another myth that has been preserved among the tablets of Ugarit. See Myth and Ritual I (KTU 1.23):30ff. Shaharu is the god of dawn.

[6] Qadmu is the deified East and therefore probably an alternative name of Shaharu (Dawn). For the reading and interpretation of the text see: The Bible World. Essays ... C. H. Gordon, New York 1980, 177, n. 29.

[7] Cf. Ps. 39:4; Luke 24:32; also 1 Cor. 7:9.

[8] From sexual excitement.

Ilu laughed in his heart
and felt expansive *in his breast.*[9]
"Go out, o Tulishu,[10] *handmaid of Yarikhu,*
o Damgayu,[11] *handmaid of Athiratu!*[12]
Take your birth-stool,[13]
your litter,[14] *your swaddling-clothes,*[15]
and go out into the plain of the demons,
into the desert of the murderous god.[16]
Dig, o handmaid,
throw up dust furiously,
position the two bricks.[17]
Writhe and bear the Devourers,[18]
crouch and bear the Rippers!"[19]
Ilu proclaimed their names.[20]

[9] The Ugaritic verb *gmḏ* is probably related to Arabic *mḏǧ* (metathesis). Cf. Isa. 60:5; Ps. 25:17; 119:32.

[10] Minor goddess, precise function unknown, forming a pair with Damgayu, cf. Aqhat, note 70. For the role of the handmaid of the moon-god Yarikhu in this particular context see W. G. E. Watson, UF 9 (1977) 282, with the pertinent comments of M. Stol, Zwangerschap en geboorte bij de Babyloniërs en in de bijbel, Leiden 1983, 29ff.

[11] Minor goddess, precise function unknown. Cf. note 10.

[12] Wife of Ilu, mother of the gods.

[13] With regard to the birth-stool see Stol, *op. cit.*, 58; G. M. Beckman, Hittite Birth Rituals, Wiesbaden 1983, 22f., 25f., 32f., 93ff.

[14] Cf. Beckman, *op. cit.*, 23.

[15] Cf. Ez. 16:4; Luke 2:7,12; Stol, *op. cit.*, 64, note 386.

[16] The desert was a place where deadly demons were roaming. Possibly "the murderous god" is the god of death Motu himself. Cf. Baal, note 377.

[17] The women had to dig a hollow above which parturition took place in a squatting position. For the pair of bricks on which the woman in labour took place, cf. Ex. 1:16; Stol, *op. cit.*, 57f.

[18] Name of dragon-like demons.

[19] Cf. Arab. *ʿaqqa* "rip open, slaughter". It is noteworthy that Ilu does not have intercourse with the two goddesses. He seems to engender the monsters by his authoritative word alone.

[20] Cf. Baal II (KTU 1.1):iv.15ff. The scribe simply skips the episode of the actual bearing.

On them were horns[21] *like bulls,*[22]
and humps like oxen,
and on them was the face of Baᶜlu.[23]
Baᶜlu was walking around and scouring (the area),
rushing along the fringes of the desert.
And he came upon the Devourers,
yes, he found the Rippers.
Surely Baᶜlu coveted them,
the son of Daganu fancied them.
Baᶜlu stalked them on foot,
yes, the god Haddu on tip-toe.

About 5 lines missing.

[ ] ... [ ]
[*the Rip*]*pers* [ ]
and eye[*s like the eyes of Baᶜlu*],
a face [*like the face of Haddu*].
Baᶜlu st[*alked them on foot*],
the god Haddu [*on* tip-toe],
step by step.[24]
Surely Baᶜlu coveted them,
surely the god fancied them,
[*his*] *br*[*east*].
One day, [*two days passed*].

[21] Cf. Dan. 7:7f.,20; Rev. 12:3; 13:1,11; 17:3,7.

[22] So they looked after their father, the Bull Ilu.

[23] They were hybrid creatures, bulls with an anthropoid face like the bull-men of ancient Syrian art, see *e.g.* G. Contenau, La glyptique syro-hittite, Paris 1922, No. 14, 22, 30, 40-45; D. Homès-Fredericq, Catalogue des sceaux-cylindres de Syrie, Bruxelles [1982], No. 13, 14, 20, 21. Of course their facial likeness to Baᶜlu was intended to provoke a mutual curiosity, cf. Gilg. I.ii.50.

[24] Literally *"coming without coming"*.

He studied [ ]
he was consumed [ ]
like a bowl [ ]
... [ ]
... [ ]
.. [ ]
.. [ ]
in [ ]
and in [ ]
Ba^{c}lu stalked them on foot,
the god Haddu on tip-toe,
step by step.
[*Ba^{c}lu*] *caught them in a* [*net*],
the son of Daganu [ ].
He put down [*his walking-stick*],
the tip [*he put*] *on* [*the ground*].[25]
He gave [*them*] *the dregs of his cup* [*to drink*].[26]
The red drink[27] *of a dignitary*[28] *they fa*[*ncied*],
the red drink of a rich man[29] *exci*[*ted them*].
Look! Ba^{c}lu took (*it*) *off his back,*
he took [*his*] *bo*[*w in* (*his*) *hand*],
the foot of Ba^{c}lu took (*position on*) [*its stave*].[30]
And he silenced the ragingly thirsty [animals],
he caught the Devourers like [ ].

[25] Cf. Aqhat, notes 228, 229.

[26] Apparently to intoxicate the beasts. Two other strange creatures engendered by Ilu in KTU 1.24 ask for wine when they come out of the desert (Myth and Ritual I (KTU 1.24):69ff.). Compare also Gilg. II.i.94-101.

[27] Literally *"redness"*, cf. Gen. 25:30; Prov. 23:31.

[28] Cf. Aqhat, note 65.

[29] Cf. Baal, note 415. The consumption of wine was a privilege of the rich, cf. Deut. 32:14; Hos. 7:5; Job 1:18; Esth. 5:6; Dan. 5:1.

[30] The bow was bent with the foot, cf. Aqhat, note 83.

(But) [Baᶜlu] fell into the marsh,
[Haddu] felt heat in his nose,
[Motu][31] *sent fever into his loins,*
[he consumed] his horns[32] *like branches,*
he himself, as when he scorches [the olives].[33]
The teeth of belly-death[34] *[him],*
surely con[sumption] pervaded him.[35]
The growth on the fields turned brown.[36]
Seven years the god[37] *completed,*[38]
eight cycles of time.[39]
Surely [his] brothers were clothed in mourning dress,[40]
in a mourning coat his kinsmen.

[31] God of death and ruler of the miry Nether World. As in the great seasonal myth of Baᶜlu, it is he who swallows Baᶜlu (line 41, cf. Baal V (KTU 1.5):ii.1ff.), causing the vegetation to die (lines 40, 43, cf. note 33 below). His relatives wear garments of mourning (lines 46-47, cf. Baal V (KTU 1.5):vi.16f.,31). And also the duration of Baᶜlu's absence is the same: seven or eight years (lines 44f., cf. Baal VI (KTU 1.6):v.7-9; Aqhat III (KTU 1.19):i.42-44). Therefore it may be concluded that our text presupposes the same basic theologoumenon, be it cast in an entirely different mould. See also notes 39 and 45 below.

[32] Baᶜlu is often depicted wearing horns, the symbols of strength.

[33] Cf. Baal V (KTU 1.5):ii.5, with Baal, note 335.

[34] Cf. CAD (M)2, 318a. Disease-causing demons come from the Nether World and are called "Biters".

[35] Cf. Aqhat III (KTU 1.19):i.10 and Arab. *trᶜ*.

[36] Cf. AOAT 16,175, n. 22.

[37] Probably Baᶜlu, as in line 9. Alternatively Ilu who had devised the whole plot.

[38] Cf. 2 Chr. 36:21, also Gen. 25:24; Ex. 23:26, etc.; Rev. 20:3,5,7; CAD (M)1, 180, 186.

[39] *I.e.* eight autumnal equinoxes marking the transition of years, cf. Ex. 34:22. At the New Year festival which fell around the time of the autumnal equinox the return of Baᶜlu was expected. See Baal, notes 18, 448, 470, 474-479; Aqhat, notes 78, 100, 269, 270; Ritual I, note 56; also notes 31 above and 45 below.

[40] Cf. note 31 as well as 2 Sam. 14:2. Because the end of the column is near, the scribe apparently shortens his account a little, avoiding the usual elaborate style of the myths and epics.

Surely his seven and seventy brothers came [upon him],[41]
yes, the eight and eighty.
The leaders of his brothers found him,
yes, they found him, the leaders of his friends.
At a crucial time,[42]
at a crucial moment,
then had Baʿlu fallen like a bull,
yes, Haddu had knuckled under like an ox,
down into the middle of the marsh.[43]

(Ritual part:)
"*Baʿlu, be poured out to give strength,*
be induced to pour out, so that there will be stability![44]
Make (it) pour out, mighty king![45]
Make the women drawing water at the well pour out!
Make the fountain of the house of Ilu pour out!
And the libation-vat[46] *of the House of Magic!*"

Myth and Ritual III

KTU 1.114

This burlesque text portrays Ilu, the head of the Ugaritic pantheon, as an incontinent drunk. His shameful conduct is indicative of his

[41] Parallelism between *ymǵy* and *ymẓ'a*, cf. I.36f. and Baal V (KTU 1.5):vi.8. The numbers 77 and 88 simply denote any large number, cf. Baal V (KTU 1.5):v.20f.

[42] Cf. Akkad. *šikin adanni*.

[43] So his fate was exactly the same as that of the monsters he had felled, cf. I.30f., II.34f.

[44] The outpouring of the life of Baʿlu (cf. 2 Sam. 14:14) as described in the mythological part of the tablet is interpreted as a life-giving sacrifice (cf. Baal, notes 37 and 335, as well as Matth. 26:28; Mark 14:24; Phil. 2:17; 2 Tim. 4:6).

[45] Possibly Baʿlu, cf. Baal, note 473. More likely, however, the king of Ugarit who was the central figure of the cult. The pouring out of water was a well-known rain-charm, cf. 1 Sam. 7:6; mSukkah IV.9-10; Dalman, AuS, Bd.1, 136ff.; M. Delcor, in: Religion d'Israel et Proche-Orient Ancien, Leiden 1976, 404ff.; Baal, note 37.

[46] The word is either related to Hebrew *m^{e}ṣūlāh* "deep (sea)" or to Arabic *ṣalata* "pour out a vessel".

impending downfall. His exalted position will soon be taken over by the younger Baˁlu.[1]

Eventually the goddesses ˁAnatu and ˁAthtartu, wives of Baˁlu who had treated their father Ilu with contempt during the banquet to which he had invited them, cure him of his delirium. Unfortunately the name of the precious herb by which they effectuate this speedy recovery is lost in a lacuna. Yet this part of the story apparently formed the reason to write down the myth. In a few lines added to the narrative there follows a magical prescription of the same herb for a patient who is presumably suffering from the effects of excessive drinking. So the myth seems to have served apotropaic purposes here.

Ilu was sacrificing in his house,
  was giving a banquet in his palace.
He called in the gods for the carving:
"Eat, gods, and drink,
  drink wine unto satiety,
    must unto drunkenness!"
Yarikhu[2] *put down its saddle-meat,*[3]
  like [ ] he tore it out.
Below the tables for the god whom he knew
  he put down bread,[4]
but whom he did not know he beat
  with a stick[5] *under the table.*
He[6] *approached ˁAthtartu and ˁAnatu.*[7]

[1] Cf. OTS 24 (1986) 1ff.

[2] Moon god.

[3] Meat of the back of the victim.

[4] Interlinear gloss: *"of the banquet"*. The lower deities had to be content with a place under the tables. Cf. Judg. 1:7; Mark 7:28.

[5] Interlinear gloss: *"with a rod"*.

[6] The rejected god.

[7] Goddesses of love and war, the naughty daughters of Ilu.

ʿAthtartu put down a haunch for him
and ʿAnatu its shoulder.
The gate-keeper of the house of Ilu rebuked them:
"One does not put down a haunch for a dog,
one does not put down a shoulder for a puppy!"
He rebuked his father Ilu:
"Ilu is sitting as though he were on the henb[ane drug[8]*],*
Ilu is sitting with his society,
he drinks wine unto satiety,
must unto drunkenness!
Let Ilu go to his house,
proceed to his residence!"
Thakumanu and Shanuma[9] *supported him*
and brought him to the steward.
He-with-the-horns-and-the-tail[10] *scolded:*
"He has fallen into his own dung and urine!
Ilu is like a dead man,
Ilu is like those who descend into the earth!"
ʿAnatu and ʿAthtartu went scouring
[ ] *they went up* [ ][11]
seven [ ]
in [ ] *ʿAthtartu*
and ʿAnatu [ ]
and with these[12] *they restored [the strength of] his hands,*[13]
when they had healed (him), look, he awoke![14]

---

[8] A powerful narcotic. Cf. UF 16 (1984) 355f.

[9] Vocalisation and function of these deities are uncertain.

[10] Apparently the house-keeper of Ilu was a faun-like demon. Cf. Hab. 3:4; Dan. 8:6,20. A term related to the one translated by "steward" would seem to occur in Ebla, cf. P. Xella, SEL 3 (1986) 17-25.

[11] Cf. Prov. 27:25.

[12] Probably herbs collected by the two goddesses. The same were administered to the patient for whom the "recipe" at the end of the tablet was meant.

[13] Cf. Ps. 76:6.

[14] Cf. Job 14:10-12.

What one should put on the brow of the unconscious patient:
Lay out the pith and the top, the node and its stalk;
put these (ingredients) together with the juice of autumn olives.[15]

Myth and Ritual IV

KTU 1.13

The greater part of this tablet is devoted to a hymn to ᶜAnatu (lines 1-23a), followed by a personal prayer on behalf of a couple whose son has an infertile marriage (lines 23b-27a). This is answered by an oracle granting them their request.[1] Next comes a mythological narrative which tells about ᶜAnatu herself having a similar problem once. Again the link between the cultic and the mythological part of the tablet is completely clear.

Possibly the mythological section of the tablet preserves a lost part of Loves II (KTU 1.10).[2] In any case both tablets contain references to the first columns of Baal I (KTU 1.101 and 1.3), the part of the myth connected with the New Year festival. This festival was also important to the fertility of women.[3]

Because in this text ᶜAnatu is urged to perform the acts described as events of the past in the myth of Baᶜlu,[4] it cannot be doubted any longer that this myth was re-enacted symbolically in the cult of Ugarit.

[15] Greenish virgin oil.

[1] Such divine pronouncements answering prayers are known from other cultures of the Ancient Near East, see Th. Booij, Godswoorden in de Psalmen. Hun funktie en achtergronden, 2 vols., Amsterdam 1978 (with an appendix on the "Umwelt").

[2] Cf. Loves II, note 29.

[3] Cf. Myth and Ritual I (KTU 1.23), 1 Sam. 1:5-20; and J. C. de Moor, New Year with Canaanites and Israelites, Vol. 1, (Kamper Cahier no. 21), Kampen 1972, pp. 14f. with note 188.

[4] See below notes 11, 27, 29, 30.

"[ ] .. [ ]
Damsel, bear [a bull to Baʿlu]![5]
Destroy under the ban[6] *for two days,*[7]
thro[w down[8] *for three] days,*
go,[9] *kill for fo[ur] days in anguish!*[10]
Make the hands pour [blood] on your girdle,
attach the heads of your warriors![11]
And fly up by the side[12] *of your eagles*[13]
and rest[14] *on your mountain Inbubu!*[15]
The throne-base of your mountain[16] *I know.*[17]
I should give you[18] *a dwelling on the roof?!*[19]
The high heaven is the cella[20] *of your throne-base!*[21]

[5] Reading: rḥm *tld* [*ʾibr.lbʿl.*], cf. Loves I (KTU 1.10):iii.1 [*rḫ*]*m ʾarḫt.tld* [*ly*] "The womb of the cow can bear for me" and iii.35 *k. ʾibr.lbʿl.yld* "For a bull is born to Baʿlu".

[6] Cf. Josh. 8:24 *lhrg ʾt kl yšby hʿy* with Josh. 8:26 *hḥrym ʾt kl yšby hʿy*.

[7] Of the seven-day New Year festival.

[8] Reading: šp[*l*], cf. Prov. 7:26.

[9] Cf. Gen. 37:20; 1 Sam. 15:18.

[10] Cf. Deut. 4:30; 2 Sam. 22:7; Isa. 25:4; 26:16, etc. The anguish of ʿAnatu may have been caused by her inability to receive Baʿlu, see below.

[11] A clear reference to Baal I (KTU 1.3):ii.11-13.

[12] Cf. Akkad. *ina aḫi*, CAD (A)1, 208.

[13] Cf. Aqhat, note 143; Incantation V, note 6.

[14] Cf. Baal I (KTU 1.101):1 (restored).

[15] Cf. Baal, note 66.

[16] Cf. 1 Ki. 8:39 (par.); Isa. 4:5.

[17] Cf. Ps. 56:10; 135:5; Job 19:25.

[18] Emphasized in the original text; for "give" with two objects cf. Josh. 15:19, etc.

[19] A reference to the booths of branches that were erected on the roof of the temple during the New Year festival. See Myth and Ritual I, note 25.

[20] Reading *prq* instead of *prẓ*. Cf. Baal, note 124. ʿAnatu soars high up in the sky according to Incantation V (KTU 1.108):7f.

[21] The singer regards such a lowly booth unworthy of the goddess. Similar statements have been recorded with regard to the Egyptian goddess Mut ("Her temple is the sky", H. M. Stewart, JEA 57 (1971) 104) and YHWH, cf. 1 Ki. 8:27; Isa. 66:1.

[S]tars fall down there[22] *like bricks,*[23]
comets like winged ash-seeds,
like [beads of sw]eat dripping from a brow.
The place of w[orship][24] *of your house is perfect,*
and the altar surpasses [everything],
the [silver] of the image is more beautiful than the stars.[25]
Let the Virgin[26] *ʿAnatu wash,*[27]
let the Breast of the Nations[28] *beautify herself!*[29]
And let her go up to Ilu, her father,[30]
may the residence—your work!—be fi[ne]!''[31]
He will listen to you, o Cow,[32]
yes, he will pay attention (to you), [Breast] of the Nations!''

(Prayer:)
''My voice is in your ears, so [an]s[wer me]![33]

[22] Cf. Isa. 34:4; Rev. 6:13.

[23] White, sun-baked bricks.

[24] Cf. Arab. *maʿābid.*

[25] Female stars, as in KTU 1.92:28.

[26] Cf. Baal, note 33.

[27] Again the poet is actualizing the Baal myth. Cf. Baal I (KTU 1.3):ii.38f.; iv.42ff.

[28] An epithet of ʿAnatu, referring to her role as the harlot of the world. Cf. Baal, note 34; Aqhat, note 218; Isa. 60:16; Ez. 23:8,21; Rev. 17:2,15; 18:3,7, all patterned after the Canaanite goddess of love.

[29] Cf. Baal I (KTU 1.3):iii.1; iv.45f.

[30] Another reference to the myth of Baal, this time to the episode where ʿAnatu goes to visit her father in order to convince him that Baʿlu should have a house of his own. Cf. Baal I (KTU 1.3):iv.57ff.

[31] Cf. Num. 24:5.

[32] Another epithet of ʿAnatu. Cf. Incantation IV, note 2.

[33] Cf. Jer. 28:7; Ez. 8:18; 9:1; Ps. 3:5; 86:1. This line introduces a short personal prayer, apparently pronounced by a priest on behalf of a couple whose son has a problem with his wife. Several other tablets from Ugarit prove that people could ask a priest to recite the appropriate text for them. See *e.g.* Myth and Ritual VI, note 35.

Because the wife is inaccessible,[34]
because the 'well'[35] *is covered up,*
let the angels from heaven[36] *fortify*[37] *the husband,*[38]
let the angels from heaven send strength!"

(Oracle:)
"*I*[39] *shall fortify your*[40] *son like a first-born,*[41]
the husband—I shall fortify (him) for you!"

(Myth:)
ᶜAnatu, the cow of Baᶜlu,[42] *was eager,*[43]
ᶜAnatu was eager to bear.
her womb[44] *had not known pregnancy,*
[*nor*] *her breasts nursing.*[45]

[34] The word *rtqt* recurs Baal IV (KTU 1.4):vii.33 for inaccessible mountains. In Arabic it may designate a woman *impervia coeunti*, cf. Lane, 1027, and compare the use of *sgr* "to close" in 1 Sam. 1:5f.; Job 3:10 as opposed to *ptḥ* "to open" in Gen. 29:31; 30:22.

[35] Euphemism for vulva and/or a fertile woman, cf. Song of Songs 4:15 (contrast 4:12); Prov. 5:15; Myth and Ritual V, note 14. 2 Sam. 17:19 explains the metaphor.

[36] Cf. Gen. 22:11; Matt. 24:36; also Luke 1-2; Gen. 18:10-15, cf. 18:21; Judg. 13, esp. 13:20, and H. Schmidt, P. Kahle, Volkserzählungen aus Palästina, Bd. 1, Göttingen 1918, 156f.

[37] As in the Legend of Aqhat the term is used in connection with fertility. Cf. Aqhat, note 23.

[38] Literally "impregnator", as in Gen. 30:20.

[39] Presumably ᶜAnatu. If so, she is taking over a prerogative of Ilu here, cf. Aqhat, note 20.

[40] Dual, referring to the parents of the husband.

[41] The first-born was thought to be the strongest, cf. KAR No. 178:i.14; Lane, 240; Gen. 49:3; 1 Sam. 16:7.

[42] Cf. Loves II (KTU 1.10):ii.

[43] Cf. Myth and Ritual I, note 28.

[44] Literally "liver".

[45] Cf. Keret, note 51; Myth and Ritual I, note 30.

[The sl]i[t of her orifice[46]*] was not one he could open,*
his 'hand'[47] *[found it* (?)*] too small.*
He rolled out [hail-ston]es,
wind, thunder-storm, clouds.[48]
He rol[led out]
he overturned [ ]
he assau[lted]
(broken)

About 5 lines are missing, but the mythological section is hardly more than an appropriate quotation from a much larger text.

Myth and Ritual V

KTU 1.24

This small tablet has been divided into two sections. The first contains a myth relating how the moon god Yarikhu obtained his bride Nikkalu. It is generally assumed that this myth was adapted from a Hurrian original. The closing lines of the mythological part (lines 34-39) suggest that it was recited while the bride-price was being weighed out.[1]

The second section of the tablet is a hymn to the Kathiratu, the goddesses supervising marital affairs.[2] It seems likely that such a text was used in connection with an ordinary marriage ceremony.

[46] Cf. Loves II, note 28.
[47] Cf. Loves II, note 33; Myth and Ritual I, note 38; V, note 15.
[48] Apparently out of frustration.

[1] A reference to this myth occurs in KTU 1.111:20f. in a context suggesting that the divine marriage was re-enacted in the cult. Cf. UF 11 (1979) 652f.
[2] Cf. Aqhat, notes 47-52; Loves II, notes 26-27; Loves III, note 3.

Let me sing[3] *of Nikkalu-and-Ibbu,*[4]
[*daughter of*][5] *Khirikhbi, the counsellor for exchange-marriages,*[6]
Khirikhbi, the counsellor for protection-marriages.[7]
When Shapshu[8] *has flown away,*
Yarikhu will strip,[9]
he will em[*brace*] *her who will bear a son to him.*[10]
Make her con[*vulse,*[11] *o Ka*]*thiratu,*
o swallows, daughters of Hilalu![12]
Look! Let the lass bear a son to him![13]

[3] Cohortative, as in Ex. 15:1; Judg. 5:3; Isa. 5:1, etc. For Babylonian parallels see K. Hecker, AOATS 8 (1974) 70; for Greek and Latin parallels, C. H. Gordon, in : Ugaritica VI, Paris 1969, 282.

[4] As appears from Ugaritic personal names Nikkalu was the Semiticized version of the Sumerian moon goddess NIN.GAL. The word *ʾib* is attested in Aqhat III (KTU 1.19):I.31 and means "blossom", cf. Song of Songs 6:11. The homograph *ʾib* "pure" would require a feminine form *ʾibt.*

[5] With Ginsberg, Herdner and others. Because in the patriarchal society of the Ancient Near East nobody but the father could give away a girl, Nikkalu must be a daughter of Khirikhbi. On the latter's name see A. Goetze, JBL 60 (1941) 358f.

[6] On this highly technical term see QS 2 (1973) 92, n. 1. It denotes an exchange of bride for bride. See for this popular and sometimes very complex type of marriage H. Granqvist, Marriage Conditions in a Palestinian Village, vol. 1, Helsingfors 1931, 109ff.

[7] Again a technical term (cf. note 6) denoting a marriage-like relationship of dependency and protection between an unprotected female and the head of the household.

Obviously both types of marriage involved difficult legal matters and required long negotions.

[8] Sun-goddess.

[9] Cf. Baal, note 326; Loves III, note 1.

[10] Cf. Aqhat, note 46.

[11] Cf. Loves II (KTU 1.10):ii.29; iii:17; Myth and Ritual II (KTU 1.12):i.25; Job 26:5.

[12] Cf. Loves II, note 27; III, note 3; Aqhat, notes 48-49.

[13] Cf. Isa. 7:14; Matt. 1:21,23; Luke 1:31; 2:7; Rev. 12:5.

Let her 'well' [14] *boil for his 'hand'*, [15]
her 'lips' for his 'flesh'! [16]
For [her] fa[ther will] let her live,
as a betrothed woman [in] his [palace]!
Listen, goddesses, Kathiratu!
[Let] the waters of her 'well' [flow], [17]
let them boil for his 'hand'!
[ ] *for her lord,*
[ ]
Daganu of Tutt[ul [18]]
[ ] a worm *for the Kathiratu,*
the daughters of Hilalu, the swallows.
Yarikhu, the Illuminator of heaven, sent (a message)
to Khirikhbi, the counsellor for exchange-marriages:
"Surrender Nikkalu! [19]
Yarikhu wants to marry Ibbu,
let her enter his mansion! [20]
And I will give as her bride-price to her father [21]
a thousand (shekels) of silver,
and ten thousand (shekels) of gold,
I will send the purest lapis! [22]

[14] Probably a euphemism for the vulva. Cf. Myth and Ritual IV, note 35. For the parallelism between "eye/well" and "lip", Prov. 10:10.

[15] Cf. Loves II, note 33.

[16] Euphemism for the penis, as in Lev. 6:3; 15:2f.,7; Ez. 16:26; 23:20.

[17] Cf. Loves II, note 25.

[18] Cf. Myth and Ritual VI, note 9.

[19] Cf. Baal III (KTU 1.2):i.48.

[20] Cf. Keret I (KTU 1.14):iv.41; CAD (E) 270b.

[21] Cf. Gen. 34:12; Ex. 22:15f.

[22] An astronomical and therefore mythological price. See Keret, note 38.

I will make her field into a vineyard,[23]
the field of her love into a flower-garden!''[24]
But Khirikhbi, the counsellor for exchange-marriages, answered:
''O most graceful among the gods,
o son-in-law of Baᶜlu![25]
Marry Pidrayu, the gi[rl of the honey-dew]![26]
I will bring you in contact with her father Baᶜlu,
he will ask ᶜAthtartu's[27] *permission.*
Marry Yabridamayu[28] *if you want,*
the Lion[29] *will arouse the house of her father!''*[30]
But Yarikhu, the Illuminator of heaven, answered,
yes, he answered:
''Only to Nikkalu do I want to be betrothed,
Yarikhu aspires after Nikkalu to marry her!''
Her father placed the standard of the balance,
her mother the scales[31] *of the balance.*
Her brothers arranged the counter-weights,
her sisters the stone-weights of the balance.

[23] Metaphorical language. ''Field'' and ''vineyard'' are ubiquitous designations of women and their pudenda, cf. Song of Songs 1:6; 2:12,15; 7:11; 8:12; Myth and Ritual I, note 18; D. Marcus, JANES 5 (1973) 281-286; S. Schott, Altägyptische Liebeslieder, 2. Aufl., Zürich 1950, 50, 56, 107; S. N. Kramer, The Sacred Marriage Rite, London 1969, 81, 100, 104; Koran II.223.

[24] Cf. M. C. Astour, in: The Bible World. Essays ... C. H. Gordon, New York 1980, 2.

[25] In according Yarikhu this epithet he anticipates his counter-offer.

[26] Cf. Baal, note 18.

[27] ᶜAnatu-ᶜAthtartu was the wife of Baᶜlu.

[28] Possibly *ybrdm* is the name of the city Yabritu in the dual, provided with the same feminine ending that characterizes the names of her sisters Pidrayu, Tallayu and Arsayu. Because this goddess is mentioned only here, it is possible that *Ybrd(m)* was a cult centre of either Tallayu or Arsayu.

[29] Another flattering epithet for Yarikhu. Cf. Kramer, *op. cit.*, 92, 99.

[30] Cf. Gen. 38:11; Lev. 21:9; Num. 30:4,17; Deut. 22:21, etc.

[31] Lit. ''palms''. The family of the bride makes preparations for weighing the bride-price.

Nikkalu-and-Ibbu of whom I sing,
shine upon Yarikhu,
and may Yarikhu shine upon you![32]

Let me sing of the goddesses, the Kathiratu,
the daughters of Hilalu, the swallows,
the daughters of Hilalu, the lord of the sickle,[33]
who descend on the jujube-trees,[34]
on top[35] *of the olives,*
those (involved in) any work whatsoever
there is with[36] *the Benevolent, Ilu the good-natured!*
Look! Their list is in my mouth,
their enumeration on my lips:
Thillukhuha and Mulugu-hiya,
Thatiqatu, with her Baqiᶜatu,
Taqiᶜatu, with Perubakhthi,
Damiqtu, the youngest of the Kathiratu.[37]

[32] Cf. Isa. 60:1; UF 11 (1979) 643; Loves II, note 21.

[33] Hilalu is the god of the crescent moon. He is identical to the Helel of Isa. 14:12. Cf. K. Spronk, Beatific Afterlife, Neukirchen 1986, 224.

[34] Descending like the birds they were. Actually the *ᶜrgz* is member of the zizyphus-family, considered a tree in Judg. 9:14f. Cf. Pal. Arab. *ᶜarqad*, Dalman, AuS I,2, 373; H. B. Tristram, The Natural History of the Bible, 4th ed., London 1875, 428-430; M. Zohary, Plants of the Bible, Cambridge 1982, 154f.

[35] Lit. "on the back".

[36] For the sake of clarity a very literal translation has been chosen. The expression may be paraphrased as "any work whatsoever the Benevolent designs", cf. Job 27:11, also Job 10:13; 23:14, and Ps. 78:7.

Only Ilu could decide on matters of childbirth, cf. Aqhat, note 20. The Kathiratu implemented his decisions.

[37] Like their Babylonian counterparts the Shassuratu the number of the Kathiratu was seven. See also the Egyptian evidence discussed by W. Herrmann, ZÄS 100 (1974) 104-108.

The names of the Kathiratu are connected with marital affairs. Their respective meanings are: "Her (*i.e.* the bride's) marriage-gift" (a present of the bride's father, cf. 1 Ki. 9:16; Mi. 1:14); "Her dowry"; "She-who-cuts-loose (the baby)"; 'She-who-forces-open (the womb)"; "She-who-blows-air-into (the baby)"; a Hurrian name of unknown meaning; "The Good One".

Myth and Ritual VI

KTU 1.100

This well-preserved tablet belonged to the private library of a priest. It consists of three major sections. First we have twelve incantations against snake-bite, couched in the form of a myth and directed to various deities, the last of which is the god of black magic Horonu. Next there follows a fragment from a myth relating how Horonu succeeded in neutralizing the poison of a snake. Finally there is an exchange between bride and groom featuring the serpent as a phallic symbol. Clearly the text was composed as an organic whole.

The mythological part of the tablet is of special interest because it seems to prove that the Canaanites knew some version of the paradise story. The subduing of the serpents is a condition to fertility and child-bearing (cf. Gen. 3:15).

I.

1 *The Mother of the He-ass, the She-ass,*[1]
the daughter of the Spring, the daughter of the Stone,[2]
the daughter of Heaven and Flood,
called to Shapshu, her mother:[3]

[1] The identity of these deified asses remains obscure. Perhaps we may compare the Greek goddess Demeter, the Mare who was mated by the stallion Poseidon. She was the mother of the horse Areion and is depicted as a goddess subduing snakes. For the snake as an enemy of the ass see the Egyptian Book of the Dead, section 40.

[2] Contrast Jer. 2:27.

[3] The sun-goddess. This text seems to presuppose a theogony differing sharply from the one generally accepted in Ugarit. According to the latter Ilu was the creator and father of all living beings. Cf. The Bible World. Essays in Honor of C. H. Gordon, New York 1980, 171-187. Here, however, it is Shapshu who is at the top of the list. She was the mother of Heaven (male) and Flood (female) who gave birth to Spring (female) and Stone (male), the parents of the She-ass representing the first animated creature.

It is possible that this theogony was derived from Hittite/Hurrian sources. In Hittite religion the sun-goddess is heading the pantheon. In any case the introduction of this text is contradicted by the main body because there it is Ilu who heads the list of twelve deities invoked against snake-bite.

"Shapshu, my mother, carry my voice
to Ilu at the fountain-head of the two rivers,
at the confluence of the two Floods.[4]
My incantation is:
'A poisonous serpent has bitten,
a serpent which has sloughed its skin![5]
Is there someone to charm for its destructive venom?
Is there someone to expel its poison?
Look! Let him bind[6] *the serpent,*
let him feed the serpent which has sloughed its skin,
let him place a chair[7] *and sit down!' "*

She called to Shapshu, her mother:
"Shapshu, my mother, carry my voice
to Baʿlu on the heights of Sapanu.[8]
My incantation is:
'A poisonous serpent has bitten,
a serpent which has sloughed it skin!
Is there someone to charm for its destructive venom?
Is there someone to expel its poison?
Look! Let him bind the serpent,
let him feed the serpent which has sloughed its skin,
let him place a chair and sit down!' "

---

[4] Variant version of the formula used in the Baal myth, cf. Baal, note 81.

[5] A serpent that has sloughed its skin in spring is more poisonous then ever. Cf. P. Bordreuil, UF 15 (1983) 299f.

[6] Cf. V. Haas, H. J. Thiel, AOAT 31 (1978) 189. A connection with Akkad. *šaqû* is unlikely (Arab. *šqw*).

[7] Cf. R. I. Caplice, The Akkadian *namburbi*-Texts: An Introduction, Los Angeles 1974, 18.

[8] Cf. Baal, note 4.

III.

She called to Shapshu, her mother:
"Shapshu, my mother, carry my voice
to Daganu in Tuttul.[9]
My incantation is:
'A poisonous serpent has bitten,
a serpent which has sloughed its skin!
Is there someone to charm for its destructive venom?
Is there someone to expel its poison?
Look! Let him bind the serpent,
let him feed the serpent which has sloughed its skin,
let him place a chair and sit down!' "

IV.

She called to Shapshu, her mother:
"Shapshu, my mother, carry my voice
to ᶜAnatu-and-ᶜAthtartu on Inbubu.[10]
My incantation is:
'A poisonous serpent has bitten,
a serpent which has sloughed its skin!
Is there someone to charm for its destructive venom?
Is there someone to expel its poison?
Look! Let him bind the serpent,
let him feed the serpent which has sloughed its skin,
let him place a chair and sit down!' "

---

[9] It is noteworthy that Daganu is mentioned *after* his son Baᶜlu. Cf. UF 2 (1970) 219.

[10] ᶜAnatu and ᶜAthtartu, goddesses of love and consorts of Baᶜlu, formed a double, cf. UF 2 (1970) 227f. For Mt. Inbubu see Baal, note 66.

She called to Shapshu, her mother:
"Shapshu, my mother, carry my voice
to Yarikhu in Larugat.[11]
My incantation is :
'A poisonous serpent has bitten,
a serpent which has sloughed its skin!
Is there someone to charm for its destructive venom?
Is there someone to expel its poison?
Look! Let him bind the serpent,
let him feed the serpent which has sloughed its skin,
let him place a chair and sit down!' "

She called to Shapshu, her mother:
"Shapshu, my mother, carry my voice
to Rashpu in Bibitu.[12]
My incantation is:
'A poisonous serpent has bitten,
a serpent which has sloughed its skin!
Is there someone to charm for its destructive venom?
Is there someone to expel its poison?
Look! Let him bind the serpent,
let him feed the serpent which has sloughed its skin,
let him place a chair and sit down!' "

---

[11] Yarikhu is the Moon-god. His city is hardly Larak in Southern Babylonia but rather Larugat mentioned in the tablets of Ebla. According to the Legend of Aqhat the city of Yarikhu would have been Abiluma.

[12] Cf. M. L. Barré, JAOS 98 (1978) 467, n. 32. KAJ 162,7 mentions a city called Bibati.

VII.

34a ⟨*She called to Shapshu, her mother:*
"Shapshu, my mother, carry my voice
to ʿAthtartu in Mari.[13]
My incantation is:
'A poisonous serpent has bitten,
a serpent which has sloughed its skin!
Is there someone to charm for its destructive venom?
Is there someone to expel its poison?
Look! Let him bind the serpent,
34e *let him feed the serpent which has sloughed its skin,*
let him place a chair and sit down!' "⟩

VIII.

35 *She called to Shapshu, her mother:*
"Shapshu, my mother, carry my voice
to Zizzu-and-Kamathu[14] *in* Hryt.[15]
My incantation is:
'A poisonous serpent has bitten,
a serpent which has sloughed its skin!
Is there someone to charm for its destructive venom?
Is there someone to expel its poison?

[13] This section was accidentally omitted. In a marginal note the scribe himself indicated his error.

Apparently this goddess ʿAthtartu (cf. lines 20 and 41) is Ishtar who had a large temple in Mari.

[14] Zizzu, also written Tittu, means "mud, clay". He forms a double (cf. note 10) with Kamathu, later on Kamosh (Chemosh), the meaning of which is unknown. According to the Bible Kamosh was the god of the Moabites but in an earlier period he must have been worshipped in a much wider area. Cf. H.-P. Müller, ZDPV 96 (1980) 10f. Even Solomon built a high place for this god according to 1 Ki. 11:7.

[15] The toponym *ḥryt* has not been identified. One wonders whether it might be an error for *qryt*, cf. Jer. 48:1,24.

Look! Let him bind the serpent,
let him feed the serpent which has sloughed its skin,
let him place a chair and sit down!' "

She called to Shapshu, her mother:
"Shapshu, my mother, carry my voice
to Maliku in ʿAthtartu.[16]
My incantation is:
'A poisonous serpent has bitten,
a serpent which has sloughed its skin!
Is there someone to charm for its destructive venom?
Is there someone to expel its poison?
Look! Let him bind the serpent,
let him feed the serpent which has sloughed its skin,
let him place a chair and sit down!' "

She called to Shapshu, her mother:
"Shapshu, my mother, carry my voice
to Kotharu-and-Khasisu in Kaphtor.[17]
My incantation is:
'A poisonous serpent has bitten,
a serpent which has sloughed its skin!

[16] Maliku, Malku or Milku was a nether world deity. He dwelt in one of the cities in Bashan related to the cult of the dead kings of Canaan. Cf. Incantation V, note 3, and K. Spronk, Beatific Afterlife, Neukirchen 1986, 187ff.

[17] Cf. Baal, notes 97, 101.

Is there someone to charm for its destructive venom?
Is there someone to expel its poison?
Look! Let him bind the serpent,
let him feed the serpent which has sloughed its skin,
let him place a chair and sit down!"

XI.

She called to Shapshu, her mother:
"Shapshu, my mother, carry my voice
to Shaharu-and-Shalimu[18] *in heaven.*[19]
My incantation is:
'A poisonous serpent has bitten,
a serpent which has sloughed its skin!
Is there someone to charm for its destructive venom?
Is there someone to expel its poison?
Look! Let him bind the serpent,
let him feed the serpent which has sloughed its skin,
let him place a chair and sit down!' "

XII.

She called to Shapshu, her mother:
"Shapshu, my mother, carry my voice
to Horonu in the fortress.[20]

[18] Cf. Myth and Ritual I, note 48.

[19] *šmmh* is hardly a city — who would give his city such a pretentious name? Moreover, Tadmor may have been the centre of the cult of Shaharu, cf. Myth and Ritual I, note 9. Since the name of Shaharu means "Dawn" heaven is an appropriate location. So the final two habitations (see also note 20) have an appellative sense, like the first two.

[20] God of black magic, master of demons. Apparently he lived in a fortified place, which is called "the city of the East" in line 62 below. Cf. note 25. Perhaps his fortress is identical to the "Palace of Confusion", cf. Incantation I, note 29.

My incantation is:
'A poisonous serpent has bitten,
a serpent which has sloughed its skin!
Is there someone to charm for its destructive venom?
Is there someone to expel its poison?' "

(Myth:)
Horonu's face[21] *turned green,*[22]
because his posterity would remain childless.[23]
He left[24] *the city of the East.*[25]
Then he headed straight
for Great Arashikh
and for Little Arashikh.[26]
He removed the tamarisk from the trees,
yes, the tree of death[27] *from the shrubs.*

[21] Cf. Aqhat, note 44.

[22] Cf. Hebr. *raʿnan* and CAD (A)2, 232.

[23] The serpent-like demons are the offspring of Horonu, cf. Incantations I (KTU 1.82). If all the gods summoned would have turned against the snakes they would have been exterminated. Therefore Horonu relents.

[24] Cf. Hebr., Akkad. *nkr*; elsewhere *tbʿ* is used in the same formula.

[25] In the Hebrew tradition the role of Horonu seems to have been taken over by Cain. Sin was couching at his door like a snake but if he wanted he could master it (cf. Gen. 4:7, cf. Ez. 29:3; Von Soden, AHw, 933), just as Horonu mastered the snakes. Cain is the first man to slay his fellow (Gen. 4:8) and in Ugarit Horonu is invoked as the archetype of an avenging murderer (cf. Baal, note 130; Keret, note 110). Cain dwelt East of Eden (Gen. 4:16) where he build a city (Gen. 4:17). Horonu dwelt in "the city of the East" which he left, presumably in a westward direction, to enter the Canaanite version of Eden. See the next notes.

[26] Arashikh is the Hurrian name of the Tigris. Here two major tributaries are meant, probably the Great Zab (Arab. Zab al-Kabir) and the Small Zab (Arab. Zab al-Saghir), east of the city of Assur on the Tigris. According to Gen. 2:14 the Garden of Eden was situated on the Tigris, east of Assur.

[27] Unfortunately the text does not indicate whether there was or had been a tree of life in that forest (cf. Gen. 2:9; 3:22f.; Rev. 22:1f.,14). So this text does not help

The tamarisk—he shook it out,[28]
the date-cluster—he put it away,[29]
the scab[30]*—he took it off,*
the wart[31]*—he carried it off.*
Horonu went to his house
and proceeded to his residence.
The poison had become weak[32] *like a wadi,*[33]
it had flowed away like a ditch.[34]

(Ritual:)[35]
(Groom:)

to resolve the old question whether or not there were two trees in the garden. In any case it is clear that the tree of Eden became a tree of death, Gen. 2:17; 3:3f.,19.

As appears from the following lines the tree of death was a hybrid, partly a tamarisk, partly a vine (like the tree of Death mentioned in another connection, see Myth and Ritual I, note 15), partly a date-palm. According to the Greek Henoch 32:4 the tree of Eden was a hybrid composed of a fir-tree, a carob-tree and a vine. The similar tree in Henoch 24:4 is also a date-palm. According to Song of Songs 7:8f. the maiden is a tree of life, both date-palm and vine.

28 In this as well as the following cola the original text has a play of words that cannot be reproduced in translation.

29 Cf. Akkad. *nesû* (which should not be compared to W. Semitic *nsᶜ*, cf. Akkad. *nasāḫu*).

30 A metaphor, cf. J. Aram. *ᶜadītā*. Apparently the tree of death was not as pleasant to the eyes as the tree of life, cf. Gen. 2:9; 3:6, probably because part of it resembled the knotty stem of a vine.

31 Cf. Hebr. *yabbelet*, in M. Hebr. also a metaphor for an outgrowth on a tree.

32 N-stem of *lʾy* "be overpowered, become weak", cf. Hebr. *lʾh*. Apparently the uprooting of the root of all evil had had a beneficial effect.

33 The water of which soon disappears, cf. Jer. 15:18; Mic. 1:14; Job 6:15-18.

34 Cf. Ps. 58:5-8; CAD (Z) 9b; Incantation I (KTU 1.82):24.

35 In the final section of the tablet a groom, an officiant and the bride take turns in speaking. Just as in the text Myth and Ritual I (KTU 1.23) and in the Song of Songs the speakers are not identified. Cf. UF 11 (1979) 649f. It is noteworthy that the marriage is concluded during a religious ceremony and that an officiant, probably the priest who owned this tablet, seems to conduct the service. Cf. Keret, note 50.

" '*Behind her the mansion*' *is my incantation.*"[36]

(Officiant:)
"*Behind her the mansion she closed,*
behind her she let down the bronze (bolt)."[37]

(Groom:)
" '*Open up the house*' *is my incantation.*"

(Officiant:)
"*Open up the house, that I may enter,*[38]
the palace that I may come in."

(Bride:)
"*Give a serpent as my bridal gift,*[39]
give a lizard as my bridal gift,
yes, a young viper as a present for my love."[40]

(Groom:)
"*I give a serpent as your bridal gift,*
a young viper as a present for your love."

[36] The groom quotes the first few words of the songs he wants the officiant to recite on his behalf.

[37] Hardly the complete song. Probably it was a love song about the universal theme of the locked out lover.

[38] Cf. Song of Songs 5:2-6.

[39] The connection between snake-charming and the solemnization of marriage has a very interesting parallel in Egypt, cf. E. Drioton, Pages d'Égyptologie, Le Caire 1957, 60f. In Babylonia pregnant women used to wear amulets of the demon Pazuzu to protect them against the child-robbing demon Lamashtu. The penis of Pazuzu is a serpent. He is often depicted next to the sacred date-palm, cf. P. R. S. Moorey, Iraq 27 (1965) 33,37; F. A. M. Wiggerman, in: M. Stol, Zwangerschap en geboorte bij de Babyloniërs en in de bijbel, Leiden 1983, 110ff. Of course the snake is understood as a phallic symbol in many cultures, but in this particular context a Sumerian parallel furnishes conclusive evidence: "he lifted his penis, brought the bridal gift", cf. S. N. Kramer, The Sacred Marriage Rite, London 1969, 53.

[40] Cf. Deut. 23:19; Mic. 1:7; Hos. 2:14.

Scribal correction on the edge of the tablet:
After Rashpu: *ʿAthtartu.*
"*...to ʿAthtartu in Mari. My incantation is*: *A serpent has bitten...*" (see the inserted lines 34a-34e).

RITUAL

Ritual I

KTU 1.41

The ritual texts of Ugarit are usually of the prescriptive type, listing in a very terse style instructions for knowledgeable people, apparently priests. Of the present text several copies are extant and this in itself bears testimony to its relative importance.

The month "First-of-the-Wine"[1] corresponds roughly to the period from the latter half of September to the first half of October in the solar calendar. However, because Ugarit observed a lunar calendar its beginning could fluctuate. In this month the New Year festival was celebrated. On this occasion the first new wine was produced and ceremonially offered to Baʿlu, the god whose victory over Death (Motu) was celebrated.[2]

Such an agrarian festival depended heavily on the state of ripeness of the grapes. Because the lunar year is about 11 days shorter than the solar year it would have become impossible to press the new wine during the New Year festival after only two or three lunar years.

Possibly the following mechanism was used to avoid this. About one month before "First-of-the-Wine" it was established whether the difference between the solar and the lunar year had become unacceptably large. If so, a leap month had to be inserted.[3] In that way the "ideal" New Year's Day, the 23rd of September, was

[1] The interpretation of the name of the month is certain, cf. AOAT 16,78, n. 16.

[2] Cf. Baal, notes 1, 15, 476; Myth and Ritual I, note 11; Incantation V; Aqhat IV.

[3] Cf. Baal, note 449.

approximately observed again and the New Year festival could be held at the beginning of the month. However, if as a result of the lunar time-reckoning it was still too early for the vintage only one bunch of grapes was cut on the first day of "First-of-the-Wine"[4] and the great festival was celebrated on and after the 15th, as in our text.[5]

From the beginning of the month it was established empirically when the autumnal equinox actually fell. According to KTU 1.104:15-24 this happened (in that particular year) on the tenth of the month,[6] so that in the preceding year the "ideal" New Year must have coincided approximately with the equinox. The next year it fell on the last day of the seven-day festival. And after that it became time again for an adjustment of the calendar. See also note 56.

The prescriptions for every day of the festival start at line 8 and are so minimal that it must be assumed that the official ceremonies and texts to be read were recorded in a different context.[7] Yet it is noteworthy that a considerable quantity of wine is sacrificed on the mountain (lines 22-23).

1 *In the month of "First-of-the-Wine",*
on the day of the New Moon,
cut off a bunch of grapes
for Ilu, as a peace-offering.[8]

---

[4] Our text, line 2. The verb is either *mtr* or dissimilated *ntr*.

[5] Incidentally this may explain the different traditions about the date of the Israelite New Year and the Feast of Booths that was directly derived from the Canaanite festival.

[6] Cf. Myth and Ritual I, note 25.

[7] Cf. next to the text of Baal also Loves II, notes 11-16; Myth and Ritual I, note 1; II, notes 39, 44, 45; IV, notes 3, 17, 19; Incantation V.

[8] Although the name of this offering is the same as in Hebrew, it is never a sacrifice of fruit in the Bible. Ilu is the head of the Ugaritic pantheon.

On the thirteenth,
the king shall wash himself clean.[9]

On the fourteenth,
the first of the tribute,[10]
and two rams for the Mistress of the Mansion.[11]
Two birds for the Most Amiable of the gods,[12] *and a ram.*
A pot (of oil) for Ilishu,[13]
a ram for Ilahuma.[14]
The king shall return[15] *clean*
and he shall wipe his face[16]
and he shall invoke the day.[17]

[9] Ritual bathing is normal in all cultures of the Ancient Near East. Cf. Keret, note 17. The king was the principal officiant but could have himself represented. Cf. Baal, note 483.

[10] It is certain that *ʾargmn* means "tribute" in Ugaritic. So it seems to denote the annual contribution to the cult here. Cf. Baal, note 476. It is possible, however, that the word had already acquired the specific meaning of "purple" attested in Akkadian, Hebrew and Aramaic. In that case cf. Baal, note 24. Such a concrete meaning would accord better with the fact that *ʾargmn* is mentioned next to two sheep and is offered precisely to the goddess ʿAnatu.

[11] ʿAnatu. She closes the doors of her mansion to go to battle in Baal I (KTU 1.3):ii, a column reflecting a sham combat during the New Year festival. Cf. Baal, note 21; Myth and Ritual IV, notes 6-11. It is interesting to note that in the latter text the fighting is said to go on for four days whereas ʿAnatu is honoured on the 14th and on all of the subsequent four days of the festival according to this ritual. The house of the goddess where the battle took place according to the myth is mentioned in lines 5, 24, 26, 32, 37.

[12] Possibly an epithet of Baʿlu. Cf. Baal, notes 40, 353; Loves I, note 4.

[13] Ilishu is a raven acting as a herald of Ilu and Baʿlu. Cf. Keret, note 96. Possibly he receives an offering because it is he who has to announce the return of Baʿlu.

[14] The same name as Hebrew *ʾelōhīm*, a designation of God. In Ugarit, however, it seems to be neither a designation of Ilu nor of Baʿlu. Rather it is a collective name for the family of Ilu. Cf. lines 16f.

[15] *Scil.* to the temple, cf. lines 54ff.

[16] The repeated wiping of the face of the king might be explained by the fact that he was thought to incorporate the god Baʿlu whose face is cared for at the beginning of the myth of Baal, Baal, fragment a (KTU 1.101):5f.

[17] New Year's Day was awaited during a nightwatch. Cf. Baal, note 478.

On the following day[18] [ ] *shall enter.*[19]
Because the ᶜAgmalu[20] *has fled*
and [the gift has been] given,[21]
he shall prepare for ᶜAnatu[22]
two ewes and a town-pigeon.
And an ox (and) a ram for Ilu.[23]
And into the lat[tice][24] *he shall pour [wine].*
A cow for Ilahuma,
Thakumanu and Shanuma,[25] *a ewe,*
Rashpu[26], *a ewe,*
as a burnt-offering.
And as a peace-offering:[27]
Two ewes for Ilahu,[28]
an ox and a ram for Ilahuma,
a cow for Ilahuma.
Baᶜlu, a ram,
Athiratu,[29] *a ram,*

[18] The 15th, the first day of the festival in that particular year. Others translate "above" which is totally unconvincing.

[19] Cf. Aqhat, notes 274-275, in the context of the celebration of the New Year.

[20] Vocalisation uncertain. Perhaps name of one of the monsters Baᶜlu had to defeat on his way back to earth. Cf. Baal, note 479. It might be a form ending in *-l*, like *ġrpl* from *ġrp*, *bṣql* from *bṣq*, *gbᶜl* from *gbᶜ*, etc. In that case Arab. *ᶜāǧim* "biter" offers a suitable etymology.

[21] Restoration very uncertain. Cf. Loves II, note 14.

[22] For ᶜAnatu's role in furthering the return of Baᶜlu, cf. Baal, notes 57, 475 and Loves II (KTU 1.10):1.

[23] On whose authority the struggle with Death was ended, cf. Baal VI (KTU 1.6):iv.25ff.

[24] A hole in graves through which offerings were presented to the spirits of dead ancestors.

[25] Cf. Myth and Ritual III, note 9.

[26] Cf. Keret, note 7; Incantation I, note 2.

[27] As in the Old Testament the peace-offerings followed the burnt-offerings. Cf. Ex. 24:5; Lev. 9:3f.; Num. 6:14; 1 Sam. 13:9; 2 Sam. 6:18, etc.

[28] The same form as Hebrew *ᵓelōᵃh*, a name of God.

[29] Wife of Ilu.

Thakumanu and Shanuma, a ram,
ᶜAnatu, a ram,
Rashpu, a ram,
the family of Ilu and the assembly of Baᶜlu,[30] *a cow,*
Shalimu (Dusk), a cow.
And in the greenery:[31] *the heart, as a roasted portion*[32]
for the Ilahuma Baᶜluma.[33]
Fill forty (jars) with fat ashes[34] *and emmer-corn.*

(The second day:)[35]
And the temple dues[36] *the house of the king*[37] *shall take:*
the sacrificial banquet,[38]
oil with myrrh,[39]

[30] Cf. Keret, note 47.

[31] Abbreviated reference to the booths that were erected for the festival. See note 60.

[32] In Israel all the fat of the intestines, the kidneys and the appendage of the liver were burnt and the blood of the victim was sprinkled around the altar (Lev. 3).

[33] Probably the same collective bodies of gods that are earlier described as "the family of Ilu and the assembly of Baᶜlu".

[34] This procedure closes a series of sacrifices. Translation uncertain. It is based on the assumption that the fat ashes were removed from the altar. Cf. Lev. 6:3-4 (transl. 6:9-10). See for the etymology: Schrift en Uitleg, Fs. W. H. Gispen, Kampen 1970, 115, n. 26. Others: "grass".

[35] Only from the fifth day of the festival the days are expressly mentioned (lines 38, 45, 47). The beginning of the prescription for the first day is fairly certain. Cf. note 18. Also its end is marked clearly by the list of peace-offerings from line 12 through line 18 as well as the closing formula in lines 18f. discussed in note 34. The end of the second and the third day is established by means of the formula "and as a peace-offering: ditto".

[36] Compare Akkad. *irbu*, *eribtu*.

[37] For the presence of the family of the king during the festivities of the New Year, cf. Myth and Ritual I (KTU 1.23) and Incantation V (KTU 1.108), also Aqhat IV, fragment c (KTU 1.22).

[38] This is the "sacrificial banquet of the king", mentioned in some administrative documents dealing with the New Year festival. See KTU 1.91:2; 4.213:24. Cf. Aqhat IV, fragment c (KTU 1.22):i.12ff.; Myth and Ritual I (KTU 1.23):6, 27.

[39] Cf. Esth. 2:12.

oil with perfume,
honey,[40]
a grain offering,[41]
and a town-pigeon,
and two unseasoned loaves.
And on the mountain,[42] *fourteen jars of wine,*
a parasu-*measure of flour.*
The steps of the altar[43] *of the house of the goddess, two birds.*
For Sapanu[44] *a ram,*
for the Lass[45] *a ram,*
for the Lad[46] *a ram,*
and for Yarikhu[47] *a cow,*
for Nikkalu[48] *a cow,*
for the Mistress of the Mansion two birds,
for the Most Amiable of the gods a cow,
a cow for Ilahuma,
a ewe for Shapshu,[49]
a cow for Rashpu,
as a burnt-offering.

[40] It is likely that oil and honey played an important part in the rituals of the festival. Cf. Baal, notes 32, 36, 45, 440, 441; Keret III (KTU 1.16):iii.

[41] The equivalent of Hebrew *minḥāh*, cf. Lev. 2:2; 23:13,18, etc.

[42] Either the mountain of Baʿlu (Sapanu, cf. Baal, note 4) or the temple mound representing that mountain (cf. Aqhat IV, fragment c (KTU 1.22):iv.24f.).

[43] Cf. Ex. 20:26; Ez. 34:17. Parts of the sanctuary and cultic objects received sacrifices in the cult of Ugarit. In this particular case the sacrifice to the altar of ʿAnatu might be related to the hymnical praise the altar received in the course of the New Year festival. Cf. Myth and Ritual IV (KTU 1.13):16.

[44] Deified mountain on which Baʿlu's victory over Death (Motu) was celebrated. Cf. note 42.

[45] Possibly an epithet of ʿAnatu.

[46] Epithet of the youthful god Baʿlu?

[47] Moon-god.

[48] Wife of Yarikhu, cf. Myth and Ritual V.

[49] Sun-goddess, intimately connected with the return of Baʿlu. Cf. Baal, note 449, 475, 478-479.

And as a peace-offering: ditto.

(The third:)
Two ewes for Ilahu,
a cow for Ilahuma,
a cow for Ilu,
a ewe for Thakumanu and Shanuma,
a ewe for the Goddess of the House,
two rams at the fountain,[50]
as a burnt-offering.
And as a peace-offring: ditto.

(The fourth:)
A cow for Ba[ᶜlu of Sapanu],
a ewe for Sapanu,
a cow for [ ],
a ram for Baᶜlu of Ugarit,
a ram for Il'ibu,[51]
.. [ ] *for Ilu,*
a ram for Athiratu
and two birds for Ri'thu.[52]
(*Invoke*) *thirty times,*
both in the house of the Mistress of the Lofty Houses
and over the altar.

On the fifth:
One full shekel of silver for the House of Ilu
and sacrifice like [ ].
[ ] *for Athiratu,*

[50] Also in other offering-texts of Ugarit wells are the recipients of sacrifices. Deified wells are known throughout the ancient world.

[51] The ancestor-god. For the relation between the ancestor-cult and the New Year festival see Baal, note 478; Aqhat, notes 240ff., 263ff.

[52] Reading uncertain. Unknown god.

two birds for the Most Amiable of the gods.
Repeat: "*Altar of Baᶜlu.*"[53]
A cow for Baᶜlu,
a ewe for Sapanu,
and a ewe for Baᶜlu of Ugarit.
(Invoke) twenty two times.
[For] a ram, a pot of oil, a cow.
And the clean king shall answer.[54]

On the sixth:
Two pots of oil,
over it a cow.
The clean king shall answer.

On the seventh:
The sun-set and the host of the day
the sun-down and the host of Maliku.[55]

And on the day of renewal:[56]
two rams for ᶜAthtartu.

[53] Probably an incantation. Cf. Myth and Ritual I (KTU 1.23).

[54] As appears from KTU 1.112:20 (a ritual for a similar festival in spring) the king had to converse with the spirits of his deified ancestors.

[55] Invocation of the innumerable celestial bodies representing the gods, including the ancestors of the royal dynasty. Cf. below lines 51ff.; Keret, notes 64, 89; Aqhat, notes 241, 242; Ritual III, note 8. On the god Maliku see Myth and Ritual VI, note 16.

[56] Here it cannot be the New Moon that is meant, as in line 1. It is the day of the renewal of the two halves of the day, *i.e.* the day of the equinox that had to fall on a day during or close to the festival. This day could not be given a date because the date had to be established empirically. See Myth and Ritual I, note 25. The spring equinox is meant in KTU 1.112:10 "and on the seventh (of the month Khiari): the day of renewal". See also KTU 1.78 for another observation of the spring equinox: *"On (day) six: the day of renewal of (the month) Khiari. (When) Shapshu went under, her 'gate' was Rashpu. They inspected the livers: it was the (correct) time."* On the cosmic 'gates' as astronomical terms see CAD (A)1,83a, 87a; (B)22; (D)55b; Henoch 72:6ff. With regard to the possibility of a second New Year festival in spring, see AOAT 16,58,61f.

Then[57] *the king shall sacrifice*
to Pirigalu of the Third Heaven[58]
on the roof, on which there are four (and) four dwellings of cut foliage,[59]
a ram as a burnt-offering,
an ox and a ram as a peace-offering.
The king shall invoke seven times with (all) his heart
the sun-set and the host of Maliku.
And clothe him with beautiful (clothes)
and let him wipe his face,[60]
and make him return to the house.
And when he is there,
he shall raise his hands to heaven.[61]

Ritual II

KTU 1.161

Whereas most of the rituals from Ugarit are of the prescriptive type, this text is a description of a spiritualistic session held in connection

[57] *I.e.* on the day of the equinox.

[58] It is assumed here that the Ugaritic *prgl ṣqrn* is a rendering of Sumerian PIRIG.GAL.NUN.GAL, a name of one of the legendary Seven Sages. Like NIN.GAL in Ugaritic *nkl*, the first part of this name was Semiticized: Pirigalu. See also Incantation I, note 38. The second part was translated as "inhabitant of the Third Heaven" (*ṣqrn*, cf. Arabic *ṣāqūrah* "Third Heaven") which tallies with the fact that NUN.GAL is a designation of the Igigi, inhabitants of heaven (cf. B. Kienast, Assyriological Studies 16 (1965) 141-158).

In the third tablet of the Babylonian series *bīt mēseri* as reconstructed by R. Borger, JNES 33 (1974) 192 we read: "Piriggalnungal who was born in Kish who angered Adad in heaven so that he let no rain and vegetation be in the country for three years". It would seem logical to appease this deity with sacrifices on the festival of Baᶜlu's return to earth.

[59] The booths on the roof were intended for the images of the gods. Myth and Ritual I, note 25; IV, note 19.

[60] Cf. note 16.

[61] In prayer, cf. Keret, note 18. Solomon prayed in the same posture on the autumnal festival according to 1 Ki. 8:22.

with the royal ancestor cult. The priests and the king took turns to invoke the spirits. In the course of the ritual the kings of old receive a throne to sit on in the Nether World (cf. Isa. 14:9).

Report on the sacrificial banquet of the shades.[1]

You invoked[2] *the Saviours of the earth,*[3]
  you summoned the Assembly of Didanu.[4]

He invoked Ulikenu,[5] *the Saviour,*
  he invoked Tarmennu, the Saviour,
he invoked Sidannu and Radanu,
  he invoked Tharru, the usurper.
    They invoked the Saviours of old.[6]

You invoked the Saviours of the earth,
  you summoned the Assembly of Didanu.

He invoked ʿAmmithtamru, the king,
  he invoked - woe! - Niqmaddu, the king.[7]

[1] The designation of the spirits of the dead as "shadows" has parallels in Homeric σκιή and Babylonian *ṣillu*. This designation as well as the large number of ancestral spirits invoked in various texts from Ugarit renders it unlikely that all the ancestors were represented by cult images. Possibly they were made visible in the form of smoke. Cf. Aqhat, note 27. There is insufficient reason to take "shadows" as a metaphor for "protectors" as proposed by B. A. Levine — J.-M. de Tarragon, JAOS 104 (1984) 649-659.

[2] Technical term for the invocation of the spirits. Cf. 1 Sam. 28:15; Job 5:1; Prov. 9:18. Probably the persons addressed are priests.

[3] Designation of the deceased members of the Ugaritic dynasty with whom the ruling king was united in communion during such a spiritualistic session. Cf. Ritual III (KTU 1.43); Keret, note 52; Aqhat, notes 275ff.; Incantation V, note 13.

[4] Probably Didanu (other texts: Ditanu) was the founder of the Amorite dynasty from which the Ugaritic line of rulers branched off. In any case he was regarded as a deified ancestor of ʿAmmurapi of Babylon and of king Kirtu (cf. ZAW 88 (1976) 324).

[5] The king (line 31) first invokes his more remote ancestors. The reading of their names is very uncertain.

[6] Cf. Gen. 6:4; 15:19f.

[7] Grandfather and father of ʿAmmurapi. Niqmaddu is Niqmaddu III who had just died.

"Throne of Niqmaddu, weep for yourself![8]
And let his foot-stool shed tears,
before him let the royal table weep!
But let it swallow its tears,
let the (tears) disappear, disappear completely!
Be hot, Sun,
yes, be hot, Great Luminary!
Let the Sun cry from above:
After your owner, o throne,[9]
after your owner descend into the earth,
descend into the earth
and lower yourself in the dust,
under Sidannu and Radanu,
under Tharru, the usurper,
under the Saviours of old,
under ʿAmmithtamru, the king,
under - woe! - Niqmaddu, the king!"

One, and he sacrificed,[10]
two, and he sacrificed,
three, and he sacrificed,
four, and he sacrificed,
five, and he sacrificed,
six, and he sacrificed,

[8] The spirits of the dead were provided with furniture by means of rituals like this one. Cf. K. Spronk, Beatific Afterlife, Neukirchen 1986, 192. Because the spirits were raised during the night, the spontaneous "weeping" of their furniture (cf. the weeping of a mountain in Keret III (KTU 1.16):i.6) may have been caused by dew. With the rising of the sun both "tears" and spirits disappeared.

[9] Cf. Epic of Gilgamesh, VIII.iii.2-3; Isa. 14:9.

[10] At the disappearance of every one of the seven ancestral spirits the king sacrifices. Finally the priests had to offer a bird.

30 *seven, and he sacrificed;*
you offered a bird.[11]

"Hail, hail[12] *to ʿAmmurapi!*
And hail to his house!
Hail to Tharyelli![13]
Hail to her house!
Hail to Ugarit!
Hail to its gates!"[14]

Ritual III

KTU 1.43

It is unknown for which month this ritual was intended. The most likely candidates are "First-of-the-Wine"[1] and Khiari,[2] both months of an equinox.[3] The text is interesting because it concerns the cult of the deified ancestors of the ruling dynasty of Ugarit.[4]

1 *When ʿAthtartu of Khurri*[5]

[11] The correct reading is *tq*d*m*, cf. Mic. 6:6 and Punic *qdmt*. Less likely is *tq*dš *ʿṣr* "you sanctified a bird" or, with reference to 2 Ki. 10:19, "may you sanctify a meeting" (so A. Kuyt — J. Wesselius, VT 35 (1985) 109-111).

[12] Cf. Isa. 57:19; Jer. 6:14; 8:11; 1 Chron. 12:19.

[13] A queen of Ugarit, cf. P. Bordreuil — D. Pardee, Syria 59 (1982) 128.

[14] Cf. Ritual IV (KTU 1.119):26ff. and Ps. 122:7.

[1] Incantation V (KTU 1.108) and KTU 1.91 would seem to agree in favour of this. See also notes 6, 11, 13, 16.

[2] KTU 1.112 and 1.148 would seem to support this hypothesis.

[3] Cf. Ritual I, note 56.

[4] Cf. K. Spronk, Beatific Afterlife, Neukirchen 1986, 157f., 181ff.

[5] Apparently a Hurrian manifestation of ʿAthtartu who formed a pair with ʿAnatu, the goddess of love and war, in the texts of Ugarit. Here it is her cult-statue which is carried around in procession.

enters the cistern[6] *of the king's house,*
serve a banquet[7] *in the house of the star-gods.*[8]
Marjoram of death,[9]
a garment and a chemise,[10]
a neck-piece of gold,
food for a three day journey,[11]
a ram, an ox and three head of small cattle,
as a peace-offering.
Seven times (he shall invoke) the gods,[12]
seven times Kotharu.[13]

On the following day[14]

[6] A cellar in which water for the summer was collected. It would seem that it is more than likely that ᶜAthtartu entered this room when it was empty or nearly empty, *i.e.* in autumn.

ᶜAthtartu's entering of this cistern may have symbolized her descent into the Nether World, the myth of which is preserved in a very fragmentary state in KTU 1.92:25ff. (cf. UF 17 (1986) 225-230). See also Baal VI (KTU 1.6):i.7ff. and Ritual IV, note 1.

[7] Apparently the royal banquet served for the spirits of the ancestors. Cf. Ritual I, note 38.

[8] For the identification of the deified dead with the stars cf. Aqhat, notes 241-242; K. Spronk, *op. cit.* (n. 4), 87ff., 157. Cf. Isa. 14:13. Even among Palestinian peasants of comparatively recent times the idea that great heroes become stars is attested, cf. G. H. Dalman, Palästinischer Diwan, Leipzig 1901, 330.

[9] Cf. Aqhat, note 26.

[10] KTU 1.148:18ff. and 1.92:25ff. render it certain that these pieces of attire were intended for ᶜAthtartu.

[11] Compare the three days it took Baᶜlu and the ancestral spirits to return from the Nether World, Aqhat, notes 270, 285.

[12] Probably the king who has to invoke the host of heaven, cf. Ritual I (KTU 1.41):52 and note 8 above. In Ritual II (KTU 1.161) the king invokes seven spirits of his ancestors.

[13] This technician among the gods played a key-role in helping Baᶜlu to vanquish his sinister opponents on his way back to earth. See Baal, note 479.

[14] Cf. Ritual I, note 18.

the two Gathru-gods[15] *will enter the house of the king.*
A shekel of gold for Shapshu and Yarikhu,[16]
for Gathru a shekel of good silver,
a snout and a throat[17] *for his ʿAnatu,*[18]
a shekel of gold for Shapshu and Yarikhu,
for Gathru two shekels of good silver,
a snout and a throat for [ ],
[*for the Goddess*] *of the House an ox and a ram.*

[ ]*s for the two Gathru-gods.*

[ ]ram *for the two ʿAnatu-goddesses.*

[ ]*male* [*first*]*lings*[19]

[ ] *for the two ʿAnatu-goddesses.*

---

[15] A pair of gods, actually called Yaqaru and Gathru, who were regarded as founders of the dynasty of Ugarit. See Incantation V, notes 2 and 5.

[16] Sun and Moon, the deities mentioned as symbolizing the eternal duration in an incantation for the New Year festival, cf. Incantation V, note 15.

[17] These parts of the victim were often sacrificed to the gods.

[18] Just as the deified king was identified with Baʿlu the Saviour (*rpʾu*), so his wife was identified with ʿAnatu/ʿAthtartu, the wife/wives of Baʿlu. As such she could be called "the ʿAnatu of Gathru", cf. Incantation V, note 5. And like Gathru she could form a pair, cf. lines 18, 20.

It is interesting to compare the Hebrew inscriptions from Kuntillet ʿAjrud mentioning "YHWH and his Asherah". See also Wellhausen's famous conjecture for Hos. 14:9 "I am his Asherah and his ʿAnat". Furthermore Isa. 8:21 where we have to read *mlkw* "his Molech". KTU 2.31:41 *ʾaṯrty* "my Athiratu".

[19] Cf. Num. 3:15-43. It is certain that firstlings were sacrificed in Ugarit. Cf. Incantation I (KTU 1.82):9; Ritual IV (KTU 1.119):31.

[ ] *for the staircase*[20]

[*And*] *he shall clothe himself with a Khurrian garment.*

The king shall go to fetch the two gods.[21]

Behind the two gods he shall walk barefoot,[22]
the king shall walk barefoot.
Seven times (*he shall invoke*)[23] *all of them.*

Ritual IV

KTU 1.119

This ritual is especially interesting since it contains a promise of deliverance from *any* enemy laying siege to the city of Ugarit.

In the month "*Where-is-the-Mistress*?",[1]
on the seventh day:

[20] Cf. Ritual I, note 43.
[21] Of course their images are meant. Cf. KTU 2.4:16-24.
[22] Cf. Ex. 3:5; Josh. 5:15; for other parallels, T. H. Gaster, Myth, Legend and Custom in the Old Testament, London 1969, 231f.
[23] Cf. note 12.

[1] As yet it is unknown which month this is. "Mistress" is an epithet of ᶜAnatu/ᶜAthtartu. Possibly it was the month in which ᶜAnatu/ᶜAthtartu's descent into the Nether World was commemorated. Cf. Ritual III, note 6 and Baal, note 446.

A ram for Baʿlu,
biscuits, *a ram for* [ ]
and in the house of Baʿlu of Ugarit [ ],
a ram [ ]

(Invoke) the sunset and the host of Maliku.[2]

On the seventeenth,
the king shall wash himself clean.[3]
The sanctuary of Ilu, a cow,
a cow for Baʿluma.
A cow for the Lad,[4]
two ewes and a cow for the two Lasses.[5]
The house of the officiant[6] *shall sacrifice.*
And roast a lamb and a town-pigeon
in the oven behind the house of the Mistress of Ugarit
as an oblation.

On the eighteenth of "Where-is-the-Mistress?",
an ox for the tower[7] *of Baʿlu of Ugarit in the greenery.*[8]
But the king should not sacrifice a wave-offering.[9]
In the house of Ilu a throat[10] *for Ishkhariyu,*[11]
a throat for Baʿlu,

[2] Cf. Ritual I, note 55.
[3] Cf. Ritual I, note 9.
[4] Cf. Ritual I, note 46.
[5] Cf. Ritual I, note 45 and Ritual III, note 18.
[6] Cf. Baal, note 483.
[7] Cf. Ritual I, note 43.
[8] Cf. Ritual I, note 31.
[9] The translation is uncertain. Cf. Ex. 29:24,26f., etc.
[10] Cf. Ritual III, note 17.
[11] An ʿAnatu-like goddess.

and a he-ass[12] *for* [ ]
(broken)

[Br]ing two [ ] *of yesterday.*
He shall honou[r]
On the fourth,
two birds.

On the fifth,
a peace-offering
and a liver
and chains[13] *for Baˁlu of Ugarit in the house.*

On the seventh,
the purification-priests[14] *shall judge.*
(*Invoke*) *the sunset and the host of Maliku.*
Look! *Baˁlu's oil of pacification*
is a libation for the former kingship.[15]

'*When a strong one attacks your gate,*
a warrior your walls,[16]
raise your eyes[17] *to Baˁlu* (*saying*):
"*O Baˁluma,*[18] *please chase away the strong one from our gate,*
the warrior from our walls!
The bull, o Baˁlu, we shall consecrate,
the vows to Baˁlu we shall fulfil,[19]

[12] Sacrifices of asses are also attested in Mari.
[13] For the chains as part of the dress of Baˁlu, cf. Baal, note 366.
[14] Class of priests?
[15] Cf. Baal, notes 32, 36, 45.
[16] Cf. Deut. 28:7, 52; Ps. 20:8; 46:6-10; 48:5-9; 76.
[17] Cf. Gen. 13:10,14; 18:2; 31:10; 33:1,5; 43:29; Ez. 18:6.
[18] *Pluralis majestatis*, as with Hebrew *ʾelōhīm*.
[19] Cf. Jer. 44:25. The same connection between the performing of vows and deliverance in Ps. 76:12f. Cf. Aqhat, note 21.

the firstlings[20] *of Baʿlu we shall consecrate,*
the ḫitpu-*sacrifice*[21] *of Baʿlu we shall fulfil,*
the tithe of Baʿlu[22] *we shall pay,*
we shall ascend the sanctuary of Baʿlu,[23]
the paths of the house of Baʿlu we shall walk.''[24]
Then Baʿlu will listen to your prayer.
He will chase away the strong one from your gate,
the warrior from your walls.'[25]

[20] Cf. Ritual III, note 19.

[21] Cf. A. J. Spalinger, JSSEA 8 (1978) 55, 59; J. L. Boyd, UF 17 (1986) 64, n. 24.

[22] Cf. Gen. 14:20; Num. 18, etc.

[23] Cf. Keret I (KTU 1.14):ii.20ff.; Judg. 16:27; Myth and Ritual I, note 25.

[24] Cf. Judg. 5:6; Job 38:20.

[25] This oracle of salvation closely resembles the theology behind the inscription of Zakkur (KAI No. 202) as well as the so-called theology of Zion, cf. Ps. 46:6-8; 48:4-9; 76:5-13, see also Ps. 20:7-10, and for criticism from the side of the prophets: Mic. 3:11; Jer. 7:4,10.

For an excellent review of the rise and ultimate fall of this theology see J. Renkema, 'Misschien is er hoop ...'. De theologische vooronderstellingen van het boek Klaagliederen, Franeker 1983, 90ff., 215, 281ff. (with a summary in English).

INCANTATION

Incantation I

KTU 1.82

In addition to the incantations embedded in rituals, a few more or less independent prayers without ritual prescriptions have been preserved. From their content, however, it is absolutely clear that they too functioned within a cultic context (see below lines 8 ff.).

It appears the people of Ugarit were very afraid of evil spirits, demons threatening their health, sanity and general well-being. They tried to exorcise them by invoking the help of the great gods, especially Baᶜlu and ᶜAnatu. They were implored to destroy the demons that took the form of marine monsters once vanquished by Baᶜlu and ᶜAnatu. Apparently their victory over the forces of evil was not considered final.

The incantations are extremely difficult to interpret so that in many cases the translation is only provisional.

May Baᶜlu smite Tunnanu,[1] *[for] my d[aughter],*
and may he appear to pour out the m[enstruation] of my [daughter] on the earth!

[1] Our word "tuna", Hebrew Tannin, a monstrous helper of Yammu, the god of the sea. Although Baᶜlu and ᶜAnatu had defeated Yammu and his helpers in the distant mythological past (Baal I (KTU 1.3):iii.40; Baal II (KTU 1.2):iv; Baal V (KTU 1.5):i.1), they continued to be a threat (Baal IV (KTU 1.4):vi.12f.; Baal VI (KTU 1.6):vi.51; Incantation II (KTU 1.83)). Cf. Baal, notes 455, 479; Keret, note 102.

Therefore people were still afraid of these demoniacal forces and held them responsible for all kinds of illness, in this case a problem with the menstruation driving a girl mad. Even in the much later Jewish Aramaic incantation bowls "Leviathan the Tannin" is still a dreaded demon. Cf. C. D. Isbell, Corpus of the Aramaic Incantation Bowls, Missoula 1975, No. 2:4; 7:7,9.

Did I not hasten to fulfil the sworn obligation?
I have no sworn obligation to fulfil!
[May] Baʿlu [st]op the arrows of Rashpu![2]
Pay attention[3] *when he shoots at her kidneys and her heart!*
Your voice [resound]s on the mountain,
your voice resounds on the hill,[4]
when [''they''[5]*] make your teeth cry out*
and ''they'' do not allow your lips to forget.
You are pledging your covenant to Death,[6]
[over] (its) repudiation I would rejoice!
Voice of Shapshu,[7] *bring to life!*
Seize the serpents, o Baʿlu![8]
I will lay out a hellebore-plant on her head.[9]
Abdomen, bleed!

[And] he[10] *shall say: ''I have cut up two fine sheep.*
Take both of us, my two rams,[11]
take both of us, and the flesh of the two firstlings!

[2] The ''arrows'' of Rashpu are the plagues and diseases this evil god is sending among mankind. Cf. Deut. 32:24; Hab. 3:5; Ps. 78:48; Job 16:13.

[3] Cf. Baal IV (KTU 1.4):v.60; Ps. 5:2; Job 34:16; Dan. 9:23; 10:1.

[4] Cf. Mark 5:5, perhaps also Judg. 11:38.

[5] The speaker avoids to mention the demons by name.

[6] Cf. Isa. 28:15,18.

[7] Because Shapshu (the Sun) visited the Nether World every night she had the power to drive away the forces of evil by her light and warmth, cf. Baal VI (KTU 1.6):vi.22ff.,45ff.; Ritual II (KTU 1.161):18ff.; KTU 1.107; JEOL 27 (1981-82) 113.

[8] Cf. Baal V (KTU 1.5):i.2; Isa. 27:1; Luke 10:19; Rev. 12:9,14f; 20:2.

[9] Compare the prescription in Myth and Ritual III (KTU 1.114):29.

[10] A son who has brought his father with him because the latter is unable to speak for himself as the result of a seizure by the spirit of his wife.

[11] Spenders and victims are identified, a clear case of substitution.

My mother leapt,
she assailed my father.[12]
[And she sai]d: I assailed you!
Go before me![13]
May Baʿlu bind [my mother],[14]
[may] ʿAnatu [fast]en (her) with a rope,
let her be bowed over like someone trus[sed up]!
[May the well of your house] dr[ive you away],[15]
may the dust of your house drive you away!
May they tie up my [mother]!
Go back, go back, creatures of Ho[ronu],[16]
[creatures of]!
O Baʿlu, seize the He[ifer of I]lu,[17]
let your hand be strong,[18]
let your hand be [ ]!"

[If] suddenly [ ] ap[pears] as a [night-de]mon,[19]
and he treats you viciously [ ]

[12] Babylonians (CAD (E) 398a) as well as Palestinians in the recent past (cf. T. Canaan, Dämonenglaube im Lande der Bibel, Leipzig 1929, 5f.) feared seizure by the spirits of dead relatives. Cf. Acts 19:16; J. Naveh — S. Shaked, Amulets and Magic Bowls, Jerusalem/Leiden 1985, Bowl 13:12 (p. 200).

[13] *I.e.*, "obey me!" The same expression occurs in Babylonian incantations against evil spirits, cf. W. Farber, Beschwörungsrituale an Ištar und Dumuzi, Wiesbaden 1977, 152:180; 192:51.

[14] Binding was what the evil spirits did to man and man retaliated by binding the spirits. The procedure is well-documented in Babylonian magical texts. See also Mark 5:3f.; Luke 13:16; Rev. 9:14; 20:2.

[15] The spirits were thought to hide in wells and dust. See also lines 40f.

[16] God of black magic.

[17] Another monster, cf. Baal I (KTU 1.3):iii.44; Incantation V (KTU 1.108):11f.

[18] Cf. Prov. 31:17. Of course the "strong hand" of a deity is a common metaphor in the Ancient Near East. Cf. Baal, notes 89f., 364f.; KTU 2.10:11f.; Ex. 3:19; 13:9, etc.

[19] See also line 33. The *ll* is the male form of the infamous Lilith (Isa. 34:14). In Babylonian incantations and Jewish Aramaic incantation bowls the male species is also attested.

[and i]f he hits you between your eyes,
sheds [your blood] with a double-headed axe,[20]
[then] you shall put the frond of a palm-tree [on] the fountain[21]
and in the [ ]
["Go back,] go [back], creatures of Agitation,
creatures of Insanity![22]
[ ]
[ ] *I will bring to life.*
I will lay out a hellebore-plant,
[ ]"

[I will recite] *an incantation [against] the susp[ect ones];*
alone I will overpower [ ].
[From the scr]een of my door I will drive away[23]
those who [ ],
[those who b]ite the poor orphan,[24]
go [ ] in [ ].
[And may] the Sons of Disease turn around,[25]
[may] the Sons of Disease [f]ly away[26] [ ],

[20] Cf. Baal III (KTU 1.2):iv.18-26.

[21] Because the spirits were always very thirsty (cf. Canaan, *op. cit.*, 9ff.), the palm-branch was obviously put over the well to prevent them from drinking. See also lines 12 and 40.

[22] More specifically the disordered state of mind of some people in autumn. It was widely believed that demons could cause madness, cf. 1 Sam. 16:14ff.; Mark 5:1ff.; Luke 8:26ff.; JEOL 27 (1981-82) 106ff.; Canaan, *op. cit.*, 45f.; Incantation III (RIH 78/20).

[23] Cf. Ex. 35:15, etc. Demons could take the form of flies.

[24] In KTU 1.107 "the Biter" is a demon next to "the Devourer".

[25] To go back to the Nether World where they belonged. Cf. Eccl. 12:5 with the name of these demons.

[26] The demons were winged.

[may they t]urn around like a door,
may they flow away like a dit[ch],[27]
[w]indow,
may they beat themselves like the ill of mind![28]
[Go back]
[go back to the] Palace of Confusion![29]
The Legions to the Legions,[30]
[the Flies] to the F[lies],[31]
those of the Flood [to the Flood],[32]
[those of] Hor[on] to Horon,[33]
[to],
the deep [Stupor] to the deep Stupor,[34]
[ ]
[ ] our wives and [children],
[ ]!
[Go back,] go back [ ]
(broken)

An unknown number of lines is missing.

[27] Cf. Myth and Ritual VI, note 34.

[28] Application of the jus talionis, cf. note 14. The demons caused the possessed to inflict injuries upon themselves, cf. Mark 5:5; 9:22; Incantation III, note 14.

[29] A designation of the home of the demons. Cf. Myth and Ritual VI, note 20; Matt. 12:44.

[30] Cf. Mark 5:9.

[31] A common designation of demons in the form of monstrous flies, cf. JEOL 27 (1981-82) 114f. The name of Baal Zebub "Fly-Lord" (2 Ki. 1:2) recalls Baᶜlu's victory over these monsters. Eccl. 10:1 mentions "flies of death". See also Baal, notes 64, 204 and Incantation III (RIH 78/20).

[32] Creatures inhabiting the ocean. Cf. Baal, notes 172, 454-456; Incantation II (KTU 1.83).

[33] See note 16 and Myth and Ritual VI, note 23.

[34] Unconsciousness was thought to be caused by demons. Cf. the literature cited in note 22.

31 [ ]
on the order of she who spends the night may go out [ ]
[ ]
[ ]
the poison by the voice of the Saviour[*s*]*!*[35]
[ ]
[ ] *night-demons.*
I will carry your crucible [ ],
[*in*] *my* [*hands*] *the plastered cup.*[36]
And may the best of g[*irls*] *live!*

---

35 [*the m*]*ale serpents*
and ri[*de*] *again on the female serpents!*[37]

[ ] *his/her dwelling the sister of Papsharru,*[38]
and Papsharratu [ ].
[I will adopt *the be*]*haviour of a carrion-vulture*
and I will sit down on the road,[39]
if the trees do not gi[*ve*] (*sound*)*!*[40]

---

[35] KTU 1.107 is an incantation against the poison spread by various demons. The "Saviours" were the good spirits who were able to neutralize the tricks of their evil counterparts and to heal the victims. See also note 40.

[36] The officiant shows his resolve to cast an apotropaic statuette of his tormentor.

[37] Probably ᶜAnatu is addressed. See line 40 and Baal (KTU 1.3):iii.39ff.

[38] Probably Papsharru is the "westernized" version of the Babylonian Papsukkal, the vizier of the Nether World.

[39] Because of the parallel in lines 42f. apparently a threat to the demons.

[40] The speaker hopes to receive a favourable omen. Cf. 2 Sam. 5:24. The rustling of the trees will be caused by the arrival of the bird-like "Saviours", the good spirits of heroes and kings. Cf. Baal, notes 478f.; Ritual II (KTU 1.161); III (KTU 1.43); Incantation V (KTU 1.108); Aqhat, notes 27f., 101, 242, 275ff.

May [ᶜAthtartu] trample on the Fugitive (Serpent)! [41]
Earth,[42] *go before her!* [43]
May Baᶜ[lu] bind[44] *[ ],*
[ ] of your house!
May ᶜAnatu also rise against your assembly,[45]
may ᶜAnatu rise [against the of] your [as]sembly!
May the well of your house drive you away,[46]
may [the dust of your house] drive you away,
o creatures of Agitation,
creatures of Intestinal Trouble,[47]
servants of Horonu,
(you who) bite [the poor orphan]! [48]
I will turn your well into a mud pond,[49]
if the arrival of the gods [does not make] the trees [trem]ble,
if the trees do not give (sound),
if the stones do not murmur! [50]

Incantation II

KTU 1.83

The general nature of this small fragment lends support to the view that it was part of an incantation comparable to Incantation I. The

[41] The full name of the "Fugitive Serpent" is found in the Myth of Baal, cf. Baal, notes 60, 323-325.

[42] "Earth" and "Heaven" were deities. "Earth" may be one of the monsters enumerated in Baal I (KTU 1.3):iii.43, with note 60. See also Isa. 11:4.

[43] Cf. note 13.

[44] See note 14.

[45] Just like the great gods the demons had their own assembly.

[46] See notes 15 and 21.

[47] The name of this demon has been preserved in the Ugaritic personal name Maᶜmaᶜa'ilu.

[48] See note 24.

[49] A formidable threat because the spirits had nothing but mud to eat in the Nether World. Cf. Baal, note 320.

[50] Cf. note 40.

lines 11 ff. seem to contain an oracle[1] for the person on whose behalf the incantation was recited. It sounds as if he has had a bad dream about drowning in a marsh from which primordial monsters rose.

“[ ]
[ ] Ilu [ ]
[*you shall go*] *out into the land of Makhanami.*[2]
Break the neck of Yammu-with-the-forked-tongue[3]
which is licking the sky!
Break the neck of Yammu-with-the-fish-tail,
put a muzzle on Tunnanu,[4]
tie (them) to the heights of the Lebanon,[5]
and the salt-marshes *will not rise (again),*
if [your] *face is not terrified,*
if you do not fa[*ll down*][6]
is the message of [ ]”
(broken)

[1] Compare Myth and Ritual IV, note 1.

[2] Biblical Mahanaim? It should be noted that according to biblical tradition it was a place where angels could be met (Gen. 32:1f.). It was close to Bashan, the land of the Rephaim (Josh. 13:26,30f.). Cf. Incantation V, note 3 and Incantation I, note 35.

[3] Reference to the dragon-like appearance of Yammu, the god of the sea. He and his helpers seem to be identified here. Cf. Baal, note 325.

[4] Compare Baal I (KTU 1.3):iii.40 with the notes 57-61, but also Baal III (KTU 1.2):iv.

[5] Compare Baal V (KTU 1.5):i. Also Job 38:8ff.; Ps. 74:13ff.; 89:10f.; Isa. 27:1; Rev. 13:1ff. (cf. J. Day, God's Conflict with the Dragon and the Sea, Cambridge 1985); and the Babylonian Epic of Creation.

[6] Cf. Baal III (KTU 1.2):i.15,31.

Incantation III

RIH 78/20

This tablet[1] has a title: "To cast out the flying demons which possess a young man".[2] The "flying demons" were monstrous flies, the supposed cause of all kinds of illness, especially mental disorders.[3] Whereas the Old Testament is very reticent about such evil spirits, the New Testament and Jewish Aramaic magical bowls prove that in folk-religion they played an important part. In Ugarit, as in other ancient cultures, exorcism was part of the official religion.

To cast out the flying demons which possess[4] *a young man.*

Let the br[eath][5] *of Baᶜlu*[6] *throw you out,*[7]
let it throw you out! And go away[8]
before[9] *the voice of the officiant,*

[1] The text is extremely difficult. See for other interpretations: P. Bordreuil, A. Caquot, Syria 57 (1980) 346ff.; Y. Avishur, UF 13 (1981) 13ff.; O. Loretz, P. Xella, MLE 1 (1982) 37ff.; B. Polentz, MLE 1 (1982) 47ff.; F. Saracino, VT 32 (1982) 338ff.; SEL 1 (1984) 69ff.; A. Caquot, Or 53 (1984) 163ff. A particularly clear photograph of the tablet was published by A. Bounni, DaM 1 (1983) Pl. 2c.

[2] The physical disposition of the tablet renders it absolutely certain that this was meant as the title.

[3] See Incantation I, note 31.

[4] Literally "those of a young man".

[5] Although the reading *r[ḥt]* "the hand of (Baᶜlu)" might be considered in view of Incantation I (KTU 1.82):14, it would presuppose that the *t* had been written on the edge. It is preferable, therefore, to read *r[ḥ]* "breath" or "wind". In that case one may compare 2 Thess. 2:8, cf. Isa. 11:4; Job 4:9. See also En.el. IV.45-47,99, 132.

[6] As in Incantation I (KTU 1.82) Baᶜlu is the champion of exorcists because he had defeated Sea and Death with their monsters. This is what the Pharisees meant when they said of Jesus: "It is only by Beelzebul (cf. Ugaritic *zbl bᶜl*), the prince of demons, that this man casts out demons" (Matt. 12:24, par.). The Arabic saint el-Khadir, in whom Baal lives on to this day (cf. AOAT 16,200), is likewise able to cure people who are possessed by demons (cf. R. Kriss, H. Kriss-Heinrich, Volksglauben

like smoke[10] *from a chimney,*
like a snake from an approaching person,[11]
like mountain-goats to the top,
like lions to the lair![12]
Wake up![13] *Get better!*
And draw near! Wake up!
You are sinning against your own back,
and are transgressing against your own pelvis.[14]
You should eat bread, fasting one![15]
You should drink purified milk and not abstain!

On the heights,[16] *in the lowland,*
in the darkness,[17] *in the sanctuary is their fury!*[18]

im Bereich des Islam, Bd. 1, Wiesbaden 1960, 160ff.), and he too was a dragon-killer.

[7] The difficult verb will be explained in a forthcoming issue of UF.

[8] Cf. CAD (A)2, 357 and Mark 5:8; 9:25.

[9] Cf. Incantation I, note 13. Interestingly enough the voice of the officiant and the breath of Baᶜlu seem to be identified.

[10] The same comparison occurs in Mesopotamian and Anatolian incantations against evil spirits, cf. V. Haas, Or 40 (1971) 426; CAD (N)2, 187b. See also Hos. 13:3.

[11] Apparently Ugar. *ᶜmd* has the same nuance of meaning as Syrian Arabic *ᶜmd* (Denizeau, 362). Cf. Aqhat, note 164.

[12] Cf. Jer. 25:38; Ps. 10:9; 27:5; 76:3; Job 38:40; Lam. 2:6.

[13] The patient appears to suffer from a cataleptic or epileptic seizure. He has periods when he loses consciousness and seems to sleep, as is the case with the patient described in R. Labat, Traité akkadien de diagnostics et pronostics médicaux, t.l, Paris/Leiden 1951, 80f. In line 6 the seizure is ascribed to the moon-god Sin, cf. the "moon-struck" of Matt. 4:24; 17:15.

[14] The possessed is hurting himself, cf. Incantation I, note 28; Mark 5:5; 9:22. Compare also the expression "to sin against his own body" in 1 Cor. 6:20 and see the similar expression in C. D. Isbell, Corpus of the Aramaic Incantation Bowls, Missoula 1975, No. 7:13,16.

[15] The young man is unable to eat during a seizure, cf. KAR No. 33:2; Mark 9:18; J. Naveh — S. Shaked, Amulets and Magic Bowls, Jerusalem/Leiden 1985, Amulet 7:16-22 (pp. 70f., 75f.).

[16] Cf. KTU 1.107:8 (par.) and Incantation I, note 4.

[17] Cf. Baal, note 297.

Let the sorcerers, the flying demons, be chased away! [19]
Let Horonu[20] *be a friend,*
and the Lad[21] *an intimate!*

Go! Do not speak scoffing language,
do not allow your tongue to stammer,[22]
do not dribble so much! [23]
May the robe of Ilu make you -[24]
may the nakedness of Ilu make you
a man, yes, someone who is awake on the earth,
(may they make) the strange one a son of man!
When the fury of the shade[25] *begins,*
look! in the soul of Lady Athiratu,[26]
in the he[art of your P]otter,[27] *may you be moulded!*
Let me observe you intently [ ] dead
And certainly do not enter!

[18] Cf. line 15. In Ps. 138:7 "the wrath of my foes" may be a designation of sinister forces ("enemies" or "foes" are common designations of demons in Egypt and Mesopotamia).

[19] *Scil.* by Baᶜlu and other good gods.

[20] For a similar wish in connection with Kotharu see Baal, note 479. Although Horonu was the master of black magic (cf. Baal, note 128; Myth and Ritual VI, note 20; Incantation I, note 16), he could be persuaded to use his considerable powers to neutralize the poison of the demons, cf. Myth and Ritual VI, note 23.

[21] Probably a name of Baᶜlu as the one able to fight off the demons, cf. Ritual I, note 46; IV, note 4.

[22] Cf. Incantation IV, note 3.

[23] Cf. Labat, *op. cit.* (n. 13), 80:2,4; Mark 9:18.

[24] Being the creator-god only Ilu could make the patient a normal human being again. Apparently the officiant touched him with a statuette of Ilu. Cf. Mark 5:28; 6:56 (par.); Aqhat, note 189.

[25] See Ritual II, note 1.

[26] Mother of the gods, wife of Ilu. Cf. Atra-hasis I.202ff.; Keret III (KTU 1.16):v.37f.

[27] Scil. Ilu, cf. Keret, note 101. Cf. Isa. 64:7, also Isa. 27:11; 43:1; 44:2,24; 45:9,11; Jer. 10:16; 51:19.

[ ]
do not turn around the head[28]
[ ]
[ ] *their wickedness like* [ ]
[ ]
[ ] true [ ]
[ ]
[ ] .. [ ]
(broken)

Incantation IV

KTU 1.93

A supplicant, apprehensive of making a slip of the tongue while reciting his incantation,[1] prays to ᶜAnatu for help.

1 *Cow!*[2] *Take away the word (spoken) in negligence,*
the stammering from my mouth,[3]
the negligence from my tongue!
Put back t[rue] words[4] *in my throat,*
the word of Baᶜlu I want to he[ed].

[28] One of the symptoms according to Labat, *op. cit.* (n. 13), 80f.:1,4.

[1] In several Babylonian prayers the supplicant begs to be forgiven unseemly words or faltering speech, cf. Shurpu II. 40ff.; M.-J. Seux, Hymnes et prières aux dieux de Babylonie et d'Assyrie, Paris 1976, 144, 207. Unseemly words are typical of the ungodly: Ps. 35:15f., 20; 36:4; 52:4-6, etc.

Different interpretations of this text have been proposed by A. Caquot, UF 11 (1979) 101ff.; S. Zevit, UF 13 (1981) 193ff.; B. Margalit, SEL 1 (1984) 89ff.

[2] An attested epithet of ᶜAnatu. Cf. Loves II, notes 22, 30, 31; Myth and Ritual IV, note 32; cf. Baal, note 421. The epithet may have Mesopotamian antecedents, cf. ANET, 580f.

[3] Cf. Isa. 32:4; Incantation III (RIH 78/20):11f.

[4] Cf. Ps. 33:4; Prov. 22:21; Eccl. 12:10; Rev. 19:9; 21:5; 22:6. Contrast Ps. 5:10.

Listen to me![5]
Let [my heart] expand![6]
Let my distress [turn into h]appiness!
Reaped corn [ ] *mil[k*]
ewe [ ] .. [ ]
(broken)

Incantation V

KTU 1.108

To ward off the machinations of the evil spirits good genies could be invoked. They were called "Saviours" (*rp'um*) like their Master, Baᶜlu the Saviour.

Long dead ancestors of the royal dynasty of Ugarit are invited to participate in the banquet of the New Year festival. The king of Ugarit has to implore Baᶜlu the Saviour to bless the city in the year to come.

[Look!] *Let the Saviour,*[1] *the eternal king, drink!*
And let [the god] Gathru-and-Yaqaru drink,[2]
the god who is dwelling in Athtartu,
the god who is judging in Hadduraᶜiyu,[3]

[5] Cf. Job 15:17; 33:31,33.
[6] Cf. CAD (N)1, 289a.

[1] Literally "Healer", a title of Baᶜlu in his role of victor over Death. Deified heroes and kings could earn the same title, just like the Greek heroes (ἰάτροι). See also note 13 and Ritual II (KTU 1.161). For "eternal king" as an epithet of Baᶜlu see Baal, note 473.

[2] A double deity, probably deified ancestors of the Ugaritic dynasty. Cf. Ritual III, note 15.

[3] Cities in Bashan, probably centres of the cult of dead kings during the Bronze Age. Cf. Aqhat, note 220. According to a tradition preserved in Deut. 1:4; 3:10f.; Josh. 9:10 (LXX); 12:4; 13:12, Og, the king of Bashan who would have been "of the remnant of the Rephaim (Saviours)", lived in both these cities. Perhaps this tradition goes back to a misinterpreted Canaanite inscription on the tomb of Og.

For the "Saviours" as judges see K. Spronk, Beatific Afterlife, Neukirchen 1986, 182.

who sings and plays,
with the lyre and the shawm,
with the tambourine and the cymbals,
with the anointed dancers,
with the merry companions of Kotharu.[4]
And may the ᶜAnatu of Gathru[5] *drink,*
the Mistress of kingship,
the Mistress of dominion,
the Mistress of the high heaven,
the Mistress of the royal cap,
and the ᶜAnatu of the Kite, the She-Kite,[6]
she who soars in the high heaven,
who devours a heifer at the banquet,
[who fills] *the horn with* new wi[ne].[7]

[4] Patron of artists and artisans. Among the Canaanites certain cultic companies or associations (called *ḥbr*, *sd* or *mrzḥ*) practised communion with the dead during sacrificial banquets and drinking bouts. These practices are attacked in Deut. 18:11; 26:14; Isa. 28:15,18; Jer. 16:5; Am. 6:7; Ps. 58:6; 106:28. For the specific connection with the New Year festival see Baal, note 479; Aqhat, notes 242ff.

[5] In the offering texts of Ugarit the dual goddess *ᶜntm* is associated with the dual god *g̱trm*, probably none other than Gathru-and-Yaqaru. See Ritual III (KTU 1.43). The goddess ᶜAnatu formed a pair with the goddess ᶜAthtartu in Ugarit. Just as the king became a manifestation of Baᶜlu-the-Saviour after his death, so the queen was identified with Baᶜlu's consort ᶜAnatu/ᶜAthtartu, the goddess of love.

[6] For ᶜAnatu as a bird of prey, more specifically a black kite, see Aqhat II (KTU 1.18):iv.20ff. It seems that Yaqaru is called a "kite" here, because the spirits of the dead could take on the form of birds or winged hybrids. Cf. Spronk, *op. cit.* (n. 3), 177ff.

[7] The new foaming wine called *ḫmr* was ceremonially produced during the New Year festival in autumn. Cf. Baal, note 15; Myth and Ritual I, note 11. This circumstance as well as the significant Assyrian parallel KAR No. 214 (cf. UF 2 (1970) 356) suggest that the text was used in the course of this festival. Also according to a Middle Assyrian ritual for the New Year festival large quantities of wine were libated (F. Köcher, ZA 50 (1952) 192-202). See also note 4. The text ends with what might be called an appropriate New Year's wish.

And let the god [ ] *drink*,
the god who sucked out *the bull-calf of Ilu*, [ᶜAtiku][8]
[*who* ---- *the* belov]ed *of Ilu*, *Shedu*.[9]
Let Maliku[10] *feed* [ ]
[ ]
[*And*] *let Ilahu drink* [ ]
[ ]
[ ] *its firm-fleshed cattle*,
[ ]
[ ] Rashpu [ ]
[ ]
[When the Saviours] *arrive*,[11]
[say to the king and] *his family*:
["Ask for grace,]
[*a*]*sk Ba*ᶜ*lu for* [strength].
[He will bless] *your coming*,
the Saviour, *the* [*eternal*] *king*, *your* [going].[12]
Surely [the grace] *of the Saviour*, *the eternal king*,
will place you, *at* [*your*] *request*,
in the strength [*of the Saviour*], *the eternal king*,
in his protection, *in his po*[*wer*],
in his patronage, *in his beneficial might*,
for the Saviours of the earth!"[13]

[8] Mythological monster, cf. Baal I (KTU 1.3):iii.44. These monsters had to be vanquished on New Year's eve, cf. Baal, note 479; Ritual I, note 20.

[9] Genius, either good or evil. Cf. JEOL 27 (1981-82) 119.

[10] Deity, perhaps identical to the Molekh of Israelite tradition. Cf. Myth and Ritual VI, note 16.

[11] Cf. Incantation I, note 40 and KTU 1.124:1.

[12] Cf. Deut. 28:6; Ps. 121:8.

[13] Designation of the members of the dynasty, both the living and the dead at this moment of communion. "Healer of the land" is a divine epithet in Mesopotamia (CT 23, No. 2:15). See also 2 Chron. 7:14 and Keret, note 52. Furthermore Amulet 3:19 in: J. Naveh - S. Shaked, Amulets and Magic Bowls, Jerusalem/Leiden 1985, 50, where the Lord is called *hrwp*ʾ *kl h*ʾ*rṣ* "the Healer of the whole earth".

(The king:)
"*Let your strength, your protection,*[14]
your power, your patronage,
your beneficial might be in the middle of Ugarit
throughout the days of Sun and Moon[15]
and the happiest of Ilu's years!"[16]

[14] Presumably this prayer was pronounced by the king himself. The combination of "your strength" and "your protection" strongly resembles the Hebrew expression in Ex. 15:2; Isa. 12:2; Ps. 118:14.

[15] *I.e.*, may it last eternally. Cf. Ps. 72:5; 89:37f.; UF 1 (1969) 179; 2 (1970) 356; S. M. Paul, JNES 31 (1972) 351-355.

[16] Cf. Ps. 90:17; Job 36:11. Ilu was older than any other active deity. Cf. Baal, note 83. For parallels with other ancient oriental blessing formulae see M. L. Barré, Maarav 3 (1982) 177-194.

LEGEND: KERET

Keret I

KTU 1.14

The Legend of Kirtu (Keret) consisted of at least four tablets, three of which have been partially preserved. It relates the tragic fate of king Kirtu who at first lost seven wives in succession before they had been able to give him offspring. Eventually the head of the Ugaritic pantheon Ilu blesses him with a wife and children, but it is likely that subsequently he lost them all again but for the youngest girl. It is the wife of Ilu, Athiratu, who takes what her husband had given. The Legend of Kirtu deals with fundamental religious questions like the supposed immortality of kings, divine justice and the destiny of man.[1] It was written by the same high-priest Ilimilku who executed the tablets of the myth of Baal and the legend of Aqhat.

Of Kirtu.[2]

[Kirtu was] *king* [of Khuburu].
[ ]
[ ]
[son] *of Ilu* [ ]
[ ] *of Naharu.*[3]

[1] For the ideas underlying the legend cf. S. E. Loewenstamm, UF 11 (1979) 505ff.; J. C. de Moor, OTS 24 (1986) 1ff.

[2] For library purposes every tablet of the series was headed by a short "title" indicating its contents: "Of Kirtu". See Baal, note 397; Aqhat, note 150.

[3] Literally "River", an epithet of the sea-god Yammu who deprived Kirtu of one of his wives (line 20). See Baal, note 57.

[Kirtu]'s clan [was w]iped out,[4]
the [k]ing's house was destroyed,
(the house) that counted seven brothers,
eight sons by the same mother.[5]
Kirtu - his authority was shattered,
Kirtu - (his) dwelling-place was a ruin.[6]
A wife (befitting) his righteousness he did not obtain,
(not) a spouse (befitting) his fairness.
He did marry a woman, but she rebelled;
he procured a mother, she was ⟨un⟩faithful to him.
A third wife died in childbirth,
a fourth in illness.
A fifth was gathered in by Rashpu,[7]
a sixth by the lads of Yammu,[8]
his seventh wife fell by Shalhu.[9]
He reviewed his authority,
Kirtu reviewed his authority:
verily it was shattered,
his dwelling was a ruin,
and the clan had been wiped out entirely,
totally those entitled to succession.[10]

[4] Literally "stripped naked", cf. Job 1:21; Lam. 1:8.

[5] For the sequence "seven-eight", see Mic. 5:4; for the standard number of seven sons, cf. Ruth 4:15; Jer. 15:9; for eight sons, 1 Sam. 17:12. Furthermore below, Keret II (KTU 1.15):ii.23. The "brothers" are identical to the "sons of the same mother", see *e.g.* Gen. 43:29; Deut. 13:7; Judg. 8:19; 9:3; Ps. 69:9; Baal VI (KTU 1.6):vi.10f.

[6] Cf. Mal. 1:4, also Isa. 64:10; Jer. 22:5.

[7] God of pestilence and other diseases. Cf. Incantation I, note 2.

[8] Yammu is the sea-god. Sea and Death are allies, cf. Baal, note 455. The satellites of Yammu came to fetch people for their cruel lord, cf. Baal III (KTU 1.2):i.

[9] Probably the deified river of the Nether World. See Baal, notes 127 and 378.

[10] Not only Kirtu's offspring, but also his brothers who could have been heirs (cf. Num. 27:9-11).

He entered his bedroom, he wept,
repeating his angry cries, shedding tears.
His tears poured forth
like shekels to the ground,
like pieces of one-fifth on his bed.
While he was weeping, he fell asleep,
while he was shedding tears, slumber (came),
sleep overpowered him and he lay down,
slumber (came) and he curled up.
And in his dream Ilu descended,
in his vision the Father of man,[11]
and he approached the questioning Kirtu.
"*What is the matter with Kirtu, that he weeps,*
(that) he sheds tears, the gracious[12] *lad of Ilu?*
Does he request the kingship of the Bull, his Father,
or dominion like the Father of man?[13]
[ ]
[ ]
[*Take silver and the yellow metal,*]
[*gold, together with its finding place,*[14]]
[*and eternal slaves, teams of three horses,*[15]]
[*chariots from the corral, bondmen!*"]
[*But Kirtu, the nobleman, answered:*]
["*Why should I (need) silver and the yellow metal,*]

[11] Title of Ilu, the head of the Ugaritic pantheon. Cf. Deut. 32:6 and Baal, notes 84, 95, 209.

[12] In the popular imagination all kings and heroes had to be extremely handsome (cf. 1 Sam. 9:2; 16:12; 1 Ki. 1:6, etc.).

[13] The poet touches here upon the theme of the divine kingship which will recur in Keret III (KTU 1.16):i.

[14] Cf. Job 28:1.

[15] Eternal slaves: cf. Baal, note 339; Deut. 15:17; 1 Sam. 27:12; Job 40:28(23). Three horses trained to cooperate were very valuable because they could be alternated before the chariot pulled by two of them. Cf. RSP II.iii.28.

II.

[gold], together with its finding place?
And eternal slaves, teams of three horses,
chariots from the corral, bondmen?
[No, s]ons I want to sire,
many boys I want to beget!"
And the Bull, his Father, approached,
Ilu, the Merciful,[16] *(approached) the weeping Kirtu,*
the tear-shedding gracious lad of Ilu.
"Wash and scrub yourself,
wash your hands, the forearms,
your fingers, up to the shoulder.[17]
Enter into the shadow of the shed.
Take a sheep in your hand,
a sacrificial sheep in your right hand,
a lamb in the two of them.
Take all your offering-bread,
fowl, a sacrificial bird.
Pour wine into a bowl of silver,
honey into a bowl of gold.
Go up to the top of the tower,
yes, go up to the top of the tower,
straddle a parapet of the wall.
Raise your hands to heaven,[18]
sacrifice to the Bull, your Father Ilu.

[16] Cf. Ex. 22:26; 34:6; Ps. 86:15; 103:8, etc. For a different restoration cf. J. P. van der Westhuizen, UF 17 (1986) 357-370.

[17] A ritual bath of the king who was the principal officiant in the Ugaritic cult is often mentioned in the liturgies. See also Ex. 29:4; 40:12, etc.

[18] Cf. Ritual I, note 61; 1 Ki. 8:22; O. Keel, Die Welt der altorientalischen Bildsymbolik und das Alte Testament, Köln 1972, 287ff.

Make Baˁlu descend by your sacrifice,
the son of Daganu by your banquet.[19]
Then Kirtu has to descend from the roof.
Let him set out food for the town,
wheat for the daughter of Khuburu.[20]
Let him bake bread of the fifth,
provisions of the sixth month.
Let an army be provisioned and let it go out,
let a mighty host be provisioned,
yes, let a strong army go out!
Let your host be a numerous force,
three hundred myriads,[21]
innumerable conscripts,
countless troopers.
Let them go by the thousands—a thunderstorm,
yes, by the myriads—like a rainshower.
After two, let there go two,
after three, all of them.[22]
Let the single man close his house,
let the widow give a generous contribution,

[19] The weather-god Baˁlu was the son of Daganu of Tuttul and through his marriage to ˁAnatu a son-in-law of Ilu. In the legend of Keret he is second to Ilu (Keret II (KTU 1.15):ii.1ff.; III (KTU 1.16):iv.10ff.), in the legend of Aqhat it is the other way round (Aqhat I (KTU 1.17):i.31f., etc.), in accordance with the fact that Kirtu's personal patron is Ilu whereas Baˁlu is the patron of Dani'ilu. At the time when these texts were written down there was a great deal of tension between the proponents of the two gods (cf. OTS 24 (1986) 1ff.) and as a high-priest Ilimilku seems to have steered a middle course.

[20] *I.e.* the inhabitants of the city; compare the Hebrew "daughter of Zion/Jerusalem". Cf. Isa. 23:10; 23:23.

[21] No army of three million warriors ever marched the roads of the Ancient Near East. We have a particularly clear example of Oriental hyperbole here.

[22] For the sequence "two-three" see Baal, note 222; Isa. 17:6; Am. 4:8; Job 33:29.

let the sick man take up his bed,[23]
let the blind one donate very generously.[24]
Let even the newly wed groom go out,
let him bring his wife to another man,
his beloved to a stranger.[25]
Let them settle like locusts[26] *on the field,*

III.

like grasshoppers on the fringes of the steppe.
Go for one day and a second,
a third, a fourth day,
a fifth, a sixth day.
And look! At sunset on the seventh[27]
you will reach Great Udumu
and Little Udumu.[28]
And attack it, the twin-city,
advance against it, the twin-town.
Assault its wood-gatherers in the fields,
(its) strawpickers at the threshing-floors.
Assault the women drawing water at the spring,
those filling (their buckets) at the well.
Stay quiet for one day and a second,
a third, a fourth day,
a fifth, a sixth day.

[23] Cf. Luke 5:25.

[24] Substantial contributions to the war-chest, even from the poorest. Cf. Mar. 12:41-44 (par.).

[25] Whereas normally he was exempted, cf. Deut. 20:7; 24:5. See also Joel 2:16, with W. G. E. Watson, UF 9 (1977) 278f.

[26] A very common simile, cf. Judg. 6:5; 7:12; Isa. 33:4; 46:23; Nah. 3:15; Ps. 105:34; H. Grapow, Die bildlichen Ausdrücke des Ägyptischen, Leipzig 1924, 98; F. Heimpel, Tierbilder in der sumerischen Literatur, Roma 1968, 446.

[27] Cf. Baal, note 264.

[28] Probably a city in the Bashan region, consisting of two more or less independent parts, like many other ancient oriental cities.

Do not shoot your arrows up to the city,
(nor) the (sling)stones of your throwing-hand.
And look! At sunset of the seventh
king Pubâla will not be able to sleep,
because of the loud roaring of his bull,
because of the loud braying of his ass,
because of the lowing of his plough ox,
the whining of his watch-dog.[29]
And he will send messengers to you,
to Kirtu in his night-quarters:
"A message from king Pubâla:
Take silver and the yellow metal,
gold, together with its finding place,
and eternal slaves, teams of three horses,
chariots from the corral, bondmen.
Take, Kirtu, peace-gifts, as many as you want,
but depart, king, from my house,
go away, Kirtu, from my residence!
Do not harass Great Udumu[30]
and Little Udumu.
Udumu is a gift of Ilu[31]
and a present of the Father of man."
And you must send back messengers to him:
"Why should I (need) silver and the yellow metal,
gold, together with its finding place?
And eternal slaves, teams of three horses,
chariots from the corral, bondmen?
No, give me what I do not have in my house,
give me the lady Hariya,
the most gracious of the family of your first-born,

[29] The cattle was suffering from thirst after seven days of siege.
[30] Cf. Deut. 2:9,19.
[31] Cf. Gen. 12:7, etc.; Deut. 32:8.

whose grace is like the grace of ʿAnatu,[32]
whose loveliness is like the loveliness of ʿAthtartu,
whose eye-shadow is the purest lapis-lazuli,
whose eyelashes form a bowl of frothing milk,[33]
(she who) girds me by them,[34]
(whom) I circle because of the clarity of her eyes,
whom Ilu gave (me) in my dream,
the Father of man in my vision,
that she bear offspring to Kirtu,
yes, a boy to the servant of Ilu!''
Kirtu awoke, and it was a dream,[35]
the servant of Ilu awoke, and it was a tremendous experience.
He washed and scrubbed himself,
he washed his hands, his forearms,
his fingers, up to the shoulder.
He entered into the shadow of the shed.
He took a sacrificial sheep in his hands,
a lamb in the two of them.
He took all his offering-bread,
fowl, a sacrificial bird.

IV.

He poured wine into a bowl of silver,
honey into a bowl of gold.
He went up to the top of the tower,
straddled a parapet of the wall.
He raised his hands to heaven,
sacrificed to the Bull, his Father Ilu.

[32] The twin-goddesses ʿAnatu and ʿAthtartu were the goddesses of love.

[33] Cf. Cant. 5:12 and for milk as a metaphor for white: Gen. 49:12; Lam. 4:7. The eyelashes of the girl form the rim of a ''vessel'' filled with the ''frothing milk'' of the white of the eye.

[34] Cf. Cant. 4:9; 6:5.

[35] Cf. Gen. 41:7; 1 Ki. 3:15.

He made Baʿlu descend by his sacrifice,
the son of Daganu by his banquet.
Then Kirtu descended from the roof.
He set out food for the town,
wheat for the daughter of Khuburu.
He baked bread of the fifth,
provisions of the sixth month.
An army was provisioned and it went out,
a mighty host was provisioned,
yes, a strong army went out!
His host was a numerous force,
three hundred myriads.
They went by the thousands—a thunderstorm,
yes, by the myriads—like a rainshower.
After two, there went two,
after three, all of them.
The single man closed his house,
the widow gave a generous contribution,
the sick man took up his bed,
the blind one donated very generously.
Even the newly wed groom was carried off,
he brought his wife to another man,
yes, (his) beloved to a stranger.
They settled like locusts on the field,
like grasshoppers on the fringes of the steppe.
They went for one day and a second.
After sunset on the third,
he reached the sanctuary of Athiratu[36] *of Tyre,*
yes, (that) of the goddess of Sidon.
There Kirtu, the nobleman, pronounced a vow:

[36] Mother-goddess, wife of Ilu. It should be noted that this incident had *not* been predicted by Ilu in column III so that Kirtu has to rely on his own (fallible) judgment.

"As surely as Athiratu of Tyre exists,[37]
yes, the goddess of Sidon:
if I take Hariya into my house,
make the lass enter my residence,
I will give twice her (weight) in silver,
yes, three times her (weight) in gold!"[38]
He went for one day and a second,
a third, a fourth day.
After sunset on the fourth
he reached Great Udumu
and Little Udumu.
He attacked it, the twin-city,
advanced against it, the twin-town.
He assaulted the wood-gatherers in the fields,
yes, the strawpickers at the threshing-floors.

V.

He assaulted the women drawing water at the spring,
yes, those filling (their buckets) at the well.
He stayed quiet for one day and a second,
a third, a fourth day,
a fifth, a sixth day.
Then, at sunset of the seventh,
king Pubâla was unable to sleep,
because of the loud roaring of his bull,
because of the loud braying of his ass,

[37] Cf. Dan. 3:17.

[38] An over-enthusiastic hyperbole (cf. note 21) to which Kirtu will be held literally. Compare Jephtah's vow, Judg. 11:29-39, as well as Shurpu II.74; BWL, 116:1f.; Prov. 20:25; Eccl. 5:4-6.

For a bride more valuable than her weight in gold see H. Granqvist, Marriage Conditions in a Palestinian Village, vol 1, Helsingfors 1931, 75. For a bride worth her own weight in gold, cf. H. Schmidt, P. Kahle, Volkserzählungen aus Palästina, Bd. 2, Göttingen 1930, 58f.

because of the lowing of his plough ox,
the whining of his watch-dog.
[*The*]*n king Pubâla*
cried aloud to his wife:
"*Now listen*, Nuᶜmayu, *wife* [*of Pubâla*]:
I shall send a message to him,
to Kirtu in his night-quarters.
[ ] *his* [ ] *surely prepare*
[ ] *between his arms*
[ ] *surely I shall send*
[ ] *his* [ ]."
He cried aloud [to his lads:]
[' the hon]our of the city[39]
[ ] ...
[ ] *my* [pe]ace-gifts
[ ] ...
[sa]crifice
you [ ]
Then head straight
for Kirtu in his night-quarters.
And say to Kirtu, the nobleman:
'*A message from king Pubâla:*
Take silver and the yellow metal,
gold, together with its finding place,
eternal slaves, teams of three horses,
chariots from the corral, bondmen.
Take, Kirtu, peace-gifts, as many as you want.
Do not harass Great Udumu
and Little Udumu.
Udumu is a gift of Ilu
and a present of the Father of man.

[39] Cf. Isa. 62:2.

Depart, king, from my house,
go away, Kirtu, from my residence!'"

VI.

[ ]
[*The messengers departed, they did not tarry.*]
[*Then they headed straight*]
[*for Kirtu in his night-quarters.*]
They raised their voices and cried:
"*A message from king Pubâla:*
Take silver and the yellow metal,
gold, together with its finding place,
and eternal slaves, teams of three horses,
chariots from the corral, bondmen.
Take, Kirtu, peace-gifts, as many as you want.
Do not harass Great Udumu
and Little Udumu.
Udumu is a gift of Ilu,
and a present of the Father of man.
Depart, king, from my house,
go away, Kirtu, from my residence!"
But Kirtu, the nobleman, answered:
"*Why should I (need) silver and the yellow metal,*
gold, together with its finding place,
and eternal slaves, teams of three horses,
chariots from the corral, bondmen?
No, give me what I do not have in my house,
give me the lady Hariya,
the most gracious of the family of your first-born,
whose grace is like the grace of ʿAnatu,
whose loveliness is like the loveliness of ʿAthtartu,
whose eye-shadow is the purest lapis-lazuli,
whose eyelashes form a bowl of frothing milk,

whom Ilu gave (me) in my dream,
the Father of man in my vision,
that she bear offspring to Kirtu,
yes, a boy to the servant of Ilu!"
The messengers departed, they did not tarry.
Then they headed straight
for king Pubâla.
They raised their voices and cried:
"A message from Kirtu, the nobleman,
a word from the gracious lad of Ilu:

Because the content of the message is known the first 20 lines of the first column of the next tablet can be reconstructed.

Keret II

KTU 1.15

[*Of Kirtu.*[40]]

["*Why should I (need) silver and the yellow metal,*]
[*gold, together with its finding place,*]
[*and eternal slaves, teams of three horses,*]
[*chariots from the corral, bondmen?*]
[*No, give me what I do not have in my house,*]
[*give me the lady Hariya,*]
[*the most gracious of the family of your first-born,*]
[*whose grace is like the grace of ʿAnatu,*]
[*whose loveliness is like the loveliness of ʿAthtartu,*]
[*whose eye-shadow is the purest lapis-lazuli,*]
[*whose eyelashes form a bowl of frothing milk,*]

40 Cf. note 2.

[*whom Ilu gave (me) in my dream,*]
[*the Father of man in my vision,*]
[*that she bear offspring to Kirtu,*]
[*yes, a boy to the servant of Ilu!"*]
[*And king Pubâla answered:*]
(broken, about 20 lines missing)

Probably the missing lines contained a negative response by Pubâla, ending in the following lines:

I.

"the hungry one—she draws (him) by the hand,[41]
the thirsty one—she draws (him) by the hand.
Should our [sla]ves bring her [to you] as a tribute,
to Kirtu in his night-quarters?
A cow moos for its calf,
recently weaned lambs (bleat) for their mothers—[42]
how (then) could the Udumites surrender her?"
And Kirtu, the nobleman, answered:

Of column II about 20 lines are missing. Apparently Pubâla eventually grants Kirtu's request. When the text becomes readable the marriage ceremony has already begun. Interestingly enough such a royal wedding seems to have been contracted in the presence of the gods who have to bless the pair.

II.

[ ]
[Kirtu invited *Ilu*], *the Bull,*
[he called] *Baʿlu*, [*the Al*]*mighty,*

[41] Pubâla is extolling the virtues of Hariya (cf. Isa. 58:7; Ez. 18:7; Hos. 7:5; Prov. 25:21; 31:20; Matth. 25:35). For some parallels from Mesopotamia see K. van der Toorn, Sin and Sanction in Israel and Mesopotamia, Assen 1985, 16.

[42] A cumulative simile, as in Isa. 1:3 and Luke 9:58. Cf. Baal VI (KTU 1.6):ii.6-9,28-30.

[he invited Tharru]*mannu, his Highness Yarikhu,*[43]
  [he called *Kotha*]*ru-and-Khasisu,*[44]
[he invit]ed *Rihmayu,*[45] *his Highness Rashpu,*[46]
  [yes,] *the Assembly of the gods in its triplicity.*[47]
Then Kirtu, the nobleman,
set a dinner *in his house.*
The entering of his house he permitted,[48]
  but leaving was not permitted.
When the Assembly of the gods had arrived,
  Baʿlu, the Almighty, spoke:
[“*How*] *do you think you can leave,*
  o Benevolent, Ilu the good-natured?
Surely you will have to bless Kirtu, the nobleman,
  surely you will have to fortify the gracious lad of Ilu!”
Ilu took the cup in his hand,
  the beaker in his right hand.[49]
Verily he blessed [his servant],
  Ilu blessed Kirtu, the nobleman,
    he fortified the gracious lad of Ilu:

[43] Tharrumannu is one of the gods worshipped in Ugarit. Cf. Baal, note 484. Yarikhu is the moon-god.

[44] The technician and musician among the gods.

[45] A name of ʿAnatu, cf. note 32.

[46] Cf. note 7. It is remarkable that he was invited in spite of the fact that he had taken away one of Kirtu's former wives.

[47] The tripartite pantheon of Ugarit: 1) the older gods like Ilu and his wife Athiratu; 2) their offspring, “the Family of Ilu”/“sons of Athiratu”; 3) the newcomers around Baʿlu, the so-called “Congregation of Baʿlu”.

[48] For the verb “to give” in the sense of “give permission” see Job 9:18; Esther 9:13; CAD (N) 1, 51.

[49] Both in the texts and in the iconography of Ugarit Ilu is usually represented with a cup of wine in one hand, his other hand raised in blessing (cf. A. Caquot - M. Sznycer, Ugaritic Religion, Leiden 1980, Plates VII, VIII, XXII). So the Jewish and Christian “cup of blessing” (1 Cor. 10:16) at the end of the meal has very ancient antecedents.

"The wife you are taking, o Kirtu,
the wife you are taking into your house,
the lass you are bringing into your residence—
may she bear you seven children,
fully eight times may she bear for you![50]
She will bear the lad Yassubu,
who will imbibe the milk of Athiratu,
who will suck the breast of the Virgin ʿAnatu,[51]
the wet-nurs[es of ....]"

About 15 lines at the beginning of column III are missing, but the blessing of Ilu still continues.

III.
"[ ]
[*Be greatly exalted,*] *Kirtu,*
[*among the Saviours*] *of the country,*
[*in the gathered*] *assembly of Ditanu.*[52]
And soon afterwards she will bear you daughters.

[50] Hariya will bear eight children within a span of six years. The poet wants to make clear that her fertility was used to the maximum: 6 times 12 months (III.20ff.) equals 8 times 9 months. So Kirtu will have only two sons, Yassubu and Iluha'u, the rest being girls. This was not exactly what he had wanted, cf. Keret I (KTU 1.14):ii.4f.

Ilu's blessing may be compared to the marriage blessing in Ruth 4:11f. See also Lev. 18:18; Deut. 22:13f.; Jer. 15:9.

[51] Both Athiratu and ʿAnatu were regarded as wet-nurses of the gods. Princelings imbibing the divine milk derived their divine status from it. The same idea is found in Sumerian, Egyptian and Assyrian literature, cf. *e.g.* M. Weippert, OBO (64) 1985, 61-64, 71-78. An ivory panel from the royal bed found in the palace of Ugarit depicts two princes sucking the breasts of a Hathor-like goddess.

[52] The title "Saviours of the country" applied to kings, both dead and alive. The former were invoked during spiritualistic sessions to confer with the living king. Cf. Ritual II and III. Both Kirtu and the dynasty of Ugarit traced their origins back to Ditanu who was possibly an Amorite king of the Old Babylonian period. See also note 54.

She will bear the girl T[........]tu,
she will bear the girl [ ],
she will bear the girl [ ],
she will bear the girl [ ],
she will bear the girl [ ],
she will bear the girl [Thatmanatu].[53]
Be greatly exalted, [Kirtu],
among the Saviours of the country,
in the gathered assembly of Ditanu.
The youngest of them—her I will make a first-born!''[54]
Having pronounced blessings, the gods went,
the gods went to their tents,[55]
the family of Ilu to their dwellings.
And soon afterwards she bore him a son,
yes, soon afterwards she bore him children.
Look! In the seventh year
the sons of Kirtu were just as the (gods) had promised,
also the daughters of Hariya just as (they had promised).
But Athiratu remembered his vow,[56]
yes, the goddess [ ].

[53] The name means ''the Eighth'', Octavia.

[54] This totally unexpected closing sentence, almost an afterthought, forms the joint on which the whole story is hinged. It is possible to read it as a promise—even the youngest girl will obtain a status comparable to that of a first-born. This is not, however, what Ilu meant. Being omniscient he knows that Kirtu will loose all his children but for the youngest girl who in this tragic way will become the first-born and sole heir to the throne. Perhaps the whole story was told to explain a weak link in the genealogy of the royal house of Ugarit.

It is interesting to observe that Thatmanatu was the eighth child and her father's favourite (Keret III (KTU 1.16):i). Stories about the youngest child becoming the legal successor to the throne are by no means rare in the Ancient Near East. In a few well-known cases it was even the *eighth* who became the first (David according to 1 Sam. 16:10, Solomon according to 2 Sam. 3 and 12).

[55] Just as in the Old Testament ''tent'' is often a synonym for ''houses''. See also IV.23 and Baal, note 82.

[56] Cf. Keret I (KTU 1.14):iv.34ff.

And she raised her voice and cried:
"Look here, alas, Kirtu, nobleman!
Woe! Two vow[s you have broken,[57]]
I [too] will break [my obligation!]
(broken)

About 12 lines are missing between the end of col. III and the remainder of col. IV. Athiratu announces that Kirtu will fall gravely ill and orders him to arrange his own funeral banquet.

IV.
[ ]
[ ]
"[You shall cry] aloud to [your wife:]
'Listen, [o lady Hariya!]
Slaughter the fattest of your fatlings,[58]
open the wine-jars!
Call my seventy Bulls,
my eighty Gazelles,[59]
the Bulls of Great Khuburu,
of Little Khuburu.
And serve a banquet,
yes, set a dinner.[60]
Arise, let [a sacrifice be sa]crificed,
let the cup-be[arers] provide [my f]riends with drink!'
The lady Hariya will obey.
She will slaughter the fattest of her fatlings,
she will open the wine-jars.

[57] The two vows made to her, cf. note 38. Cf. Num. 30:13f.,16, etc.
[58] Cf. Aqhat I (KTU 1.17):v.16ff.
[59] Metaphors for the leaders of Khuburu, vassals of Kirtu. Cf. Deut. 33:17; Isa. 23.9.
[60] A funeral banquet served in advance, cf. IV.22f, V.14f. Compare Jer. 16:7f.

She will bring in his Bulls to him,
she will bring in his Gazelles to him,
the Bulls of Great Khuburu,
of Little Khuburu.
They will enter the house of Kirtu,
they will go to the dwelling of weeping,
yes, they will proceed to the tent of bitterness.[61]
They will extend their hand to the bowl,
they will put the knife into the meat.
[*Then*] *lady Hariya* [*will*] *say*:
'[*To ea*]*t, to drink I have called you,*
[*yes, there is a sacrifice for*] *Kirtu, your lord*!' "[62]

About 17 lines missing. Athiratu's instructions are carried out.

[ ]
[ ] house [ ]
[ ] *of the Saviou*[*rs*]
[ ] *the young man.*
[*They ente*]*red* [*the house of*] *Ki*[*rtu*],
[*they went*] *to the dwelling of weeping,*
[*yes, they proceeded to the tent of bitterness*].
They extended their hand to the bowl,
they put the knife into the meat.
Then lady Hariya said:
"*To eat, to drink I have called you,*
yes, to bless the offering of the produce (of the land).
(*But*) *you are weeping over Kirtu,*
like braying bulls!

[61] For the pair "weeping"//"bitter(ness)" cf. Isa. 22:4; 33:7; Jer. 31:15.
[62] Cf. 2 Ki. 10:19; KTU 1.91:2.

You weep over him as if he were dead,
and in your heart you are burying him!
[*Yes,*] *he is only a finger-breadth removed from death,*
Kirtu is going to join Ilu.[63]
Kirtu will reach the sun-set,
our lord the sun-down,[64]
and [*Yas*]*subu will become king over us.*"
But Kirtu, the nobleman, answered:
"*Should a young man* [*become king*] *over us?*[65]
He will [*at*]*tach himself to your wife on* [the roof],[66]
he will force [your daughter] *to leave Great Khuburu,*
(*and*) *Little Khuburu.*
May Ilu the [*Merciful* deliver] *you,*
may he [save you] *by the friendliness* [*of his face*]![67]
Fill [ ]
[ ]."
(broken)

About 18 lines are missing. Probably the guests let themselves be reassured all too soon by Kirtu's scornful words.

VI.

They obeyed their own bowels, their bellies,
again they ate, they drank.
And lady Hariya said:
"*To eat, to drink I had called you,*
there was a sacrifice for Kirtu, your master.

[63] Expressing the belief that the king becomes a god after his death. Cf. K. Spronk, Beatific Afterlife, Neukirchen 1986, 145ff.

[64] The souls of the deceased travelled to the West with the setting sun. There they found the entrance to the Nether World, cf. Baal, note 374.

[65] Cf. Isa. 62:5.

[66] Cf. 2 Sam. 16:22.

[67] Cf. Ps. 37:40.

They went in to Kirtu,
their braying was like the braying of bulls.
In their vision Kirtu was (already) dead,
[ ].''
(broken)

About 45 lines are missing now. The hypocrite bunch of diners is sent home and only the children of Kirtu remain to bewail their father.

Keret III

KTU 1.16

Of Kirtu.[68]

''*Like dogs we prowl through your house,*
like puppies - ah! - through your basement.[69]
Ah father! Woe! Should you die like mortal men?
Alas! Should moaning pass through your basement?
Dirges of father's wife on the heights?[70]
For you, father, the mountain of Baʿlu weeps,[71]
Sapanu, the holy bastion,[72]

[68] Cf. note 2.

[69] The simile is attested in T I, Pl.II.ii.9f.; OIP 2,54:54.

[70] ''Heights'' is in antithetical parallelism to ''basement''. Women used to go out into the mountains to bewail their beloved. See also lines 35 and 43, as well as Judg. 11:37-40.

[71] Weeping mountains are also attested in Gilg. VIII:i.11. See furthermore Am. 1:2 and M. Feghali, Contes, Légendes, Coutumes populaires du Liban et de Syrie, Paris 1935, 107, 116.

[72] Cf. Lam. 2:8.

the mighty bastion groans,
the bastion with its wide crests.
Ah! Is not Kirtu a son of Ilu,
a child of the Benevolent and Qudshu?'' [73]
He entered into (the presence of) his father,
he wept and gnashed his teeth,
he made his voice heard in weeping:
''In your life, our father, we rejoiced,
in your immortality we exulted.
(Now), like dogs we prowl through your house,
like puppies - ah! - through your basement.
Ah father! Should you die like mortal men?
Alas! Should moaning pass through your basement?
Dirges of father's wife on the heights?
How can they say: Kirtu is a son of Ilu,
a child of the Benevolent and Qudshu?
Alas! Do gods die? [74]
Does not a child of the Benevolent live?''
But Kirtu, the nobleman, answered:
''My son, do not weep for me,
do not mourn for me!
Do not use up, my son, the fountain of your eyes,
the marrow of your head for tears. [75]

[73] According to the royal ideology of the ancient world the king was the ''son'' of the highest god. In the Old Testament only rudiments of the idea have been preserved: 2 Sam. 7:14; Ps. 2:7; 45:7f.; 89:27f., and about the divine kingship of foreign rulers: Isa. 14:13; Ez. 28:2,6,9,13f.,16. Qudshu was a name of Athiratu.

[74] The immortality of kings was another element of the royal ideology (cf. 1 Ki. 1:31) and outside Israel it was derived from the divine nature of the office of the king, as it is here. Although the concept of ''dead'' gods was not unknown in the Ancient Near East (cf. Baal, note 403) and although the poet of Ps. 82:6f. mocks at such ideas, the question of the children of Kirtu must have sounded rather provocative, because the central theme of the myth of Baʿlu concerned his death.

[75] Some propose to read ''the water of your head'' on the basis of Jer. 8:23. See, however, P. Xella, SEL 1 (1984) 28-33.

Call your sister Thatmanatu,
the daughter whose passion is strongest:
let her weep and mourn for me![76]
Come back![77]
Do not (yet) talk to your sister!
Speak by night,
for I know how compassionate your sister is.
Let her not (yet) turn on her water-works[78] *in the fields,*
the outpouring[79] *of her soul on the heights.*
[*You*] *should await the setting of lady Shapshu,*[80]
and the turning in of the great Lamp.[81]
Then speak to your sister Thatmanatu:
'*Kirtu has sacrificed a sacrifice,*
the king has served a banquet.
Take your nose in your hand,
your windpipe in (your) right hand.[82]
Go! Sing on the heights!
Bring your Lord[83] *silver*
as your personal gift, and gold for all (of us)!'"
Then the hero Iluha'u
took his nostrils in his hand,
his throat in his right hand.
And he drew near to the pool.

[76] The youngest daughter had a special status as a weeping woman, cf. Dumuzi's Dream, 12-14.

[77] The boy is already running to fulfil the wish of his father. Cf. Ps. 9:4.

[78] For tears as water, cf. Jer. 8:23; Ps. 119:136; Lam. 1:16; 2:18f.; 3:48.

[79] The metaphor of the first colon is elaborated in the second one, cf. Gen. 2:10; Ex. 17:6; 2 Ki. 2:21; Isa. 41:18; 58:11; Ps. 107:33,35; 2 Chr. 32:30.

[80] The Sun-goddess.

[81] Cf. Gen. 1:16.

[82] A universal gesture of anguish.

[83] "Lord" is a designation of the personal god of Thatmanatu here. Cf. Isa. 51:22. Perhaps this personal god was Baᶜlu, cf. Baal, note 435.

When he arrived, it had darkened.
(*When*) *his sister went out to draw water*,[84]
he directed his nostrils towards the tell.
(*When*) *her face came out of the gate*,
her brother hit his nose.
And she let her [*jug*] *shatter on the ground*,[85]
[*before*] *her brother she wept.*[86]
"[*Do you know that*] *the king is ill*?
[*That*] *Kirtu, your lord, is sick*?"
[*And*] *the hero Iluha'u* [*answered*:]
"[*I know that*] *the king is ill*,
[*that K*]*irtu, your lord, is sick.*
[*Kirtu has sa*]*crificed a sacrifice*,
[*the king has*] *served a banquet.*

II.

"*Enter* [ ]
and go into [ ]
you go into [ ]
and [ ]
the girl [ ]
for K[*irtu*]
like Ilu [ ]
and that he would [*live*]
Who [ ]
wife [ ]
your brother [ ]

Refresh [*your*] *si*[*re with wine*][87]
and pour [*oil of pacification*]."

[84] At dusk, Gen. 24:11,13.
[85] Cf. Isa. 21:9; Eccl. 12:6.
[86] Cf. Deut. 1:45; Judg. 20:23; 2 Ki. 13:14; 22:19, etc.
[87] Cf. Gen. 19:32ff.; Ps. 36:9; 1 Tim. 5:23.

She offered [Kirtu, her father,] drink,
she refreshed [her] sir[e with wine,]
and with mixed wine she refreshed [the servant of Ilu].
She drew near to her brother Iluha'u:
"*Why did you bring me [to our father?]*
How many months is it that he has been ill?
How many that Kirtu has been sick?"
And the hero Iluha'u answered:
"*It is three months (now) that he has been ill,*
four that Kirtu has been sick.[88]
Perhaps Kirtu has reached
[sunset] *and grave.*"[89]
She shrieked with a [loud v]oice,[90]
she shrieked, raised [her] cry.
Like women pounding the gate [she beat her breast],
like women in labour [she wailed].
Nakedly, without [her garment] of linen [she went],
wretchedly [she], without a vest.[91]
And until her orphan-brother was sated with her weeping,
she wept before the hero Iluha'u.
She raised her voice, shrieked,
she raised her cry,
she wept and gnashed her teeth,
made her voice heard in weeping:
"*In your life, our father, we rejoiced,*
in your immortality we exulted.
(Now), like dogs we prowl through your house,
like puppies - ah! - through your basement.

[88] For the sequence "three-four" cf. Am. 1:3, etc.
[89] Cf. Job 3:22.
[90] Cf. Deut. 27:14, also Gen. 39:15,18; Isa. 40:9; 58:1, etc.
[91] Gestures of mourning, cf. Mic. 1:8.

Ah father! Should you die like mortal men?
Alas! Should weeping pass through your basement?
Dirges of father's wife on the heights?
Alas! Do gods die?
Does not a child of the Benevolent live?
For you, father, the mountain of Baʿlu weeps,
Sapanu, the holy bastion,
the mighty bastion groans,
the bastion with its wide crests.
Ah! Is not Kirtu a son of Ilu,
a child of the Benevolent and Qudshu?"
Then she entered into (the presence of) her father,
she entered [his bedro]om.
Again she [ ]
the neighbours [ ]
Weeping [ ]
the mountain [ ]
he mourned [ ]
Then [ ]
[ ]
(broken)

About 33 lines are missing between col. II and col. III. As a result of the mortal illness of king Kirtu nature is suffering from drought (the death of prince Aqhatu has a similar effect according to the Legend of Aqhat, III:i). An unknown person is performing magic to make it rain.

III.

He poured out oil of [pacification]
and said: "*Please refresh earth*[92] *and heaven!*"

[92] Cf. Isa. 34:7; 55:10.

He went around to the fringes of the land,
to the emmer of the furrowed lowland.[93]
There was rain of Baʿlu on the earth,
yes, rain of the Most High on the field!
The rain of Baʿlu was sweet on the earth,
yes, the rain of the Most High on the field!
Sweet to the wheat in the furrow,
like perfume in the tilth,
like fragrant herbs on the ridge.
The ploughmen raised their heads,
upwards the growers of grain.[94]
Spent was the grain on the bottom of their buckets,
spent was the wine in their skins,
spent was the oil in their [ ].[95]
The house of Kirtu [ ]
(broken)

About 43 lines are missing between the end of col. III and the beginning of col. IV. The long awaited rain is a good omen reflecting a favourable development in the world of the gods. It is probably Baʿlu who proposes to convene the assembly of the gods to resolve Kirtu's problem.

"Ilu listens to your word,
your utterance [is wise] like that of Ilu,
you are wise like the Bull, the Benevolent.

[93] Emmer-corn was sown at the fringes of the field because it was less valuable than wheat so that a little damage due to traffic and animals was not a serious loss. Cf. Isa. 28:25.

[94] Compare the "growers of flax" in Isa. 19:9.

[95] Cf. 2 Ki. 4:2; Hos. 2:10,24; 1 Chr. 2:14.

Call Ilishu, the herald of Ilu,
Ilishu and his wife, the heraldess of the goddesses.[96]
Like gravel, like crumbs [let the (gods) be gathered![97]]"
He called Ilishu, the herald of Ilu,
Ilishu the herald of the house of Baʿlu,
and his wife, the heraldess of the goddesses.
Then the Benevolent, Ilu the good-natured said:
"*Listen, o Ilishu, herald of Ilu;*
Ilishu, herald of the house of Baʿlu,
and (*let listen*) *your wife, the heraldess of the goddesses*:
Go up to a parapet of the building.
Croak, announcer, three times to the defiled (*earth*),[98]
likewise you, little bird, [*to*],
call loudly to the mountain.
[*fa*]*tlings* [ ]
(broken)

In the next 27 lines the convening of the gods must have been described in great detail.

V.

Entered [(names of deities)],
entered [ ],
entered [ ].
And [ ] stood up [and spoke]
in the Assembly of [*the gods*:]

[96] These so-called "heralds" took the shape of ravens, cf. lines 14f. Cf. Baal, notes 100, 133; Eccl. 10:20; Hos. 8:1.

[97] Cf. Baal II (KTU 1.1):iv.11 and also Hab. 1:9. The simile points to the very large number of gods, like the simile "sand" in the Bible: Gen. 22:17; Josh. 11:4; Ps. 78:27; Rom. 9:27; Hebr. 11:12; Rev. 20:8.

[98] Cf. Num. 35:33; Jer. 3:1,9; Mic. 4:11; Ps. 106:38. The earth had been "defiled" by the drought, cf. Isa. 24:4f.

"O Athiratu [ ]
in your hand [ ].
Twice her (weight) [in silver I will give],
three times her (weight) [in gold]!"[99]
And the Benevolent, Ilu the good-natured, said:
"Who among the gods is able to cast out the disease,
to expel the illness?"
None of the gods answered him.
For the second, for the third time he asked:
"Who among the gods is able to cast out the disease,
to expel the illness?"
None of the gods answered him.
For the fourth, for the fifth time he asked:
"Who among the gods is able to cast out the disease,
to expel the illness?"
None of the gods answered him.
For the sixth, for the seventh time he asked:[100]
"Who among the gods is able to cast out the disease,
to expel the illness?"
None of the gods answered him.
And the Benevolent, Ilu the good-natured, said:
"Return, my children, to your dwellings,
to your exalted thrones.
I myself shall perform magic and shall create,[101]
I shall create a female being able to cast out the disease,
to expel the illness!"

[99] Cf. Keret I (KTU 1.14):iv.42f. Apparently a god (Baʿlu ?, cf. note 83) is offering Athiratu satisfaction.

[100] Cf. Baal, note 264.

[101] Ilu was the creator-god, cf. Baal, notes 81, 95, 209. Here he is shaping a good genius from clay, cf. Baal, note 320 and Job 33:6. See also Incantation III, notes 24, 27.

He filled his palms with the best of loam,
he pinched off [clay] such as is used by the potter.
[He formed] one able to remove [the disease],
one able to [ ] the Tunnanu,[102]
[ ] the Tunnanu.
[ ]
[ ]
[ ]
In the bre[ast of Lady Athiratu she] was moulded,
[in the heart of Ilu she was formed.]
[Ilu took] a cup [in his hand],
a bea[ker in his right hand].
"*You, Sha[ᶜtiqtu,*[103] *drive out],*
drive out [the disease of K]irtu,
dr[ive out his illness]!"
He put a primrose in her hand,
in the mouth of Sha[ᶜtiqtu (he put) a powerful charm[104]].
"*[Go into the c]ity,*
[let your charm fly] through the town,
let the flow[erstalk fly through the city]!
The disease [ ]
the illness [ ]."
(broken, about 8 lines missing)

VI.

"*Motu*[105] *be the one who is shattered,*
Shaᶜtiqtu the one who prevails!"

[102] Sea-monster, cf. Baal, notes 59 and 480. Here the incorporation of the demoniacal power of the disease, cf. Incantation I.

[103] The name of the winged creature means "She-who-causes-to-pass" and there is an apparent play of words in the Ugaritic text.

[104] Cf. En.el. IV.61f.

[105] God of death.

And Shaʿtiqtu departed,
soon she would enter the house of Kirtu.
Weeping she appeared and went in,
shrieking she went inside.
Through the town she let her charm fly,
through the city she let her flowerstalk fly.
She rolled the primrose into a brush,
whenever the illness was on his head,
she washed him clean of sweat.
She opened his throat so that he would eat,
his gorge so that he would dine.
Motu was the one who was shattered,
Shaʿtiqtu the one who prevailed.
And Kirtu, the nobleman, called out,
he raised his voice and cried:
"*Listen, o lady Hariya!*
Slaughter a lamb, for I want to eat,
a special one, for I want to dine!"
Lady Hariya obeyed.
She slaughtered a lamb, and he ate,
a special one, and he dined.
Look! After one day and a second,
(then) Kirtu returned to his dais,
he sat down on the throne of his kingship,
on the seat of the throne of (his) dominion.
Yassubu also returned to the palace.
And his soul instructed him:[106]
"*Go to your father, Yassubu,*
go to your father and speak,
repeat to the gr[acious lad of Ilu]:
'*Listen and let ⌊your ear⌋ be attentive!*

[106] Cf. Ps. 16:7.

The most munificent you drive away,
but the usurer you allow to stay!
You have let your hand fall down in slackness:
You do not judge the case of the widow,
you do not try the case of the impatiently waiting.
Ah! You are a brother of the bed of sickness,
you are a companion of the bed of illness.[107]
Abdicate the kingship, let me be king!
(Abdicate your) dominion, let me sit (on the throne)!' "
The lad Yassubu departed,
he entered into (the presence of) his father.
He raised his voice and cried:
"Now listen, o Kirtu, nobleman,
listen and let your ear be attentive!
Ah! The most munificent you drive away,
but the usurer you allow to stay!
You have let your hand fall down in slackness:
You do not judge the case of the widow,
you do not try the case of the impatiently waiting,[108]
you do not drive the robbers away for the poor!
Before your (eyes) you do not let the orphan eat,
(nor) behind your back the widow.
Ah! You are a brother of the bed of sickness,
you are a companion of the bed of illness.
Abdicate the kingship, let me be king!
(Abdicate your) dominion, let me sit (on the throne)!"
But Kirtu, the nobleman, answered:
"O son, Horonu[109] *break -*
Horonu break your head,
(and) ʿAthtartu, consort of Baʿlu, your skull!

[107] Cf. Isa. 53:3; Ps. 41:4; Job 17:14; Prov. 31:8.
[108] Cf. 2 Sam. 15:2-4, also Judg. 16:16; Zech. 11:8.
[109] God of black magic, master of demons. Cf. Myth and Ritual (KTU 1.100):61ff.

May you fall down at the height of your years,
in the prime of your strength, and yet be humbled!"[110]

At least one tablet must have followed, otherwise this tablet would have been provided with a full colophon, as is the case with Baal VI (KTU 1.6). Now there is only a marginal note: "*Scribe*: *Ilimilku, the officiant*", as wịth the tablets Baal IV (KTU 1.4) and Aqhat I (KTU 1.17).

It has to be assumed that the death-curse on Yassubu became effective and that Kirtu eventually lost all his other children but one (Thatmanatu). Thus the youngest girl became his sole heir, as had been predicted beforehand (Keret II (KTU 1.15):iii.16). Kirtu may be termed a tragic sufferer, victim of the whims of the gods. What Ilu had given him was taken by Athiratu as a result of one over-enthusiastic vow. Kirtu refused to accept the gold of Ilu and Pubâla, but in the end he did not have the gold to pay Athiratu her due. Kirtu was a favourite of the highest god of the Ugaritic pantheon, a "son" of Ilu even. But Ilu uses his power as a creator only to make Kirtu a witness of the destruction of his family all over again.

[110] Cf. Baal III (KTU 1.2):i.7-9, with notes 128-130.

LEGEND: AQHAT

Aqhat I

KTU 1.17

Like the legend of Keret the legend of Aqhat (Aqhatu)[1] deals with questions of life and death, and with the fate of man who all too often appears to be the victim of divine caprice. The scribe was Ilimilku, the same high-priest who wrote the myth of Baal and the legend of Keret. Although he gave the poem the title "Of Aqhatu", the main personage is king Dani'ilu who obtains a son, Aqhatu, at the intercession of Baᶜlu, but eventually loses the lad as the result of a vicious plot of ᶜAnatu, the wife of Baᶜlu. Dani'ilu is a righteous sufferer who in the end has no alternative but to invoke the spirits of the dead to embrace his son once more.[2]

The Aqhat-series consisted of at least four tablets. Three have been partially preserved; of the fourth only fragments from two different tablets are known.[3] About 10 lines are missing from the first column of tablet I.

I.

1* [ ]

[1] Both may be classified as "heroic poetry". For a number of parallels to themes of the legend of Aqhat see C. M. Bowra, Heroic Poetry, London 1952; T. H. Gaster, Thespis, 2nd ed., Garden City 1961, 330-376; J. C. L. Gibson, SVT 28 (1975) 60-68; P. Xella, Problemi del mito nel Vicino Oriente Antico, Napoli 1976, 61-91.

[2] For an attempt to evaluate the religious ideas underlying the legend of Aqhat see OTS 24 (1986) 1ff.

[3] Formerly these fragments (KTU 1.20-22) were often regarded as belonging to a different text.

And then Dani'ilu,[4] *the Saviour's man,*[5]
then the hero, the Harnamite man,[6]
gave the gods consecrated oblations[7] *to eat,*
gave the sons of Qudshu[8] *consecrated oblations to drink.*
In his sackcloth[9] *he went up*[10] *and lay down,*
in his loincloth[11] *- and so he spent the night.*[12]

4 Cf. Ez. 14:14,20; 28:3; Jub. 4:20; 1 Henoch 6-7, with J. Day, VT 30 (1980) 174ff.

5 "Saviour" or "Healer" was an epithet of Baʿlu, the weather-god, as the leader of the deified spirits rising from the Nether World when he returned to his mountain. Cf. notes 275ff.; Incantation V, note 1; K. Spronk, Beatific Afterlife, Neukirchen 1986, 145ff.

The title "the Saviour's man" characterizes Dani'ilu as a special protégé of Baʿlu.

6 Aqhat III (KTU 1.9):iv.22-25,29-31 proves that *hrnmy* is an epithet of Dani'ilu (*pace* M. Dietrich - O. Loretz, UF 10 (1978) 69f.) because there we have the following equations:

VERB	OBJECT	INDIRECT OBJECT
yqry/qry	*dbḥ*	*ʾilm/lʾilm*
yšʿly/šʿly	*dġṯh*	*bšmym*
	dġṯ hrnmy	*dkbkbm*

so that *hrnmy* is a genitive. As a result we have *mt hrnmy* next to *hrnmy* just as we have *ʾyš ʿbry* next to *hʿbry*, *ʾyš yhwdy* next to *hyhwdy*, *ʾyš knʿny* next to *hknʿny*, etc., in Hebrew.

Probably *hrnm* is Harnam/Arnam mentioned in Egyptian sources. It has been identified as modern Hermil on the Orontes, cf. W. Helck, Die Beziehungen Ägyptens zu Vorderasien, 2. Aufl., Wiesbaden 1971, 200, 317 (following W. F. Albright). For less likely identifications see D. N. Freedman - F. I. Andersen, BASOR 198 (1970) 41 (*hhrmwnh* in Am. 4:3); M. C. Astour, RSP II:viii.37 (*byt hrm/n* in Transjordan, cf. Num. 32:36,43; Josh. 13:27); M. H. Pope, in: Ancient Near Eastern Studies in Memory of J. J. Finkelstein, New Haven 1977, 166 (valley of Hinnom near Jerusalem); B. Margalit, in: G. D. Young (ed.), Ugarit in Retrospect, Winona Lake 1981, 141f. (somewhere in the vicinity of Kinnereth).

7 Cf. UF 7 (1975) 172f. Others translate: "girded" which results in an unusual syntactic construction, necessitates the assumption of a suppressed object, and is morphologically dubious (cf. S. Segert, Basic Grammar, 54.28).

8 Qudshu was a name of Athiratu, mother of the gods and wife of the supreme god Ilu.

9 It follows from Baal III (KTU 1.2):iii.20 that under normal circumstances people used to undress and wash for the night. Therefore it must be regarded as a token of self-neglect when people went to bed fully dressed.

A close parallel may be found in the Hittite tale of Appu. He too does not have

Look! For one day and a second,
Dani'ilu gave the gods consecrated oblations,
gave the gods consecrated oblations to eat,
gave the sons of Qudshu consecrated oblations to drink.
For a third, a fourth day,
Dani'ilu gave the gods consecrated oblations,
gave the gods consecrated oblations to eat,
gave the sons of Qudshu consecrated oblations to drink.
For a fifth, a sixth day,
Dani'ilu gave the gods consecrated oblations,
gave the gods consecrated oblations to eat,
gave the sons of Qudshu consecrated oblations to drink.[13]
In his sackcloth Dani'ilu,
in his sackcloth he went up and lay down,
in his sackcloth — and so he spent the night.
Then, on the seventh day[14]
Ba^{c}lu drew near in his mercy:[15]

a son and sacrifices to mollify the gods. Then he lays down "with his boots on", an outrageous act expressing total indifference. Cf. J. Siegelová, Appu-Märchen und Ḫedammu-Mythus, Wiesbaden 1971, 4f.

The Ugaritic *ṣt* indicates a garb of coarse fabric, like the Arabic *ṣaydān* (Kazimirski I, 1390; the root is attested in Ugaritic and we have to assume the development **ṣīdtu* > **ṣittu* or **ṣītu*). The same garb is called *śaq* in Hebrew, see especially 1 Ki. 21:27; Isa. 58:5; Joel 1:13; Esth. 4:3.

[10] His bed, cf. Gen. 24:21; 49:4; Deut. 28:29, etc.

[11] Loincloth was a mourner's garb, cf. Baal, note 390; Keret, note 91.

[12] Apparently hoping for a revelation, cf. Baal VI (KTU 1.6):iii.1-13; Keret I (KTU 1.14):i.31ff.; Gen. 28:11-17; 1 Sam. 3:9, etc.

[13] Apparently such monotonous repetitions were not considered bad style.

[14] See for the seven-day pattern, Baal, note 264.

[15] A similar construction occurs in Keret I (KTU 1.14):i.37f. Nevertheless it is likely that *bḥnth* means "in his mercy", cf. UF 7 (1975) 172; 14 (1982) 160, with Ex. 22:26; 34:6; Ps. 77:10; Jonah 4:2; Neh. 9:31, etc. and also, in this case, Prov. 14:31.

"Is Dani'ilu, the Saviour's man, miserable?[16]
Is the hero, the Harnamite man, sighing?[17]
Because he has no son[18] *like his brothers,*
nor root[19] *like his kinsmen?*
He has no son like his brothers,[20]
nor root like his kinsmen!
He has given the gods consecrated oblations to eat,
has given the sons of Qudshu consecrated oblations to drink.[21]
Please bless him, o Bull Ilu, my father,[22]
fortify[23] *him, o Creator of creatures!*[24]
And let him have a son in (his) house,
a root within his palace,

[16] Unintroduced direct oration is a frequent phenomenon in the literature of Ugarit. The parallel in Keret I (cf. note 15) suggests that the verse has to be read as a question. The term "miserable, poor" is a conventional description of the situation of any supplicant, cf. G. J. Botterweck, ThWAT I, 38ff.

[17] Cf. Ps. 6:7.

[18] Cf. Num. 27:4; 2 Sam. 18:18; 1 Chr. 4:27.

[19] A common metaphor for offspring, cf. KAI No. 14:11; 43:16; 222:C.24f.; Isa. 5:24; 11:1,10; 53:2; Dan. 11:7.

[20] The repetition indicates that Baʿlu is now addressing his father-in-law Ilu who as the Creator-god is the only one able to bless people with children. Cf. Keret II (KTU 1.15):ii.14ff.

In the O.T. El blesses the patriarchs with offspring: Gen. 12:2; 16:11; 17:2,5; 35:11; 49:25. It is noteworthy that Hos. 9:10-16 mocks at Baal's inability to bless his followers with offspring.

[21] Sacrifices as an argument for blessing, as in Ritual IV (KTU 1.119):29ff. Cf. Nah. 2:1; Ps. 50:14f.; 76:11f.

[22] See note 20 as well as Baal, notes 75 and 77.

[23] *Pace* D. Pardee, UF 10 (1978) 249ff., cf. W. A. Ward, UF 12 (1980) 357ff. The semantic development may be reconstructed as follows: "to be bitter" (attested), metaphorically "to be painful" (attested) and "to prevail" (cf. Akkad. *marāru*), which gave rise to "to expel" (attested) and "to be/make strong" (attested). So there is only one root *mr(r)* in Ugaritic.

[24] Cf. Baal, note 209; also 2 Sam. 18:18.

someone to set up the stelae of his ancestral gods,[25]
in the sanctuary the marjoram[26] *of his clan,*
someone to make his smoke come out from the earth,[27]
from the dust the Protectors[28] *of his place,*
someone to put the lid on the abuse of his revilers,[29]
someone to chase away those who do something to him,[30]
someone to grasp his hand when he is drunk,
someone to support him when he is sated with wine,[31]
someone to serve his emmer-corn[32] *in the house of Baʿlu,*
and his portion[33] *in the house of Ilu,*[34]

[25] See for this translation, The Bible World. Essays in Honor of C. H. Gordon, New York 1980, 184f., n. 66.

[26] Flowers on cane-like stems, the biblical "hyssop". It was an apotropaic against evil forces, especially death. Cf. Ex. 12:22; Lev. 14:4,6, 51f.; Ps. 51:9; John 19:29; UF 17 (1986) 407-409.

[27] In the spiritualistic rituals performed at Ugarit the spirits were possibly made visible as "shadows" (KTU 1.161:1) or "smoke" (cf. Aqhat II (KTU 1.18):iv.24f.,36; RIH 78/20:3). Kings and other members of the royal family were buried in subterranean vaults.

[28] Protective genies, the Lares of Ugarit. The Nether World was a place where dust abounded.

[29] The sea-god Yammu has to perform this filial duty for his father Ilu according to Baal II (KTU 1.1):iv.23f. and later on the same may have been true of Ilu's other son Motu, cf. Baal V (KTU 1.5):iv.25 with note 362. Compare also Ps. 63:12; Prov. 27:11.

An alternative translation is: "one who shuts the jaws of his revilers", cf. Ps. 63:12.

[30] Cf. Gen. 20:9; 22:12; 31:43; Ex. 14:11; Deut. 22:26; 1 Sam. 3:17; 2 Sam. 3:35; Mic. 6:3; Ps. 56:5; Job 35:6, etc., against Y. Avishur, UF 17 (1986) 54f.

[31] This filial duty is performed for Ilu by Thakumanu and Shanuma in Myth and Ritual III (KTU 1.114):15-19. See also Isa. 51:18 and Gen. 9:18f. as well as Wisdom of Amenenope, Ch. 26.

[32] Alternatively: "his share, slice".

[33] Cf. 1 Sam. 1:4f.

[34] The poet pressupposes two major temples in the city of Dani'ilu, one of Ilu and one of Baʿlu. This reflects the situation in Ugarit itself (the so-called temple of Daganu is actually the temple of Ilu). This may be an indication that Ilimilku was not merely the scribe, but also the author of the legend of Aqhatu.

someone to plaster his roof on a day when it is muddy[35]
someone to wash his equipment on a foul day!''[36]
Ilu took the cup in his hand.[37]
He blessed Dani'ilu, the Saviour's man,
fortified the hero, the Harnamite man:
''(*By*) *my soul*![38] *May Dani'ilu, the Saviour's man, live*!
(*By*) *my life*! *May the hero, the Harnamite man*, (*live*)!
[*May he tra*]*vel smoothly*![39]
Let him go up and lay down.[40]
While he is kissing his wife, there will be conception,
while he is embracing her, there will be heat.[41]
She who is going to bear will ach[*ieve conception*],
heat for the Sa[*viour's man*]!
And he will have a son in (*his*) *house,*
a root within his palace,
someone to set up the stelae of his ancestral gods,
in the sanctuary the marjoram of his clan,
someone to make his smoke come out from the earth,
from the dust the Protectors of his place,

[35] Roofs were plastered with mud and had to be rolled with a cylinder of stone after a heavy shower. Cf. Prov. 27:15 and for Rabbinic parallels: Y. Avishur, UF 17 (1986) 56.

[36] Cf. Baal, note 208, and W. G. E. Watson, UF 8 (1976) 376.

[37] Cf. S. B. Parker, Maarav 2 (1979) 19-22 and Keret, note 49.

[38] Abbreviated formula introducing an oath, cf. PRU 3, RS 8.333:20-23 (pp. 7f.); Am. 6:8. Cf; J. Pedersen, Der Eid bei den Semiten, Strassbourg 1914, 136, 141.

[39] Aqhat III (KTU 1.19):iv.39 has the same formula in the feminine form. The word *ʾarḫ* is an absolute infinitive, a form peculiar to blessings. Literally the formula means ''may he/she travel marrow-like'', *i.e.* be successful on the way of life. Compare the following phrases from Hittite texts: ''Your ways should be anointed for you with oil'' and ''I have spread out marrow (and) fine oil. now walk over it'' (V. Haas, Or 45 (1976) 210). See furthermore Job 29:6.

[40] Echo of lines 4ff.

[41] A term for orgasm which was thought to be a sure sign of conception. The same is said of Ilu himself in Myth and Ritual I (KTU 1.23):51,56. For ''to be in heat'' cf. Isa. 57:3; Ps. 51:7.

someone to put the lid on the abuse of his revilers,
someone to chase away those who do something to him,
someone to grasp his hand when he is drunk,[42]
someone to support him when he is sated with wine,
50 *someone to serve his emmer-corn in the house of Baˁlu,*
and his portion in the house of Ilu,
someone to plaster his roof on a day when it is muddy,
someone to wash his equipment on a foul day.''
(broken)

About 12 lines are missing between the reconstructed end of column I and the reconstructed beginning of column II. Probably it is Baˁlu who announces the good news to his protégé.

II.

1a ''*You will have a son in (your) house,*
a root within your palace,
someone to set up the stelae of your ancestral gods,
1 *in the sanctuary the marjoram of your clan,*
someone to make your smoke come out from the earth,
from the dust the Protectors of your place,
someone to put the lid on the abuse of your revilers,
someone to chase away those who do something to you,
someone to serve your emmer-corn in the house of Baˁlu,
5 *and your portion in the house of Ilu,*[43]
someone to grasp your hand when you are drunk,
someone to support you when you are sated with wine,
someone to plaster your roof on a day when it is muddy,
someone to wash your equipment on a foul day.''

[42] From this line on the rest of the column has been reconstructed.
[43] Note that this verse and the next have changed places as compared to the earlier versions of the same speech.

Dani'ilu's face rejoiced,
and his brow above radiated.[44]
His frown disappeared, and he laughed,
he placed his foot on the footstool,
he raised his voice and cried:
"*I can sit down now and rest,*
and my soul can rest in my breast,[45]
for a son will be born to me[46] *like my brothers,*
and a root like my kinsmen,
someone to set up the stelae of my ancestral gods,
in the sanctuary the marjoram of my clan,
someone to make my smoke come out from the earth,
from the dust the Protectors of my place,
someone to put the lid on the abuse of my revilers,
someone to chase away those who do something to me,
someone to grasp my hand when I am drunk,
someone to support me when I am sated with wine,
someone to serve my emmer-corn in the house of Baʿlu,
and my portion in the house of Ilu,
someone to plaster my roof on a day when it is muddy,
someone to wash my equipment on a foul day!"
Dani'ilu arrived at his house,
Dani'ilu proceeded to his palace.
The Kathiratu[47] *entered his house,*
the daughters of Hilalu,[48] *the swallows,*[49]

[44] For a similar description of the opposite reaction see Baal I (KTU 1.3):iii.32-35. Cf. Ps. 104:15.

[45] Cf. Baal, note 443.

[46] Cf. Myth and Ritual V, note 13; Gen. 4:18; 10:1,21; 17:17, etc., also 1 Ki. 13:2; Isa. 9:5; Luke 2:11.

[47] Goddesses of matrimony, see Myth and Ritual V, notes 12, 33-37.

[48] Hilalu was the god of the crescent moon, cf. Myth and Ritual V, note 33 and Isa. 14:12.

[49] Like many other divine beings in the pantheon of Ugarit, the Kathiratu could take the shape of birds, in this case swallows who in Syria as elsewhere seek the neighbourhood of man.

And then Dani'ilu, the Saviour's man,
then the hero, the Harnamite man,
slaughtered an ox for the Kathiratu,
he gave the Kathiratu to eat,
and gave the daughters of Hilalu, the swallows, to drink.
Look! For one day and a second,
he gave the Kathiratu to eat,
and gave the daughters of Hilalu, the swallows, to drink.[50]
For a third, a fourth day,
he gave the Kathiratu to eat,
and gave the daughters of Hilalu, the swallows, to drink.
For a fifth, a sixth day,
he gave the Kathiratu to eat,
and gave the daughters of Hilalu, the swallows, to drink.
Then, on the seventh day,
the Kathiratu left his house,
the daughters of Hilalu, the swallows,
those who measure[51] *the happiness of the bed of conception,*[52]
the delight of the bed of childbirth.
Dani'ilu sat down [to] count her months.[53]
One month, a second month passed,
a third, a fourth.[54]
[*Then, the t*]*e*[*nth*] *month arrived,*[55]
[*and the*] *wo*[*m*]*b* [*of Danatiya*[56] *was opened.*[57]]
(broken)

[50] Note the antithetical correspondence with column I.

[51] A metaphor for apportioning, cf. Isa. 65:7. Compare Loves II, note 27; Loves III, note 3.

[52] Cf. Ez. 23:17, also Appu (cf. note 9), Obv. II.6-8.

[53] Cf. Atra-hasis I.278f.; Job 39:2.

[54] Cf. Appu, Rev. III.6-8; V. Haas, Hethitische Berggötter, Mainz 1982, 161.

[55] The restoration of "tenth" rests on the traces and the parallels Atra-hasis I.281; Appu, Rev. III.8f.

[56] Wife of Dani'ilu,

Unfortunately the columns III and IV have been destroyed entirely. In all 150-160 lines of poetry are missing between the end of column II and the beginning of column V. Probably they contained an elaborate account of the birth, naming, blessing and early youth of the son Aqhatu.[58] Then one day Kotharu-and-Khasisu, the technician among the gods, appears to Dani'ilu in a dream.[59]

"[ ]
I shall bring you a loaded *bow*,[60]
  I shall take four arrows with me."[61]
And look! On the seventh day,
then Dani'ilu, the Saviour's man,
  then the hero, the Harnamite man,
arose,[62] *sat in front of the gate*,[63]
  before[64] *the dignitaries*[65] *on the threshing-floor.*
He judged the case of the widow,
  he tried the case of the orphan.[66]

[57] The restoration rests on the traces and the parallel Atra-hasis I.282, cf. Gen. 29:31; 30:22.

[58] His name may mean "the very obedient" which is not exactly an apt description of his independent behaviour in column VI.

[59] Cf. Keret I (KTU 1.14):i.35ff.

[60] Restoration based on the traces and Isa. 5:28; 21:15. See also notes 83 and 84 below. With the reading *ṯmn* possibly "as a present".

[61] Cf. the Egyptian phrase "he grasped his bow and gripped four arrows at the same time" (UF 1 (1969) 227; 7 (1975) 181).

[62] Cf. Num. 23:24; Prov. 30:32 and as said of YHWH rising to act as Judge: Isa. 33:10; Ps. 7:7; 94:2.

[63] Cf. 1 Ki. 22:10; Job 29:7. The threshing-floor served as a city-square, market-place and court of justice (cf. Am. 5:10).

[64] Literally "under" because they were standing while the judge was seated (cf. Job 29:7-17). Compare the expression "standing over" for "standing by" a seated person (*e.g.* Baal III (KTU 1.2):i.21; 1 Ki. 22:19).

[65] The title is also attested in non-literary texts from Ras Ibn Hani. Cf. Judg. 5:13; Jer. 14:3; Ps. 16:3, etc.

[66] The typical task of a righteous king, cf. Keret III (KTU 1.16): VI.33,46-50; 2 Sam. 15:2-4; Isa. 1:17, also Ps. 72:2,4,12-14; Isa. 11:4; etc., and for other parallels from the Ancient Near East RSP I:i.47; F. C. Fensham, JNES 21 (1962) 129-139.

When he raised his eyes, he saw,
over a thousand acres,
ten thousand square miles,[67]
he was sure he saw Kotharu coming,
and saw Khasisu approaching.
Look! He brought the bow!
Look! He had the four arrows with him!
And then Dani'ilu, the Saviour's man,
then the hero, the Harnamite man,
cried very loudly to his wife:
"Listen, o lady Danatiya![68]
Prepare a lamb from the stock[69]
for the appetite of Kotharu-and-Khasisu,
to the liking of the Skilful Craftsman.
Give the god[70] *something to eat, give (him) something to drink,*
regale, honour him,
the lord of all Divine Egypt!"[71]
Lady Danatiya obeyed.
She prepared a lamb from the stock
for the appetite of Kotharu-and-Khasisu,
to the liking of the Skilful Craftsman.
Then Kotharu-and-Khasisu arrived.
In the hands of Dani'ilu he layed the bow,
he put the arrows on his knees.[72]

[67] See Baal, note 68.

[68] Compare Keret II (KTU 1.15):iv.1-5,15f.; III (KTU 1.16):vi.15ff., and also Gen. 18:6-8.

[69] Literally "a lamb from the ram(s)", cf. Num. 15:11 for a comparable expression and M. Dietrich-O. Loretz, UF 17 (1986) 100f.

[70] The text has duals because Kotharu-and-Khasisu was a double god, a kind of two-unity, a type of gods frequently attested with the Canaanites.

[71] Cf. Baal, note 101.

[72] Possibly this scene is depicted on a Syrian seal published by C. H. Gordon, Iraq 6 (1939) Pl. V, no. 39, where ʿAnatu is already waiting in the background to take possession of the bow.

Then lady Danatiya
gave the god something to eat, gave (*him*) *something to drink,*
she regaled, honoured him,
the lord of all Divine Egypt.
Kotharu departed to his tents,[73]
the Skilful departed to his dwellings.
And then Dani'ilu, the Saviour's man,
then the hero, the Harnamite man,
named (*and*) *blessed the bow,*[74]
yes, for Aqhatu[75] *he named it*:
"*The first spoils of your chase, o son,*
[*bring me*] *the first spoils of your chase,*[76]
look, the first spoils of your chase in my palace!"
(broken)

About 20 lines are missing between the end of column V and the beginning of column VI. Dani'ilu has invited the gods to a banquet in celebration of the naming of the bow.[77] During the meal the splendid weapon excites the envy of ʿAnatu who is a great huntress herself.

There is a deep symbolism in the putting of the bow on the lap of Dani'ilu. Doubtlessly the poet has described in the lost preceding columns how the newly born Aqhatu was placed on the knees of his father. This was the formal way of accepting a child (cf. *e.g.* Appu, Rev. 10; M. Weippert, OBO (64) 1985, 61-64, 71-78; Gen. 30:3; Num. 11:12; Ruth 4:16). The bow that is placed on his lap now will take the place of his son, in a way it becomes a "daughter" of Dani'ilu (cf. En.el.VI. 87). See also the ensuing naming-ceremony, with note 74.

[73] See Baal, note 82; Keret, note 55.

[74] Cf. Baal, note 178.

[75] Cf. Gen. 30:28 for the construction.

[76] Cf. Gen. 27:1-4.

[77] Compare Baal II (KTU 1.1):iv.28ff., a dinner in honour of the naming of Yammu.

VI.

"[ ]...[ ]
[Eat of any b]read,
[and drink of] any [foaming wine]!"[78]
Aga[in they ate, the gods drank],
[with] a salted knife [they carved a fatling].[79]
[They drank beakers of] wine,
from golden cups [the blood of trees].[80]
[They fille]d [the cups of silver],
beaker after beaker.[81]
[And look! The c]up-bearers [came again],
and they brought up must [to the house of Baʿlu],
[to the house of Ilu until n]o ready-made wine was left,[82]
on the carrying-net [ ].
[Aqhatu l]owered an arrow,[83]
[the bow, the creation of Kotharu,] was loaded.[84]
When she[85] *raised her eyes, she saw (it).*

[78] The formula has been taken over from a ritual for the New Year festival, cf. Myth and Ritual I (KTU 1.23):6. The references to the carving of a fatling (note 79), to the counting of the years (note 100), to the revivification of the dead (note 101) and to the part of the myth of Baʿlu containing the mythological prototype of the celebration of Baʿlu's return from the Nether World (note 102) are further indications that the poet wanted to situate this episode at the New Year festival.

[79] Cf. Baal I (KTU 1.3):7f., in the part of the myth describing the prototype of the New Year festival. Also, however, Baal V (KTU 1.5):iv.12ff.

[80] Cf. Baal, note 227.

[81] For the construction cf. Jer. 4:20. In KTU 4.279, a list of rations of wine for the first five days of the New Year festival, the ration for the first day is stated to be "jar after jar" (in KTU 4.279:1 the word *yn* accidentally dropped out, see PRU 2, no. 86).

[82] Cf. Baal, note 361.

[83] To load the bow that was bent with the foot, cf. Ps. 11:2; 18:35; 58:8. Cf. note 60.

[84] Cf. Lam. 3:12.

[85] ʿAnatu.

[How beautiful it was!]
  [*Beautiful the sh*]*ape of its stave,*[86]
    [*its arrow*] *like lightning.*[87]
[*Its string shook*],[88]
  just as the lightning makes the Flood shudder.[89]
[*ʿAnatu would like to lower*] its [*arrow*],
  would like to load the bow, the creation of Ko[*tharu-and-Khasisu*],
    [*the ti*]*ps of which were curved like a snake.*[90]
[*She threw her beaker*] *on the ground,*
  she spilled her cup [*in the dust*].
She raised her voice and cried:
''*Now listen, o hero Aqhatu*!
Ask for silver and I shall give it to you,[91]
  gold and I shall send it to you,
but give your bow to the Virgin ʿAnatu,
  your arrows to the Wanton Widow of the Nations!''[92]
But the hero Aqhatu answered:
''*The ash trees from the Lebanon are excellent,*[93]
  the sinews from wild oxen are excellent,
    the horns from mountain-goats are excellent,
      the tendons from the hocks of a bull,[94]
        the canes from the divine[95] *marshes are excellent.*

[86] Cf. En.el., VI.84.

[87] Cf. STT 19:54; Ps. 18:15; 144:6; Zech. 9:14.

[88] For vibrating strings see Isa. 14:11; 16:11, and for the same root in connection with the roaring of the sea or the Flood: Isa. 17:12; 60:5; Jer. 5:22; 6:23; 50:42; 51:42,55; Ps. 46:4.

[89] Cf. Ps. 77:17-19.

[90] Curved tips are characteristic of composite bows.

[91] Cf. 1 Ki. 3:5; Ps. 2:8; Matth. 7:7 (par.); Mark 6:23; 11:24; Luke 6:30.

[92] Cf. Baal, notes 33-34.

[93] What follows is an enumeration of the materials used in the construction of a composite bow with arrows. Cf. myth of Anzû, ANET, 516a.

[94] The text should not be emended arbitrarily at this point. The translation ''most splendid of'' is impossible, because it would require *ʾadrt qrnt, ʾadr mtnm* and *ʾadr qnm*.

Give (them) to Kotharu-and-Khasisu;[96]
let him make a bow for ᶜAnatu,
arrows for the Wanton Widow of the Nations!"[97]
And the Virgin ᶜAnatu answered:
"Ask for life, o hero Aqhatu!
Ask for life and I shall give it to you,
immortality and I shall send it to you![98]
I shall make you count the years with Baᶜlu,
with the son of Ilu[99] *you will count the months!*[100]
Just as when Baᶜlu brings to life,[101] *he is served—*
(when) he has brought to life, then one serves and gives him to drink,

Too many irregularities have to be assumed by the proponents of such a translation. See also note 96.

[95] Possibly "divine" is used in the sense of "vast", but it may just as well describe the area as "marvellous". Cf. Baal I (KTU 1.3):vi.12f. (par.); VI (KTU 1.6):i.65; Ps. 36:7; 80:11.

[96] In a command following a list of objects the objects may be omitted because they are self-evident, cf. 2 Ki. 4:42 (after a list of victuals).

[97] The impudence of Aqhatu's reply is characteristic of the spiritual attitude of the time. Cf. OTS 24 (1986) 1ff.

[98] On this ultimate offer and its implications see K. Spronk, Beatific Afterlife, Neukirchen 1986, 151ff. Furthermore Ps. 21:5; John 10:28; 17:2; 1 John 5:11,16.

[99] Cf. Baal, note 75.

[100] A reference to time-reckoning according to the New Year festivals celebrating Baᶜlu's return to his throne, cf. Baal, note 474.

With the Hittites a festival for the Weather-god marked the beginning of the year (H. Otten, RLA 3, 483). According to KAR no. 174:Rev. III.26 it is "Adad who measures the year" (for the root in connection with time-reckoning see CAD (M)1,8; Hebr. *middāh*). According to a late Phoenician-Greek tradition Zeus (= Baal) had received from Kronos (= El) "all the measures of the whole creation", because it was he who was "the originator of times" (R. A. Rosenberg, Bibl 53 (1972) 108).

[101] A reference to the revivification of the spirits of dead kings and heroes in the course of the New Year festival. Cf. Baal, note 478, Keret, notes 52 and 63, also notes 5, 27-28, and below the fragments of Aqhat IV. Furthermore K. Spronk, *op.cit.* (note 98), 158, also for the important formula "(to be) with Baᶜlu". As in many other respects these ideas reached the N.T. through the channels of the folkreligion of Palestine. Cf. Rev. 20:4,6, also Matth. 20:21-23; 26:27-29.

a gracious lad who answers his (wishes)[102]
improvises and sings before him—
so I too can bring to life
the hero Aqhatu!"
But the hero Aqhatu answered:
"Do not fabricate (lies), o Virgin,
because to a hero your fabrications are rubbish![103]
Death in the future, what can take (it) away?
What can take away death in the days to come?[104]
Glaze[105] *will be poured on my head,*
potash[106] *on top of my skull,*
[then] I too shall die the death of every man,[107]
o yes, I too shall certainly die!
And I have still something else to say:
The bow is a warrior's [weapon],
shall womenfolk now go hunting [with it]?"[108]
ᶜAnatu laughed [al]oud,
but in her heart she devised [a vicious plan].[109]

[102] It is absolutely clear that the goddess is referring here to Baal I (KTU 1.3):i. (see also note 177). What she is offering Aqhatu is nothing less than a place in the divine world comparable to that of Ganymedes, cf. Baal, note 17.

See for the formula "answer his (wishes)" 1 Ki. 12:7; Hos. 2:17, and for the long parenthesis Isa. 55:10f.

[103] Cf. Baal, note 309.

[104] Cf. Prov. 24:11 as well as Num. 23:10; Eccl. 6:12. Contrast 1 Cor. 3:22; 15:19,37; 1 Tim. 4:8; 6:19.

[105] The word denotes both a bluish-grey glaze (cf. Prov. 26:23) and a vessel covered with this substance. Here it is used in the first meaning as a metaphor for greying hair, cf. Hos. 7:9.

[106] Metaphor for white hair. See note 158 below.

[107] Cf. Num. 16:29; Ps. 82:7.

[108] On the bow as an unsuitable weapon for women, cf. N. Oettinger, Die militärischen Eide der Hethiter, Wiesbaden 1976, 11. It is noteworthy that ᶜAthtartu/ᶜAnatu, though being a great huntress, only uses spear and shepherd's club to kill the game (KTU 1.92 and ANEP, 473).

[109] Cf. Isa. 32:6; Job 36:13.

"Return to me, o hero Aqhatu,
return to me, and I shall return to you![110]
If ever I encounter you on the path of transgression,[111]
[find you] on the path of presumption,
I myself shall make you fall beneath my feet,[112]
o gracious lad,[113] *strongest of men!"*[114]
She shuffled her feet and flew up from the earth.[115]
Then she headed straight
for Ilu at the fountain-head of the two Rivers,
in the middle of the bedding of the two Floods.
She appeared in the encampment of Ilu
and entered the camp of the King, the Father of Years.
At the feet of Ilu she bowed and fell down,
prostrated herself and honoured him.
She railed at the hero Aqhatu,
[cursed[116] *the child*[117] *of Dani]'ilu, the Saviour's man.*
And [the Virgin ʿAnatu] said,
[she raised] her voice and cried:
"That one [ ]
may Aqhatu ...[ ]!
[ ]...[ ]
(broken)

Edge: [*Scribe: Ilimilku, the Shubanite, pupil of Attanu,*] *majordomo.*[118]

110 Cf. Baal, note 77.

111 Cf. Deut. 25:18; Jer. 12:1; Ps. 107:17; 119:101,104,128; Prov. 4:14; Matth. 7:13 (par.).

112 Cf. Ps. 18:39; 110:1; Matth. 22:44 (par.).

113 Clearly a reference to her earlier words, line 32.

114 Obviously mocking at his boastful words of lines 40f.

115 See with the following passage Baal, notes 81-84.

116 Cf. Prov. 30:10.

117 Akkad. *kudādu*, Von Soden, AHw, 925; Hebr. *kydwd*, Job 41:11 (HAL, 449f.).

118 Cf. Baal, notes 481-484.

Aqhat II

KTU 1.18

About 13 lines are missing. ʿAnatu is still denouncing Aqhatu before her father Ilu.

"[ ]
[ ]
[ ]
[ ] his [ ]
I shall break [his bow]!"[119]
[And the Bull Ilu,] her fa[ther, answered:]
"*Are [you] an[gry, Virgin ʿAnatu, my daughter?*"][120]
And [the Virgin ʿAnatu] answered:
"*Let not the sons of your mansion, o Ilu,*[121]
let not the daughters of your mansion rejoice,
let not [the children of your palace re]joice!
I shall make sure I seize them with my right hand,
I myself shall strike (them) with my long, mighty arm!
I shall strike you on your skull,
make your grey hair run with blood,
the grey hair of your old age with gore!
Then let Aqhatu [save you, o Ilu],
and let the son [of Dani'ilu] deliver you, [my father],
and let him help you from the hand of the Virgin [ʿAnatu, o Ilu]!"[122]

[119] Cf. Aqhat III (KTU 1.19):i.3f. The breaking of a bow is a favourite theme in the literature of the Ancient Near East, cf. N. M. Waldmann, JQR 69 (1978) 82-88.

[120] Cf. Baal II (KTU 1.2):i.38,43; VI (KTU 1.6):v.21; RIH 78/20:15.

[121] With this and the following lines cf. Baal I (KTU 1.3):v.20-25, with the notes 88-90.

[122] Cf. Ps. 37:40 for the parallelism between the verbs. ʿAnatu's contempt for her father, the nominal head of the pantheon, betrays the eroded esteem for the gods in general which is characteristic of the Ugaritic religion towards the end of the Late Bronze Age. Cf. OTS 24 (1986) 1ff.

And the Benevolent, Ilu the good-natured, answered:
"*[Depart, my daughter]!*
I know you, my daughter, (I know) that you are like a man,[123]
and that among goddesses your scorn is unequalled.
Depart, my daughter!
[Execute] the vicious plan of ⌊your⌋ heart,[124]
seize what is in your bosom,[125]
realize[126] *what is in your breast.*
Surely your opponent will be threshed,[127]
⌊your], Virgin ʿAnatu!"
Then she headed straight
for [the house] of the hero Aqhatu.
Over a thousand a[cres she],
[ten thousand] square miles,
and the Virgin ʿAnatu laughed.
She raised her voice and cried:
"*Now listen, o hero Aqhatu!*
You be my brother,
and I shall be ⌊your⌋ si[ster]![128]
[You, brin]g your seven groomsmen.[129]

[123] Cf. Baal, note 91.

[124] Cf. 2 Sam. 7:3 and note 109 above.

[125] Cf. 1 Sam. 2:16.

[126] Cf. Ex. 10:1f.; Ps. 104:20, also Ps. 13:3; Prov. 26:24.

[127] Cf. Mic. 4:13, also Am. 1:3; Hab. 3:12 and for other parallels from the Ancient Near East: M. Dijkstra, Gods voorstelling, Kampen 1980, 324, n. 20.

[128] A formal proposal of marriage, cf. Baal, note 69; KTU 1.96:2; KAI, No. 264; Song of Songs 4:9ff.; 8:1; Tobit 7:12; UF 7 (1975) 194; M. H. Pope, Song of Songs (AB, 7C), Garden City 1977, 481f., 657.

Neither the context (cf. I.25, 28;IV.15) nor the passages cited in support of it favour the proposal of H. H. Dressler, UF 11 (1979) 211-217.

[129] Seven trusted friends who assisted the groom with regard to the arrangements to be made in connection with the wedding. It is certain that this custom existed at Ugarit as well as in Mesopotamia, cf. UF 7 (1975) 194. Among the Arab peasants of Palestine it is still the bridegroom who arranges and pays for the meal in the bride's house. His friends help him to transport the supplies to the village of the bride. Cf.

Let [them] not [come near the house of] my father,
I have fled [from my father],
[I am living in Abi] luma.[130]
Come, you should come to hunt,
[ ]
a happy man[131] [ ]
[ ]
I shall teach you to h[unt],
[ ]
[Go] to the city of Abiluma,
Abiluma, the city of his Highness Yarikhu,[132]
the tower of which is [a thousand acres on hig]h,[133]
[ten thousand square m]iles their town.
[ ]
I shall make my[self up]
[Aqhatu],
[I want to c]har[m the son of Dani'ilu]''
(broken)

A very large portion of text, about 173 lines, is missing now. It must have contained much more than a mere description of the journey of Aqhatu to the city of Abiluma. In addition to this the poet may have given an account of the preparations for the wedding and perhaps a description of an encounter between the lovers during the hunting party.

H. Granqvist, Marriage Conditions in a Palestinian Village, vol. 2, Helsingfors 1935, 18ff.

[130] *Nomen est omen*, cf. notes 135, 217, 218, 223, 230. Although the name probably meant something like ''meadows'', it could be understood to mean ''mourners'', cf. Gen. 50:11. No certain identification of the town is possible at the moment.

[131] Cf. Aqhat IV:fragm. 3, iv.19 (KTU 1.22:I.19); Ps. 1:1; etc.; Gen. 30:13.

[132] Moon-god.

[133] Cf. CAD (E) 111a.

IV.

[ ] … [ ]
[ ] *broke* [ ]
[ ] *red lumps of two spans,*
[pieces of two cubits][134]
[the Virgi]n ʿAnatu for all [ ].
The Virgin ʿAnatu departed.
Then she headed straight
for Yattupanu,[135] *the warrior of the Lady.*[136]
She raised her voice and cried:
"*Yattupa,*[137] *the hero Aqhatu is staying*[138]
in the city of Abiluma,
Abiluma, the city of his Highness Yarikhu!
How can Yarikhu fail to renew himself
with the h[orn of his (left) side],
with the horn of his right side,
with the friendly [horns] on his skull?"[139]
And Yattupanu, the warrior of the Lady, answered:

[134] Cf. Baal V (KTU 1.5):i.5f.

[135] *Nomen est omen.* The name probably means "He will tear out" (W. G. E. Watson, UF 8 (1976) 373), cf. lines 23ff. and note 130.

[136] Outside this formula the title designates ʿAnatu in Aqhat III (KTU 1.19):iv.59 and KTU 1.24:61. See also KTU 1.13:7 "your warriors" and KTU 1.22:'I'.9 "the warriors of ʿAnatu".

An alternative translation was proposed by B. Margalit, UF 8 (1976) 181ff.; 15 (1983) 97 ("Sutaean warrior"). One would expect **sty* instead of *št* though.

[137] Shorter form of the name.

[138] Cf. 2 Sam. 11:1; 16:3, etc.

[139] For the cusps of the moon see CAD (Q) 137f. Usually weddings were celebrated around the time of the Full Moon which was needed for illumination, cf. Granqvist, *op.cit.* (n. 129), 32f. To plan such a feast at the New Moon is in itself an indication of sinister intentions. But ʿAnatu does not even want to wait for the slightest waxing of the moon, everything has to happen in pitch-darkness. All this explains why Yattupanu sees through her plot immediately.

"Listen, o Virgin ʿAnatu!
(Now) you can slay him for his bow!
Do not let him live, (for) his arrows!
The gracious hero has set the banquet,
and [his lads] have stayed behind in the encampment,
so let us celebrate the wedding [with him]!"
And the Virgin ʿAnatu answered:
"Return, Yattupa,
and [I shall return] to you! [140]
I shall put you like an eagle in my game-bag,
yes, like a kite in my pouch. [141]
When Aqhatu sits down to eat,
yes, the son of Dani'ilu to dine,
eagles will hover over him, [142]
a flock of kites will be watching.
Between the eagles I (myself) shall be hovering. [143]
I shall release you over Aqhatu.
Strike him twice on the skull,
three times above the ear. [144]
Pour out (his) blood like a murderer, [145]
like a butcher on to his knees.

[140] Cf. note 110.

[141] Hunting with partially tamed birds of prey is attested in the Ancient Near East. See also Baal III (KTU 1.2):iv. Just as in Egypt and Israel the different species of prey-birds were not distinguished properly in Ugarit.

[142] ʿAnatu could transform herself into a black kite, cf. Incantation V (KTU 1.108):7.

[143] Cf. Gen. 1:2; Deut. 32:11.

[144] *I.e.* on the temple, the most tender spot of the skull. Cf. Aqhat III (KTU 1.19):ii.38.

[145] Designation of evil demons roaming in the desert, cf. A. H. Mustafa, AcOr 29 (1975) 104; J. C. de Moor, JEOL 27 (1981-82) 111f.

Let his soul depart like wind,[146]
his life like spittle,
like smoke[147] *from his nose!*
Woe! Alas! his heart
I cannot let live!"
She took Yattupanu, the warrior of the Lady.
She put him like an eagle in her game-bag,
like a kite in her pouch.
When Aqhatu sat down to eat,
the son of Daniʾilu to dine,
eagles were hovering over him,
a flock of kites was watching (him).
Between the eagles ʿAnatu was hovering.
She released him over Aqhatu.
He did strike him twice on the skull,
three times above the ear.
He poured out his blood like a murderer,
like a butcher on to his knees.
His soul departed like wind,
his life like spittle,
like smoke from [his nose].
ʿAnatu [ ] at the silencing of his heart,
[at the] of Aqhatu.
And she wailed for the bo[y of Daniʾilu]:
"I can[not] create,[148]
yet [have slain you] for [your bow],
(for) your arrows, [you] could not be allowed to l[ive]!

[146] The simile seems to indicate that the Canaanites were aware of the fact that they were using metaphorical language when they talked about "spirits" (*rḥm*). Cf. Gen. 35:18; Ps. 146:4; Song of Songs 5:6.

[147] Cf. note 27.

[148] Only Ilu was able to create (cf. Keret, note 101) and, to a far lesser extent, Baʿlu according to Aqhat III (KTU 1.19):iii.12f.

[ ]
and the birds that have s[lain you] have vanished!''

Nothing is missing between tablet II and tablet III. The first column of tablet III is notoriously difficult and many different translations have been proposed.[149]

Aqhat III

KTU 1.19

Of Aqhatu.[150]

[*ᶜAnatu*] *was distressed,*
[*she let herself fa*]*ll amidst the* [*ce*]*lestial beings,*[151]
ᶜA[*natu*] *fell* [*flat on*] (*her*) [*b*]*reast.*
The bow broke,
[*and the ly*]*re*[152] *broke* [*too*].
There the Virgin ᶜAnatu [*wept*],
she sat down [*on the ground*].[153]
''*Raise,*[154] (*o*) *furrow,*[155] *a cry*: '*How bitter!*'[156]

[149] Of the more recent attempts to make sense of the passage we mention: B. Margalit, UF 16 (1984) 119-128; G. del Olmo Lete, Interpretación de la mitología cananea, Valencia 1984, 125-131; A. Caquot, SEL 2 (1985) 93-114.
[150] Heading for library purposes. Cf. Baal, note 397; Keret, notes 2,40,68.
[151] The gods, Aqhat III (KTU 1.19):iv.23f. Cf. note 241 below.
[152] ᶜAnatu's beloved instrument which she used to press to her breast, cf. Baal I (KTU 1.3):iii.4f. (restored, cf. Baal, note 39).
[153] Cf. Ps. 137:1 (also v.2!) and Baal, note 388.
[154] Cf. Jer. 7:29; Ez. 19:1; 27:2; 28:12; 32:2.
[155] Cf. Gilg. VIII.i.13 and Job 31:38. Alternatively: ''*hills*'', cf. Keret, note 71.
[156] Cf. Isa. 33:7, also Ez. 27:30f.; Esth. 4:1.

He whose hands were like a singer's,
whose fingers were like a musician's,[157]
whose 'mouth-stones' were like potash,[158]
his teeth have been affected,
and decay has taken over the whole body,[159]
rotting[160] *like the heart of old trees.*
And two young men[161] *are repeating*[162] *a recitation,*[163]
his two young men are singing about Aqhatu,
they are saying: 'How bitter, how bitter!'
Like a dangerous viper from a wall,[164]
like a dog deserving the stick,[165] *I have slain him.*
Thus I have slain him for his bow,
for his arrows, I did not allow him to live.
Yet his bow has not been given me ...
And through [his] death the young ear of corn is parched,[166]
the first of the summer-fruit droops,
the ear in its sheath!''[167]

[157] Singers were not subjected to manual labour and ordinary people raved about their delicate hands. Cf. G. R. Castellino, Two Šulgi Hymns, Roma 1972, 48f.:168.

[158] As white as potash. Cf. note 106.

[159] Reading *bʿmm*.

[160] Pun on the word for ''potash'' in the preceding verse.

[161] The two personal attendants of Aqhatu who are on their way to Dani'ilu. Cf. col. II.27-44.

[162] With regard to the form *ṯn*, see Baal IV (KTU 1.4):vi.3 (// *ʿny* in line 1).

[163] Masculine *mn* next to feminine *mnt*.

[164] Cf. Incantation III (RIH 78/20):3; Am. 5:19; Eccl. 10:8.

[165] Cf. Myth and Ritual III (KTU 1.114):7f. + 12f. Alternatively, one might consider the emendation *lḥṭ⟨ʾi⟩h* (haplography): ''*for his sin*''.

[166] Syr.Arab. *ḥammeṣ* ''dry up, be parched'' (Denizeau, 123f.). The term used for the young ear of corn is a highly technical one indicating an ear having leaves but no farina. At this stage it is extremely vulnerable to heat. If the extremity of the ears becomes too dry and tough, the corn will remain unproductive. Therefore farmers hope the latter rains of March and April will arrive exactly on time so that the hot and dry sirocco will not destroy their standing crop. Cf. Gen. 41:6 as well as the references in AOAT 16,151,175.

[167] As appears from the sequel (lines 30ff., 39ff., II.12ff.) the passage describes the

And then Dani'ilu, the Saviour's man,
then the hero, the Harnamite man,
arose, sat in front of the gate,[168]
before the dignitaries on the threshing-floor.
He judged the case of the widow,
he tried the case of the orphan.
[*When*] *he* [ ],
[*over a thousand acres*],
[*ten thousand square mile*]*s*,
[*he was sure he saw Pughatu*[169] *approaching*],
[*saw Pughatu*] *coming.*
When she raised her eyes, she saw,
[*the barley*] *on the threshing-floor was drying up,*
[*the*] *wilted,*
the blossom of the vi[*neyards*] *drooped.*[170]
Over the house of her father
eagles were hovering,
a flock of kites was watching.[171]

severe drought setting in as a result of the death of prince Aqhatu. Nature mourns, just as in the case of the mortal illness of Kirtu (cf. Keret III (KTU 1.16):iii). Compare 2 Sam. 21:1.

[168] See the notes 62-66 with this passage.

[169] Daughter of Dani'ilu. Her name simply means "Girl".

[170] All this is possible only if the poet wanted to situate this episode in spring when spells of sirocco threaten the fruit-trees. Cf. note 166 and Baal, notes 288, 335. Additional proof for a dating in spring: the grain is still standing in the field (II.13), which excludes summer and autumn, and the black kite, a migratory bird, is in the country, which excludes the winter.

Consequently, about half a year has elapsed since the first exchange between ᶜAnatu and Aqhatu (Aqhat I (KTU 1.17):vi, cf. notes 78, 79, 100-102). In other words, there is a certain correspondence between the time of the year reflected in the narrative about the death of Baᶜlu and the present episode of the legend of Aqhat. The fear expressed in lines 42ff. betrays that this correspondence has been woven into the story quite deliberately. See also the notes 177, 210, 236, 240, 242, 249, 263.

[171] Obviously the very same birds that had killed Aqhatu. Yet the father still knows nothing. Pughatu, however, interprets the birds of prey as a sure sign of death. Cf. Matth. 24:28.

Pughatu wept from her heart,[172]
she shedded tears from her bosom.
The garment of Dani'ilu, the Saviour's man, was rent,[173]
the mantle of the hero, the Harnamite man, (was rent)!
Then Dani'ilu, the Saviour's man,
adjured the clouds,
cast a spell[174] *on the heat:*
"Let the clouds pour rain on the summer-fruit,[175]
let dew fall on the grapes!
Would Baʿlu fail[176] *for seven years?*
For eight the Rider on the Clouds?[177]

[172] *I.e.* spontaneously, cf. 1 Ki. 12:33; Ez. 13:2, 17; Neh. 6:8.

[173] Because mourners used to rend their own clothes (cf. Gen. 37:29,34; Num. 14:6; 2 Ki. 5:7; Ezra 9:3, etc.) Pughatu cannot be the subject of the verb. The poet describes the succession of ominous signs Pughatu notices while she is approaching her father. Only at close range she sees the rent in her father's mantle.

[174] Cf. UF 6 (1974) 495f. According to a multilingual vocabulary from Ugarit the Akkadian *arratu* "curse" is the equivalent of the Ugaritic *ṣlt* "incantation" (attested in KTU 1.119:34). This does not exclude a translation "to adjure", as B. Margalit, RB 89 (1982) 418ff. seems to think.

The word translated by "spell" may occur in Hos. 10:8; 1 Sam. 15:23; Zech. 10:2. Normally, however, its magic overtones made it tantamount to "wickedness" in the Bible. Cf. HAL. 21f.

[175] In spring the so-called latter-rains were eagerly awaited. If they failed to come in time and if the heat of the sirocco prevailed, the consequences were dire. Cf. notes 166 and 170 as well as Baal, notes 240, 256, 278.

[176] Alternatively "bind you", cf. W. G. E. Watson, UF 8 (1976) 377, with reference to Job 26:8. In that case one would expect *yṣrkm* however. Moreover Prov. 30:4 and Eccl. 11:3 suggest that it was normal for the rain to be bound up in the clouds. See also the next note.

[177] Again Ilimilku, the scribe of these tablets, betrays that he is also the author of the seasonal myth of Baʿlu (cf. note 102). The reference is to the seven years Baʿlu was confined to the realm of death, Baal VI (KTU 1.6):v.8f. During that period he was powerless (*ʾill*, cf. Baal, note 376). So Dani'ilu expresses the fear that the disasters of the pristine age of myth will repeat themselves in his time.

Without dew,
without drizzle,
without surging of the two Floods,[178]
without the delight of the voice of Baʿlu?''[179]
Surely the garment of Dani'ilu, the Saviour's man, was rent,
the mantle of the hero, the Harnamite man.
Dani'ilu cried aloud to his daughter:

''Listen, Pughatu, (you) who carry water on your shoulder,[180]
who scoop up dew from the wool,[181]
who know the course of the stars![182]
Saddle a he-ass,
harness a male (animal).

[178] For dew and drizzle as gifts of Baʿlu see Baal I (KTU 1.3): ii.38-41. With regard to the two Floods see Baal, note 81. Abundant rain was explained as an overflowing of the Upper Flood. At the same time wells and rivers seemed to indicate an upsurging of the Lower Flood (cf. Gen. 49:25; Deut. 33:13). It is a matter of dispute whether the same word ''upsurging'' may be read in 2 Sam. 1:21, cf. J. P. Fokkelman, ZAW 91 (1979) 290-292 *versus* T. L. Fenton, VT 29 (1979) 162-170. With the parallel in Deut. 32:2 see BiOr 31 (1974) 5f.

With the typical Oriental love of hyperbole Dani'ilu deliberately exaggerates the situation. Not only the latter rains, but also the dew of summer, the drizzle of autumn and the surging of sources and wells of winter might fail, and that for seven years.

[179] His thunder which heralded showers, cf. Baal, notes 280-281.

[180] A task of women in the evening, cf. Keret I (KTU 1.14):iii.9f. (par.); III (KTU 1.16):i.49-54; Gen. 49:15; John 4:7.

[181] Early in the morning, before the sun could evaporate it, dew was collected with the help of fleeces of wool (for *šʿr* ''wool'' next to *šʿrt* see M. Liverani, OrAnt 11 (1972) 193f.), as attested by Judg. 6:36-38 and Galen, Opera omnia, ed. C. G. Kühn, VI.738ff. This dew was collected because of its sweetness (''honey-dew'', cf. UF 7 (1975) 590ff., with reference to Ex. 16:13f.,31; Num. 11:9; 1 Sam. 14:25). For a slightly different interpretation see M. Dietrich-O. Loretz, UF 17 (1986) 95-98.

[182] Somebody who comes home late (note 180) and rises very early (note 181) has an excellent opportunity to study the stars. It is likely that especially the phases of the Pleiades were observed intently because their disappearance from the night sky heralded the dry season. Cf. Baal, note 372.

Put on my reins[183] *of silver,*
my straps of gold!"
Pughatu obeyed, (she) who carried water on her shoulder,
who scooped up dew from the wool,
who knew the course of the stars.
Then she saddled the he-ass,
then she harnessed the male (animal).
Then she lifted up her father,
put him on the back of the he-ass,
on the most comfortable part[184] *of the male (animal)'s back.*
Dani'ilu u⟨rged⟩ it on,
he went around[185] *his* cracked *land.*[186]
He saw a bulging shoot[187] *in the* cracked *land,*
he saw a shoot among the lean stalks.[188]
He embraced the bulging shoot and kissed (it).[189]
"I beseech (you gods)![190]
May (this) bulging shoot rise from the cracked *land,*
may (this) bulging shoot rise from the lean stalks!
Herb, may the hand of the hero Aqhatu collect you,
put you within the granary!"[191]

[183] Cf. Baal, note 229.

[184] Cf. Hos. 10:11.

[185] In the technical sense of making a regular inspection tour around a corn field. Cf. Baal V (KTU 1.5):vi.3-5; Keret III (KTU 1.16):iii.3.

[186] The translation is uncertain. Cf. Baal, note 444.

[187] This word enabled scholars to restore the original text of 2 Ki. 4:42, cf. UF 7 (1975) 203f. See also Isa. 53:2.

[188] Cf. Gen. 41:6.

[189] Magic by touching, cf. H.-P. Müller, UF 1 (1969) 92; 1 Ki. 17:21; 2 Ki. 4:29, 34f.; Mark 6:56 (par.); Acts 20:10, etc.

[190] Cf. Ex. 32:11; 1 Sam. 13:12, etc., with B. Margalit, UF 16 (1984) 140f. The elliptic expression became a petrified form in Biblical Hebrew: 2 Ki. 5:3; Ps. 119:5.

[191] The picture of the totally unsuspecting father who is embracing a promising young plant instead of his son is a masterful touch in this tragic tale. In the end Dani'ilu will only be granted the right to kiss the intangible spirit of his boy, see Aqhat IV, fragm. c, iv.4 (KTU 1.22:I.4).

He urged his (animal) on,
he went around his fissured field.[192]
He saw an ear of corn in the fissured field,
an ear of corn rose from the shriveled stalks.
He embraced the ear of grain and kissed it.
"*I beseech (you gods)*!
May (this) ear of corn rise from the fissured field,
may (this) ear of corn rise from the shriveled stalks!
Herb, may the hand of the hero Aqhatu collect you,
put you within the granary!"
The word had scarcely left his mouth,
his speech, his lips,
when she raised her eyes[193] *and saw*:
there was no p[eace] in the walking of the two lads![194]
They came back[195] *alone*![196]
[*Surely*] *they came back, but he*[197] *did not come back*!
Twice they struck (their) skull,
three times above the ear.[198]

[192] Actually a field with "clods or similar undesirable formations" which is in need of irrigation, cf. CAD (A)1, 275f.

[193] *I.e.* Pughatu, presumably leading the ass of her father (cf. Baal IV (KTU 1.4):iv.15ff.). Grammatically within the realm of possibility is the translation: "or when he (Dani'ilu) raised his eyes."

[194] From a great distance she saw that they were deeply disturbed. Cf. Isa. 48:22; 57:21; Jer. 6:14; 12:12; 30:5; Ez. 7:25; 13:10,16; Ps. 38:4; 2 Chr. 15:5, as well as 1 Sam. 20:13,42; 2 Ki. 5:19.

[195] For the nuance "to appear, come forth", as said of messengers, cf. CAD (A)2, 365b as well as Zech. 5:5; 6:1.

[196] Cf. 2 Sam. 18:24-26.

[197] *Scil.* Aqhatu.

[198] With vivid gestures the lads recount the murder of their master (cf. Aqhat II (KTU 1.18):iv.33f.), but they are still too far away for their voices to be heard.

The locks of th[eir] head were not bound,[199]
from the locks a band was mi[ssing],[200]
surely the tresses had been sh[aved off]![201]
And did they not pour forth tears
that weig[hed] as much as quarter shekels?[202]
"By the hand of Sapanu[203] *some*[204] *are victorious,*
[by Sa]panu some are with[out] triumph![205]
[My tas]k is arduous!
What good news could I possibly bring you, Dani'ilu?
What (news) now that the head has been struck on the temp[le]?[206]
Under (the feet) of ʿAnatu he fell,[207]
she could not make him rise.[208]

[199] Men in action had their long hair tied up by a head-band. Unkempt hair was a token of sorrow, cf. Lev. 10:6; 21:10.

[200] Cf. Eccl. 9:8.

[201] Cf. Judg. 16:19. Shaving off the hair was a rite of mourning: Isa. 22:12; Jer. 16:6; 47:5; 48:37; Ez. 7:18; Am. 8:10; Mic. 1:16; Sargon 8, 412; Gilg. VIII.i.40, ii.21, etc.

[202] Cf. Keret I (KTU 1.16):i.28-30.

[203] Unintroduced direct oration of the two lads, opening with a proverbial saying of the type "Man proposes, God disposes". Obviously the name of Sapanu is used to mask the name of Baʿlu, cf. Baal, note 188. And it was a question indeed whether Baʿlu, the patron of Dani'ilu, could not have prevented his wife ʿAnatu from killing Aqhatu. Cf. OTS 24 (1986) 1ff.

For Oriental parallels of the saying see *e.g.* En.el. IV.8; A. W. Sjöberg, ZA 65 (1975) 194f.; Deut. 32:39; 1 Sam. 2:4-9; Ps. 75:7; 113:7-9.

[204] Cf. Josh. 8:22; Isa. 49:12; Ps. 20:8; Dan. 12:2.

[205] Cf. Isa. 63:6; Lam. 3:18,26, also 1 Sam. 11:13; 2 Sam. 23:10; Prov. 21:31.

[206] Reading: *m bh[lm] rʾiš . rq[t]h*. Cf. Judg. 5:26.

[207] This and the two following cola were accidentally omitted. Later on the scribe wrote them on the edge of the tablet.

Unwittingly the messengers refer to ʿAnatu's earlier threat (Aqhat I (KTU 1.17):vi.45f.). Cf. the parallel expressions in Ps. 18:39; 47:4.

[208] Namely, from the Nether World, cf. Aqhat II (KTU 1.18):iv.41; III (KTU 1.19):i.15f. as well as 1 Sam. 2:6; 28:8,11; Ez. 37:12f.; Ps. 30:4. The reading *tšʿ[ly]* was proposed by B. Margalit, UF 15 (1983) 115.

She made his soul depart like wind,[209]
(his) life like spittle,
like smoke from his nose!"
They arrived.
They raised their voices and cried:
"Listen, o Dani'ilu, (you) Saviour's man!
The hero Aqhatu is dead![210]
The Virgin ʿAnatu made his soul depart like wind,
his life like spittle,
like smoke from his nose!"
With him,[211] *the feet began to totter,*
his face above began to sweat,
at his back the spine loosened,
the joints of his spine shook,
the small of his back too.[212]
He raised his voice and cried:
[ ]
slayer [ ]
... [ ]
[ ]
[ ]
[ ]
[ ]
[ ]
When he raised his eyes he saw,
he saw eagles in the clouds.

[209] Cf. notes 146-147. Apparently the lads have learnt somehow that ʿAnatu was the real murderess. Still they avoid mentioning the name of Aqhatu.

[210] Note the parallelism with the announcement of the death of Baʿlu, also by two messengers, in Baal V (KTU 1.5):vi.9. Cf. note 170.

[211] *Scil.* Dani'ilu.

[212] Cf. Baal I (KTU 1.3):iii.32-35.

III.

1 *He raised his voice and cried:*
"Let Baˁlu break[213] *the wings of the eagles,*
let Baˁlu break their pinions!
Let them fall down at my feet![214]
I shall rip open their entrails and look:
if there is fat,
5 *if there is bone,*
I shall bewail and bury him,
put (him) into a grave of the earth-gods."[215]
The word had scarcely left his mouth,
his speech, his lips,
when Baˁlu broke the wings of the eagles,
Baˁlu broke their pinions.
10 *They fell at his feet.*
He ripped open their entrails and looked:
there was no fat,
there was no bone.
He raised his voice and cried:
"Let him re-create[216] *the wings of the eagles,*
let Baˁlu re-create their pinions!
Eagles, flap your wings and fly!"

[213] Cf. Adapa, EA 356:5f., ANET, 101. The Arabic cognate referred to by W. G. E. Watson, UF 8 (1976) 372 does not seem to exist. So we have no choice but to emend the text: *y̱tb⟨r⟩*. Nevertheless Watson's reference to the legend of Etana would seem pertinent, cf. J. V. Kinnier Wilson, The Legend of Etana, Warminster 1985, 38f.:7, 98f.:118.

[214] Again a pun on the metaphor mentioned in note 207. Symbolically Dani'ilu wants to trample the goddess who trampled his son.

[215] Cf. Baal, note 403.

[216] Cf. Baal, note 209; Keret, note 101; above, note 20. The reversable miracle was regarded as proof of ultimate power, cf. En.el. IV.19-32; Ex. 4:2-9; Judg. 6:36-40; S. Bertram, HistRel 3 (1964) 323-327. Its introduction into the legend of Aqhatu may indicate the tendency to replace Ilu by Baˁlu as the supreme god of the pantheon.

When he raised his eyes he saw,
he saw Hargubu,[217] *the father of the eagles.*
He raised his voice and cried:
"*Let Baˁlu break the wings of Hargubu,*
let Baˁlu break his pinions!
And let him fall down at my feet!
I shall rip open his entrails and look:
if there is fat,
if there is bone,
I shall bewail and bury him,
put (him) into a grave of the earth gods."
The word had scarcely left his mouth,
his speech, his lips,
when Baˁlu broke the wings of Hargubu,
Baˁlu broke his pinions.
And he fell at his feet.
He ripped open his entrails and looked:
there was no fat,
there was no bone.
He raised his voice and cried:
"*Let Baˁlu re-create the wings of Hargubu,*
let Baˁlu re-create his pinions!
Hargubu, flap your wings and fly!"
When he raised his eyes he saw,
he saw Samlu,[218] *the mother of the eagles.*

[217] *Nomen est omen*, cf. note 130. The name recalled that of Argob, a region in Bashan known for its connection with the Canaanite cult of the dead Saviours (spirits of the royal dead, *rpʾum*, cf. Deut. 3:13) and located not far from Kinnereth where Aqhatu will be buried eventually (cf. Deut. 3:17). With regard to the etymology of the name of Argob itself the most likely explanation is "(the land) with many clods", a term used for the covering of a grave in Job 21:33.

[218] *Nomen est omen*, cf. note 130. The word *ṣml* is attested in the meaning of "ripe fig". In the Mishna fully developed breasts are compared to this fruit (mNiddah V.7, a passage J. C. Greenfield, JCS 21 (1967) 90 aptly describes as "an earthy folk tradi-

He raised his voice and cried:
"Let Baᶜlu break the wings of Samlu,
let Baᶜlu break her pinions!
Let her fall at my feet!
I shall rip open her entrails and look:
if there is fat,
if there is bone,
I shall bewail and bury him,
put him into a grave of the earth-gods."
The word had scarcely left his mouth,
his speech, his lips,
when Baᶜlu broke the wings of Samlu,
Baᶜlu broke her pinions.
She fell at his feet.
He ripped open her entrails and looked:
there was fat,
there was bone!
And he took Aqhatu from her.
He yelled, (but) he did not awake.[219]
He bewailed and buried (him),
he buried him in a mausoleum in Kinnereth.[220]

tion" which may be "Canaanite" in origin). "The Ripe Fig", then, is a pun on another name of ᶜAnatu: "The Breast (of the Nations)", cf. Myth and Ritual I, note 58; IV, note 28; UF 12 (1980) 308.

219 Reading and interpretation are uncertain. Cf. Judg. 5:28; 1 Ki. 18:27 as well as note 221 below.

220 Reading and interpretation are dubious. In any case a translation like "in the fishing-grounds of Kinnereth" (Barton, Ullendorff, Margalit) is unacceptable because Dani'ilu wanted to give his son a decent burial "in a grave of the earth-gods" and because the lines 42-44 would become meaningless.

The grave in Kinnereth must have been a historical note in the legend of Aqhatu. Possibly it did still exist when the tale was written down. The literature of Ugarit contains several indications of close ties with the Bashan region (cf. Keret, note 28) which abounded in megalithic monuments inviting an etiological explanation.

He raised his voice and cried:
"Let Baʿlu break the wings of the eagles,
let Baʿlu break their pinions,
if they fly over the grave of my son,
causing him to loose his sleep!"[221]
The king struck[222] *Qoru-Mayima:*[223]
"Woe to you, Qoru-Mayima,
(you) who are responsible for the slaying of the hero Aqhatu![224]
Always be a stranger in the house of Ilu,[225]
a fugitive now and forever,[226]
now and to all generations!"[227]
He put down the tip[228] *of his walking-stick.*[229]

[221] With a slight emendation the translation would be "wake him up from his sleep". Of course it is the sleep of death that is meant here, cf. Jer. 51:39,57; Eph. 5:14; note 219. For Sumerian and Akkadian parallels see K. Spronk, Beatific Afterlife, Neukirchen 1986, 98f.

[222] The Arabic cognate specifically means "to strike with a staff or stick", cf. line 49. At the same time it is clear that we are dealing with a symbolic gesture (cf. Isa. 11:4).

[223] *Nomen est omen*, cf. note 130. The literal meaning of the name is simply "well of water". However, in a figurative sense it was a standard metaphor for the weeping eye, cf. Keret III (KTU 1.16):i.26f. No certain identification of the town is possible at the moment.

For the cursing of cities with the "woe! "-formula cf. Isa. 29:1; Jer. 13:27; Nah. 3:1; Zeph. 3:1; Matth. 11:21-24 (par.).

[224] Literally "on whom is the slaying", etc. Cf. Lev. 20:9; Josh. 2:19; 2 Sam. 1:16, etc. When a murder was committed by an unknown person the towns nearest to the place of the crime were held responsible. Cf. CH par. 23-24; Deut. 21:1-9; 2 Sam. 1:21, etc. Here the problem is that the murderers are known but, as far as ʿAnatu was concerned, inviolable.

[225] *I.e.*, seek asylum in the sanctuary, cf. Ex. 21:14; 1 Ki. 1:50; 2:28, etc., and for other parallels: T. H. Gaster, Myth, Legend and Custom in the Old Testament, London 1969, 490f.

[226] Cf. Gen. 4:12.

[227] Cf. Ex. 3:15; 17:16, also 20:5.

[228] Cf. 2 Sam. 2:23.

[229] Dani'ilu had raised his stick while cursing the city. Cf. note 222.

He arrived at Mirartu-Taghallilu-Binuri.[230]
He raised his voice and cried:
"*Woe to you, Mirartu-Taghallilu-Binuri,*
(you) who are responsible for the slaying of the hero Aqhatu!
May your root not rise from the earth,
may (your) top wilt in the hand of him who plucks you![231]
Be a fugitive now and forever,
now and to all generations!"
He put down the tip of his walking-stick.

IV.

He arrived at the city of Abiluma,[232]
Abiluma, the city of his Highness Yarikhu.
He raised his voice and cried:
"*Woe to you, city of Abiluma,*
(you) who are responsible for the slaying of the hero Aqhatu!
May Baʿlu render you blind,[233]
from now on and forever,
from now on and to all generations!"
He put down the tip of his walking-stick.
Dani'ilu arrived at his house,
Dani'ilu proceeded to his palace.

[230] *Nomen est omen*, cf. note 130. The noun *mrrt* is attested as "gall-bladder" so that the name seems to mean: "the gall-bladder that brings into the fire", *i.e.* that sets the patient on fire. It hints at the bitterness of the sorrow this town would cause by letting the murder of Aqhatu happen in its vicinity. Cf. note 156. Also KTU 1.12:I.10f. *ʾiš // mrm*.

[231] A widely attested metaphor, cf. Erra IV.125; KAI, no. 14:11f.; 2 Ki. 19:30; Am. 2:9, etc., cf. W. G. E. Watson, UF 8 (1976) 374f.; 14 (1982) 274-276.

Now that Dani'ilu does not have a "root" anymore (cf. note 19) those who are responsible should be deprived of their roots too.

[232] Cf. note 130.

[233] Cf. KAI, no. 222:A.39; Gen. 19:11; Deut. 28:28; 2 Ki. 6:18; Acts 13:11, and for more parallels: Gaster, *op.cit.* (n. 225), 158f.

The weeping women[234] *entered,*
women pounding their breasts[235] *into his palace,*
men bruising their skins[236] *into his residence.*[237]
They wept for the hero Aqhatu,
they shed tears for the child[238] *of Dani'ilu, the Saviour's man.*
Days became months,
months became years,[239]
until the seventh year[240]
they wept for the hero Aqhatu,
they shed tears for the child of Dani'ilu, the Saviour's man.
Then, in the seventh year,
Dani'ilu, the Saviour's man answered,
the hero, the Harnamite man, replied,
he raised his voice and cried:

[234] Wailing was a task of women, sometimes professionals (as in this case, since it lasted seven years), cf. Baal VI (KTU 1.6):i.9ff.; Keret III (KTU 1.16):i.25ff.; Jer. 9:16ff.; Am. 5:16; 2 Chr. 35:25; John 11:31, and for more parallels: Gaster, *op.cit.* (n. 225), 610.

[235] Cf. Keret III (KTU 1.16):ii.27 (restored); Eccl. 12:5.

[236] Cf. Baal, note 392. As we saw earlier (note 170) the Legend of Aqhatu more or less follows the seasonal pattern of the myth of Baʿlu. Therefore the weeping and lacerating may mirror the rites of mourning for Baʿlu. Cf. Baal, note 398.

[237] The lines IV.8-11 have been composed in apparent contrast to Aqhat I (KTU 1.17):ii.24-27, the passage describing the joyful entering of the goddesses overseeing the conception of Aqhatu. Whereas the latter stayed only for seven days, the mourners will stay for no less than seven years. Cf. note 239. The deeply pessimistic message is clear: it is the tragic fate of man that sorrow prevails over happiness. Cf. note 2.

[238] Cf. note 117.

[239] Cf. Baal, note 429.

[240] Normally a period of mourning lasted seven days, cf. ANET, 562a; Gen. 50:10; Num. 19:11f.; Job 2:12f.; Judith 16:24, etc. The hyperbole of seven years has been chosen not only to indicate the depth of Dani'ilu's sorrow, but also to underline the parallelism between the death of Aqhatu and that of Baʿlu. The latter stayed away for seven years, cf. note 177. The New Year festival when his return was celebrated is impending, however. Cf. notes 242-246, 249, 263.

"De[part from[my [house], weeping women,
from my palace, women pounding your breasts,
from my residence, men bruising your skins!"
And he brought the gods a sacrifice,
he made his incense rise to the celestial beings,[241]
the incense of the Harnamite (to) the beings of the stars.[242]
He praised [his] child,
[Dani'ilu] praised his child.[243]
The cymbals returned [to his] palace,
the anointed dancers to [his house].[244]

[241] It is unwarranted to equate the singular *šmym* with *šmm* "heaven". Cf. Loves II (KTU 1.10):i.3-5 where the "sons of Ilu", "the assembly of the stars" and "the race of heaven" are mentioned side by side. Also the biblical "host of heaven" may be compared—it is often equated with the stars (cf. Deut. 4:19; Jer. 8:2 LXX; Dan. 8:10; also Jer. 33:22 as compared to Gen. 22:17 and Isa. 40:26 as compared to Ps. 147:4).

[242] For "the Harnamite" see note 6. The lords of the stars are the gods, cf. En.el. V.2. According to the ancestor cult of Ugarit the members of the royal family became gods after their death. They are called "star-gods" in Ritual III (KTU 1.43):2f. As saviour-spirits (*rpʾum*) they rose with Baʿlu from the Nether World on the New Year festival. See Baal, note 478, and the comments on Aqhat IV, Ritual II (KTU 1.161), III (KTU 1.43) and Incantation V (KTU 1.108).

For these reasons the sacrifice of Dani'ilu may be interpreted as a first sacrifice to the spirit of his deified son. The incense he is burning happens to be of a type burnt during the New Year festival (Myth and Ritual I (KTU 1.23):15). It reminds us of Dani'ilu's hope that after his own death his son would make his smoke rise from the earth (notes 25-28 above). Now it is the father who has to perform the ancestral rites for his son. The message is dire: a world governed by the gods is a world turned topsy-turvy. Cf. note 2.

Next to this passage Ilimilku wrote a note in the margin: "*The recitation of this (passage) should be repeated.*" Probably he meant to instruct the reciting priest to extend the sacrifices of Dani'ilu over a period of seven days. In this way the connection with the beginning of the legend would have been made even more explicit.

[243] Reading uncertain. Although the verb involved may be used for the praise of mortals (*e.g.* Gen. 49:8) the object is usually God in the Hebrew Bible.

[244] Cf. Incantation V (KTU 1.108):4f. where the anointed dancers are the ancestral spirits raised in connection with the New Year festival. Cf. "the anointed ones of the earth" in Ps. 22:30. For the anointing itself also Ps. 23:5.

And Pughatu, who carried water on her shoulder, said:
"So my father has brought a sacrifice for the gods,
he has made his incense rise to the celestial beings,
the incense of the Harnamite (to) the beings of the stars.
Please bless me, (that) I may go blessed,
fortify me, (that) I may go fortified![245]
I want to slay the slayer of my brother,
I want to destroy the destroyer of my kin!"
And Dani'ilu, the Saviour's man, answered:
"(By) my soul! May Pughatu, who carries water on her shoulder, live!
She who scoops up dew from the wool,
who knows the course of the stars,[246]
may she travel smoothly![247]
May she slay the slayer [of her brother],
may she destroy the destroyer of [her] kin!"
She made a fish come up from the sea.[248]
She washed and reddened herself,
reddened herself with the sea-whelk,
whose habitat covers a thousand acres in the sea.[249]

[245] Echo of Aqhat I (KTU 1.17):i.23f.

[246] In this connection the standard epithets of Pughatu acquire a special meaning. She is the ideal person to pose as the rain-bride ʿAnatu at the New Year festival. Cf. Baal, notes 37-38 and notes 249, 263 below.

[247] Echo of Aqhat I (KTU 1.17):i.37f. The daughter executes the blood vengeance for her father. Cf. Num. 35:19; Deut. 19:12; 2 Sam. 14:7, etc.

[248] Cf. Isa. 63:11; Ez. 29:4; 32:3; Hab. 1:15.

[249] Pughatu rouges herself with a purple-snail in exactly the same way as ʿAnatu in Baal I (KTU 1.3):ii.38-iii.2. Note that this took place in autumn, especially in connection with the New Year festival. See Baal, note 24. So the scribe connects his narrative once more with the seasonal myth of Baʿlu. See notes 102, 177, 240.

Under[neath] she dressed in a man's clothes,[250]
she put a d[agger] in her plaited bag,
she put a sword in her pouch,[251]
and on top she dressed in a women's clothes.
[At] the setting of Shapshu, the Lamp of the gods,[252]
Pughatu entered the meeting-place in the fields.
At the going-down of Shapshu, the Lamp of the gods,
Pughatu arrived at the tents.
Word was brought to Yattupanu, the warrior of the Lady:[253]
"Our employer has come to your camp,
[ᶜAnatu] has come to your tents!"
And Yattupanu, the warrior of the Lady, answered:
"Bring her in and let her give me wine to drink![254]
Let her take the cup from my hand,[255]
the goblet from my right hand!"
They brought Pughatu in and she gave him drink.
She took the cup from his hand,
the goblet from his right hand.
And Yattupanu, the warrior of the Lady, said:
"Through wine, o Lady, I become strong![256]

[250] Like the Babylonian Ishtar, the Hurrian Shauska and the Phoenician Tinnit the goddess ᶜAnatu/ᶜAthtartu used to wear male clothes along with female garb. It is clear that Pughatu wants to disguise herself as Yattupanu's employer ᶜAnatu.

[251] Part of ᶜAnatu's equipment in which she had concealed her "weapon" (the eagle), cf. Aqhat II (KTU 1.18):iv.18,29.

[252] The sun-goddess. Obviously Pughatu prefers to arrive in the dusk.

[253] Cf. notes 135-136.

[254] Like many a hired murderer Yattupanu grossly overrates his power over his employer. He wants the goddess to serve him as a hand-maid. For girls serving wine cf. Keret III (KTU 1.16):ii.12-16; Gen. 19:32ff., and scenes of Egyptian banquets. Judg. 4:19-21 and Judith 12:11-13:8 offer partial parallels.

[255] Cf. Isa. 51:22; Jer. 25:15,17,28.

[256] A drunk's bragging. Compare the following saying in Tanhuma, section Noah: "Has he drunk moderately, he is strong like a lion'".

I can scol[d][257] (*even*) *Ilu, the owner of the encampment*![258]
The hand that slew the hero Aqhatu
will slay a thousand foes of the Lady!''
She put a spell on the tents.[259]
Then [*she carried*] *out the wish of her heart.*
When for a second time [*she po*]*ured*[260] *w*[*ine*] *for him,*
for the second time she gave him mixture to drink,
she gave [*him*] *a d*[*rug*] *to drink.*[261]

Marginal note, beginning next to line IV.23:
''*The recitation of this* (*passage*) *should be repeated.*''[262]

Unfortunately only fragments of the next tablet have been preserved. Probably Pughatu succeeded in killing the murderer of her brother.[263] The great goddess ᶜAnatu, however, will have remained inviolable even though it was she who planned the crime.

Apparently Dani'ilu did not find rest. It seems he asked his patron Baᶜlu for help. In the first fragment of tablet IV Baᶜlu answers that there is only one possibility to see Aqhatu again. Dani'ilu has to invite the spirits of the dead heroes into his house to celebrate the New Year festival with him. He may lure them with the promise that if they decide to come Baᶜlu will revive them when

257 Like the house-keeper of Ilu when the latter was dead-drunk, cf. Myth and Ritual III (KTU 1.114):20. The implication being that Yattupanu expects to hold his liquor better than the head of the pantheon—a blasphemous assumption.

258 Cf. Baal, note 82. See also Gen.25:10; Lev. 27:24.

259 Cf. Baal II (KTU 1.1):ii.3f., 10 (restored).

260 Reading [*tm*]lᶜah, cf. Gen. 21:19.

261 Cf. Hab. 2:15.

262 Cf. note 242 and Baal, note 251.

263 It may be noted that the poet situated this episode around the time of the New Year festival (cf. notes 242, 244, 246, 249 and the commentary on Aqhat IV below). During this festival enormous quantities of wine were consumed and a girl, impersonating ᶜAnatu, ''killed'' many soldiers (*mhrm*) in a sham combat. See Baal, notes 15, 21; Myth and Ritual IV, notes 6-11.

he returns to his palace "on the third day" to celebrate his victory over Death.[264]

Aqhat IV, fragment a

KTU 1.21

II.

"[*Then Dani'ilu must say*:] ,
'[*Come to the house of*] *my drinking society*,[265]
  go into my house [*for the Saviours*[266]]!
I invite you [*to*] *my* [*hou*]*se*,
  I call [*you to*] *my* [*pa*]*lace*.
May the Saviours flutter[267] *to the holy place*,[268]
  may the ghosts flutter [*to*] *the* [*holy place*],
    [*may they come to the house of my*] *drinking society*!
Then he will hea[*l you*],
  the Shepherd will [*revive you*]!'[269]

[264] Cf. notes 98-102 above.

[265] Men formed cultic societies called *mrzḥ* or *mrzᶜ* in which they practised communion with their ancestors over a cup of wine. Wealthy men fitted up a special room or hall for this purpose. The institution of the *mrzḥ* is already attested in Ebla and continued to exist until comparatively recent times (Palmyra). See K. Spronk, Beatific Afterlife, Neukirchen 1986, 196ff.; P. Xella, SEL 3 (1986) 22, n.2.

[266] Literally "Healers", epithet of dead kings and heroes, like the Greek ἰατρός. See Baal, note 478 and Keret, note 52. Being the Victor of Death Baᶜlu was the first among the Saviours, see note 5.

[267] The spirits could take the physical form of birds. Just as the moment of Baᶜlu's descent into the Nether World coincided with the vernal migration of birds (Baal, note 301), so his return was marked by the autumnal migration.

[268] Birds resorting to sacred edifices enjoyed protection. See Ps. 84:3 and Spronk, *op.cit.* (n. 265), 100, n. 3, 134, 167, 184ff.

[269] "Shepherd" was an epithet of Baᶜlu/Haddu. Cf. the place name *hdrᶜy*. His resurrection from the Nether World "on the third day" (see note 270) gave life to the dead. See notes 101, 242, and especially Aqhat IV, fragment c (KTU 1.22:II).

Apparently the myth of Baᶜlu influenced not only Hos. 6:1f. and Am. 4:4 (cf. 5:6), but also early Christian traditions about the resurrection of Christ. Cf. Matth. 20:21-23; 26:27-29; 1 Cor. 15:20-27; 1 Thess. 4:14; Rev. 20:4,6.

Now I shall go, [for one day and a second],
[on the] third I shall arrive at the house,
[I shall come] to my palace.''[270]
And Dani'ilu[271] *said:*
''*[Come to the house of] my [drinking society],*
go into my house for the Saviours!
[I inv]ite you [to my house],
I call you [to] my [pala]ce.
May the Saviours [flutter] to the holy place,
may the [ghosts] flutter to the [holy place]!''
(broken)

Aqhat IV, fragment b

KTU 1.20

This fragment of tablet IV is a partial duplicate of KTU 1.22: II [= III]. The gap between the fragments a and b cannot be very large because Dani'ilu is still invoking the spirits of the dead. Eventually he succeeds. Spiritualistic sessions like the one described here were part of the actual cult of Ugarit.

''[... *may the Sa]viours take part in the sacrifice,*[272]
[... *may] the ghosts be served,*
[may they ea]t like the long dead.[273]

[270] Baʿlu's triumphant return is announced in Baal VI (KTU 1.6):vi.32-34 and the mythological prototype of the New Year's banquet is described in Baal I:i (KTU 1.101 + KTU 1.3:I). Cf. John 14:2-5; K. Oberhuber, Fs. L. R. Palmer, 261-272.

[271] The tablet has *wyʿn ʾil*. This is either a scribal error for *wyʿn* ⟨*dn*⟩*ʾil* (homoioteleuton) or we have to translate ''And the god said'' which would imply that Dani'ilu had been deified (see for a similar case Aqhat III (KTU 1.19):ii.12).

[272] Cf. KTU 1.161:1; 1 Sam. 28:24; Ps. 106:28. Also Isa. 25:6-8 (''He will swallow up Death''); Ez. 39:17-20; Rev. 19:17.

[273] Literally ''the dead of dead''. The dead were supposed to suffer insatiable hunger and thirst if they had no relatives on earth who could take care of their regular offerings.

[May they draw nea]r and enter the company,[274]
[may they ....] on the day of the summer fruit![275]
May [the ghos]ts eat,
[yes,] may the [Sa]viours drink!
[May they descend], the god of the jujube-trees,
[the goddess] who is sitting on a twig![276]
[I have sacrific]ed the sacrifice of Amurru,[277]
[ ] day [ ]."
(broken)

II.

1* "*[... seven ... in my house]*,
1 *eight within my palace.*[278]
May the Saviours flutter to the holy place,
may the ghosts flutter to the holy place!"
They tied up [the chariots],
harnessed the horses,
[raised] the ban[ners].[279]

[274] Cf. Gen. 49:6; Ps. 89:8, also note 265.

[275] During the New Year festival the spirits were regaled with the first of the summer fruit, especially grapes and gourds. See fragment c below as well as Baal, note 476; Myth and Ritual I, note 11; Ritual I, notes 8 and 10.

[276] Cf. note 267.

[277] Probably Amurru was the name of the country over which Dani'ilu ruled. See also fragment c, III.17 (KTU 1.22:II.17). The early Israelite New Year festival also had a definitely tribal aspect.

[278] Compare the seven apparitions of Ritual II (KTU 1.161). Also Mark 16:9; Luke 11:26. For the pair seven-eight: Keret I (KTU 1.14):I.8f.; Aqhat III (KTU 1.19):i.42f.; Micah 5:4; Eccl. 11:2.

[279] The abrupt change from theriomorphic to anthropomorphic representation of deities is not unusual in the religious literature of Ugarit. For a Phoenician parallel of an evil spirit tying up his chariot to visit the earth see JEOL 27 (1981-82) 111. For some interesting Aramaic parallels see C. D. Isbell, Corpus of the Aramaic Incantation Bowls, Missoula 1975, No. 12:16; J. Naveh-S. Shaked, Amulets and Magic Bowls, Jerusalem/Leiden 1985, Bowl 13:6 (p. 198). For other parallels: K. Spronk, *op.cit.* (n. 265), 167f. Perhaps 2 Ki. 2:11f. rests on a tradition according to which Eliah was taken up among the celestial beings by the chariots of the blessed ones.

They mounted their chariots,
cam[e to their stallions].
They went for one day and a second.
After sun[set on the third]
the Saviours arrived at the threshing-floors,
the gh[osts at] the plantations.[280]
And Dani'ilu, the Saviour's man, said,
the hero, the Harnamite man, replied:
"*[The Saviours] at the threshing-floors,*
the gods at the plan[tations],
[the ghosts] who came, let them be fed,
feed the An[cient Ones],
[ ] apples, ambrosia.
Go round [with],
[am]brosia [ ]
(broken)

Aqhat IV, fragment c

KTU 1.22

This fragment supplies us with a number of lines preceding the second column of fragment b (III.1-18 = KTU 1.22:II.1-18), duplicates the first part of that column (III.19 ff.) and finally gives part of the sequel in column IV (= KTU 1.22:I).

"*And let them co[me to my house],*
[go into] my palace.
[Go into the house of my drinking society],
come to my house for the Savi[ours]!

[280] Flocks of migrating birds descending on places where they could feed. Cf. note 267 and G. H. Dalman, Palästinischer Diwan, Leipzig 1901, 28.

[I call] you [to my house],
I invi[te you to my palace].
[May the Saviours flutter] to the holy place,
may the ghosts flutter [to the holy place]!
[May they rise up[281] *there, the Saviour*[282]*],*
the soldiers of Baʿlu,
[may they rise up there, Baʿlu],
[the soldiers] of ʿAnatu.
Come to [my house, Saviours],
I call you [to my house],
[I invite you to] my palace!
[May the Saviours flutter to] the holy place,
may [the ghosts flutt]er to the holy place!
May the host [of the filth[283]*] rustle*[284] *[there],*
[the highness, the king, the usurper].
Listen, you [Saviours],
[pay attention, you ghos]ts!
Why do you cower?
[Why do you bow down?]"
[He poured out] oil of decision,
[Dani'ilu] made a vow:
"If [my son Aqhatu becomes ki]ng over Amurru,
gras[ps the throne of his kingship],
the seat of the throne of his do[minion],
I will [always] *call the Saviours [to my house],*
[invite the ghosts] to [my palace]!

[281] Literally "tower, become tall". Deities were taller than men. Probably the Canaanite traditions about the giant *rpʾum* gave rise to the Israelite stories about tall Rephaites dwelling in Canaan before the people of God wandered in. Cf. *e.g.* Deut. 2:20f.; 2 Sam. 21:18-22.

[282] Cf. notes 266, 269.

[283] The Nether World was a place of mire. Cf. Baal, note 309.

[284] The verb denotes the specific sound of rustling wings. Cf. note 267.

May [the Saviours] flutter [to the holy place],
[may the ghosts flutter] to the holy place!"
They tied up the chariots,
harnessed the horses.
They mounted their chariots,
came to their stallions.
They went for one day and a second.
After sunset on the third[285]
the Saviours arrived at the threshing-floors,
the ghosts at the plantations.
(broken, but see fragment b, II.7ff.)

[he]aven
[ ]
[ ] *his* [ ].
"*Look! Your son,*
Look! [He will protect your holy pla]ce,[286]
your grandson, your holy place!
Look! [Your] off[spring],
[he who will gras]p your hand,[287]
your lips will kiss the boy!"[288]
There, shoulder to shoulder, were the brothers
whom Ilu made stand up in haste.[289]

285 See note 269 and also fragment b, II.5f. (duplicate).

286 A tragic reminder of Aqhat I (KTU 1.17):i.28 (par.) and a cold comfort because Dani'ilu had hoped for more (Aqhat IV, fragm. c:iii.15ff.).

287 A tragic reminder of Aqhat I (KTU 1.17):i.30 (par.). See note 294.

288 Cf. note 191.

289 The kind of revivification with Baʿlu Aqhatu had refused haughtily (Aqhat I (KTU 1.17):vi.25-38) has nevertheless become his share.

It is highly interesting that the verb *qwm* "stand up" is used here, cf. Isa. 14:21; 26:14; Ps. 88:11; Eph. 5:14, etc.

There the name of Ilu gave substance to the dead,
the blessing of the name of Ilu[290] *gave substance to the heroes.*
There rose up Baʿlu the Saviour,
the soldiers of Baʿlu and the soldiers of ʿAnatu.
There rustled the host of the filth,
the highness, the king, the usurper,
as when ʿAnatu chases the game,
causes to fly up the birds of heaven.
He slaughtered oxen,
and small stock as well.
He slew bulls,
and the fattest of rams,
yearling calves,
sheep, a multitude of lambkins.
To those who came over[291] *the olives were like silver,*
to those who came over the gourds were like gold,
among the fruit on the table in the hall,
in the hall of kings.
Look! For one day he poured wine of Thamuka,
must-wine, fit for rulers,[292]
wine with no after-thirst,
wine of happiness,
the purple necklace of the Lebanon,[293]
must-dew grown by a god.
Look! For one day and a second they ate,
the Saviours drank,

[290] Cf. Ps. 72:19; 96:2; 100:4; 113:2; 145:1,21; Job 1:21; Neh. 9:5.

[291] Those who had crossed the waters of death. Cf. Spronk, *op.cit.* (n. 265), 175.

[292] Cf. Gilg. VII:iii.37.

[293] Wine as an ornament of the Lebanon. On the quality of the wines of the Lebanon in antiquity see Hos. 14:6-8. In the course of the New Year festival wine was libated for the *rpʾum*, cf. Baal, notes 1, 15, 476; Ritual I, note 42; Incantation V, note 7.

for a third, a fourth day,
a fifth, a sixth day they ate,
the Saviours drank,
in the dining room on the summit,
on the crest, on the flank of the Lebanon.
Then, on the seventh [*day*],
*Ba*ʿ*lu the Almighty* [*came*],
[*he approached*] *his friend* [*with merc*]*y*:[294]
"[*Is Dani'ilu, the Saviour's man,*] *miserable*?
[*Is the hero, the Harnamite man, c*]*rying*?"
(broken)

[294] A tragic return to the situation of Aqhat I (KTU 1.17):i.15-18, also after seven days of sacrificing. As in the other major works of Ilimilku (Baal and Keret) the end of the story links up with its beginning. For an attempt to evaluate this cyclic principle see OTS 24 (1986) 1ff.

INDEX OF SCRIPTURAL REFERENCES

SUBJECT INDEX ARTU

1856